The Fullness of Trinitarian Love

VERITAS

Series Introduction

"The truth will set you free" (John 8:32)

In much contemporary discourse, Pilate's question has been taken to mark the absolute boundary of human thought. Beyond this boundary, it is often suggested, is an intellectual hinterland into which we must not venture. This terrain is an agnosticism of thought: because truth cannot be possessed, it must not be spoken. Thus, it is argued that the defenders of "truth" in our day are often traffickers in ideology, merchants of counterfeits, or anti-liberal. They are, because it is somewhat taken for granted that Nietzsche's word is final: truth is the domain of tyranny.

Is this indeed the case, or might another vision of truth offer itself? The ancient Greeks named the love of wisdom as *philia*, or friendship. The one who would become wise, they argued, would be a "friend of truth." For both philosophy and theology might be conceived as schools in the friendship of truth, as a kind of relation. For like friendship, truth is as much discovered as it is made. If truth is then so elusive, if its domain is *terra incognita*, perhaps this is because it arrives to us—unannounced—as gift, as a person, and not some thing.

The aim of the Veritas book series is to publish incisive and original current scholarly work that inhabits "the between" and "the beyond" of theology and philosophy. These volumes will all share a common aspiration to transcend the institutional divorce in which these two disciplines often find themselves, and to engage questions of pressing concern to both philosophers and theologians in such a way as to reinvigorate both disciplines with a kind of interdisciplinary desire, often so absent in contemporary academe. In a word, these volumes represent collective efforts in the befriending of truth, doing so beyond the simulacra of pretend tolerance, the violent, yet insipid reasoning of liberalism that asks with Pilate, "What is truth?"—expecting a consensus of non-commitment; one that encourages the commodification of the mind, now sedated by the civil service of career, ministered by the frightened patrons of position.

The series will therefore consist of two wings: (1) original monographs; and (2) essay collections on a range of topics in theology and philosophy. The latter will principally be the products of the annual conferences of the Centre of Theology and Philosophy (www.theologyphilosophycentre.co.uk).

Conor Cunningham, *Veritas Series Editor*

Available from Cascade Books

Nathan Kerr	*Christ, History, and Apocalyptic: The Politics of Christian Mission*
Anthony D. Baker	*Diagonal Advance: Perfection in Christian Theology*
D. C. Schindler	*The Perfection of Freedom: Schiller, Schelling, and Hegel Between the Ancients and the Moderns*
Rustin Brian	*Covering Up Luther: How Barth's Christology Challenged the* Deus Absconditus *That Haunts Modernity*
Timothy Stanley	*Protestant Metaphysics After Karl Barth and Martin Heidegger*
Christopher Ben Simpson	*The Truth Is the Way: Kierkegaard's* Theologia Viatorum
Richard H. Bell	*Wagner's Parsifal: An Appreciation in the Light of His Theological Journey*
Antonio Lopez	*Gift and the Unity of Being*
Toyohiko Kagawa	*Cosmic Purpose*, translated and introduced by Thomas John Hastings
Nigel Zimmerman	*Facing the Other: John Paul II, Levinas, and the Body*
Conor Sweeney	*Sacramental Presence After Heidegger: Onto-theology, Sacraments, and the Mother's Smile*
John Behr et al. (eds.)	*The Role of Death in Life: A Multidisciplinary Examination of the Relation Between Life and Death*
Eric Austin Lee et al. (eds.)	*The Resounding Soul: Reflection on the Metaphysics and Vivacity of the Human Person*
Orion Edgar	*Things Seen and Unseen: The Logic of Incarnation in Merleau-Ponty's Metaphysics of Flesh*
Duncan B. Reyburn	*Seeing Things as They Are: G. K. Chesterton and the Drama of Meaning*
Lyndon Shakespeare	*Being the Body of Christ in the Age of Management*
Michael V. Di Fuccia	*Owen Barfield: Philosophy, Poetry, and Theology*
John McNerney	*Wealth of Persons: Economics with a Human Face*
Norm Klassen	*The Fellowship of the Beatific Vision: Chaucer on Overcoming Tyranny and Becoming Ourselves*
Donald Wallenfang	*Human and Divine Being: A Study of the Theological Anthropology of Edith Stein*
Sotiris Mitralexis	*Ever-Moving Repose: A Contemporary Reading of Maximus the Confessor's Theory of Time*
Sotiris Mitralexis et al. (eds.)	*Maximus the Confessor as a European Philosopher*
Kevin Corrigan	*Love, Friendship, Beauty, and the Good: Plato, Aristotle, and the Later Tradition*
Andrew Brower Latz	*The Social Philosophy of Gillian Rose*
D. C. Schindler	*Love and the Postmodern Predicament: Rediscovering the Real in Beauty, Goodness, and Truth*
Stephen Kampowski	*Embracing Our Finitude: Exercises in a Christian Anthropology Between Dependence and Gratitude*

William Desmond	*The Gift of Beauty and the Passion of Being: On the Threshold Between the Aesthetic and the Religious*
Charles Péguy	*Notes on Bergson and Descartes*
David Alcalde	*Cosmology Without God: The Problematic Theology Inherent in Modern Cosmology*
Benson P. Fraser	*Hide and Seek: The Sacred Art of Indirect Communication*
Philip John Paul Gonzales	*Exorcising Philosophical Modernity: Cyril O'Regan and Christian Discourse After Modernity*
Caitlin Smith Gilson	*Subordinated Ethics: Natural Law and Moral Miscellany in Aquinas and Dostoyevsky*
Michael Dominic Taylor	*The Foundations of Nature: Metaphysics of Gift for an Integral Ecological Ethic*
David W. Opderbeck	*The End of the Law? Law, Theology, and Neuroscience*
Caitlin Smith Gilson	*As It Is in Heaven: Some Christian Questions on the Nature of Paradise*
Andrew T. J. Kaethler	*The Eschatological Person: Alexander Schmemann and Joseph Ratzinger in Dialogue*
Emmanuel Falque	*By Way of Obstacles: A Pathway Through a Work*
Paul Tyson (ed.)	*Astonishment in Science: Engagements with William Desmond*
Darren Dyk	*Will and Love: Shakespeare and the Motion of the Soul*
Matthew Vest	*Ethics Lost in Modernity: Reflections on Wittgenstein and Bioethics*
Hanna Lucas	*Sensing the Sacred: Recovering a Mystagogical Vision of Knowledge and Salvation*
Philip John Paul Gonzales et al. (eds.)	*Finitude's Wounded Praise: Responses to Jean-Louis Chrétien*
Martin Koci et al. (eds.)	*God and Phenomenology: Thinking with Jean-Yves Lacoste*
Steven E. Knepper (ed.)	*A Heart of Flesh: William Desmond and the Bible*
Tyler Dalton McNabb	*An Analytic Theology of Evangelism*
Duncan Reyburn	*The Roots of the World*
Rachel M. Coleman	*Matter as an Image of the Good: Ferdinand Ulrich's Metaphysics of Creation*
Pablo Irizar et al. (eds.)	*To Die of Not Writing: Doing Philosophy of Religion with Emmanuel Falque*
John Milbank, et al. (eds)	*New Trinitarian Ontologies, Volume I*
Christine Stephenson	*Remembering Augustine: The Symphonic Forms and Fundamental Affordances of Memory in His Theology of Memoria*
Aimé Forest	*Consent to Being*

The Fullness of Trinitarian Love

The Convergence of Kenotic Love and Plerotic Fecundity in the Holy Trinity

CAMERON B. CRICKENBERGER

CASCADE *Books* • Eugene, Oregon

THE FULLNESS OF TRINITARIAN LOVE
The Convergence of Kenotic Love and Plerotic Fecundity in the Holy Trinity

Cascade Books
An Imprint of Wipf and Stock Publishers
199 W. 8th Ave., Suite 3
Eugene, OR 97401

www.wipfandstock.com

PAPERBACK ISBN: 979-8-3852-4407-2
HARDCOVER ISBN: 979-8-3852-4408-9
EBOOK ISBN: 979-8-3852-4409-6

Cataloguing-in-Publication data:

Names: Crickenberger, Cameron B., author.

Title: The fullness of trinitarian love : the convergence of kenotic love and plerotic fecundity in the holy trinity / Cameron B. Crickenberger.

Description: Eugene, OR : Cascade Books, 2026 | Series: Veritas | Includes bibliographical references and index.

Identifiers: ISBN 979-8-3852-4407-2 (paperback) | ISBN 979-8-3852-4408-9 (hardcover) | ISBN 979-8-3852-4409-6 (ebook)

Subjects: LCSH: Trinity. | Jesus Christ—Person and offices. | Trinity—History of doctrines.

Classification: BT111.3 .C75 2026 (paperback) | BT111.3 (ebook)

VERSION NUMBER 04/14/26

To my wonderful wife, Julia.
Our life together is teaching me the truth of this divine love.

Lovers are the ones who know most about God;
the theologian must listen to them.

Hans Urs von Balthasar
Love Alone Is Credible

Contents

Acknowledgments

THE DIFFICULTY OF COMPILING a list of those to whom I owe thanks underscores the immense importance of doing just that. It is safe to say that while any project of this length requires assistance from others, and that doctoral dissertations in particular pose unique challenges, there is no question that whatever merit this thesis possesses is due more to the love and friendship of others rather than my own effort and capability. Their encouragement has represented the steadfast love of the Lord, from whom my help comes.

I am immensely grateful to my supervisory team, Professors Judith Wolfe and Simon Oliver, who graciously stepped in when my first supervisor, Professor Christoph Schwöbel, suddenly passed away. For their availability, critiques, praise, and confidence in me, which carried this project through many difficult moments, I am a better theologian and pastor.

While Professor Schwöbel's careful guidance gave this project its initial direction in the first year of my program at the University of St Andrews, the example of his life shaped me much more. Though a thinker of rare caliber, Christoph showed his students genuine interest and respect. Though constantly beset by academic demands, Christoph maintained an unswerving commitment to serving the church of Jesus Christ, refusing to let theology be torn asunder between two worlds. And though surely encountering the temptation to surround himself by admirers, Christoph's heart resided in the home he shared with his wife, the Rev. Katrin Bosse, and his two young sons. I am grateful for his example; may the Lord's perpetual light shine upon him.

My gratitude goes to two colleagues and friends from the University of St Andrews, Parker Haratine and Cody Warta, along with their families. While the feedback I received from Parker and Cody was genuinely helpful and thought-provoking, it was the love and care of these two families that enriched me and my family most during those two years.

Three churches have been invaluable to me during this period. The rector of St Andrews Episcopal Church, the Revd. Canon Professor Trevor Hart, allowed me to preach and encouraged me to continue pursuing both the academic and ecclesial paths. After moving home in the middle of my program, Christ Church in Murrells Inlet, South Carolina, gave me the gift of time to focus on my dissertation and finish it well. And finally, the love and encouragement of my friends at Church of the Ascension, my current parish, has sustained me through the last leg of this project. It is an honor to walk along with you as pastor and friend.

Then there are those whose friendship has granted me persistence. I am thankful to Steven and Elizabeth McCain, who graciously opened their home to me time and time again when I traveled to Durham, North Carolina, to use the library at Duke Divinity School. Jack and Paige Hannigan have my gratitude for keeping me grounded in the concrete details of true friendship; they have embodied the sacrificial love of God to me and my family. Tyler Holley, Joe McCulley, and Matt Klem, along with their wives and children, who have traveled with me through the better part of my theological education, have been a community of friends in which I have found solace, comfort, wisdom, and rest. I am grateful for their comments on sections of this work as well. Christian Kalmbach and Madeline Larson were with my family through the entirety of the doctoral process, first as our only friends in the flesh during the pandemic and then sharing our home with us. For Christian's penetrating insight, wide-ranging knowledge, and intellectual generosity, I am deeply grateful to him. This project (and I) would be far worse off apart from his friendship.

Both my parents and my wife's parents supported us through the long journey of higher education with their love, prayers, confidence, encouragement, and willingness to always open their doors to us and share their tables with us. I am grateful to live once more in the same place as them.

Finally, I am grateful for my wife and children. Julia, without your love and encouragement, this book would never have come to fruition. In your willingness to move so many times, in your care for me in my times of discouragement and fear, and in your embrace of my weaknesses, you have embodied the very heart of the divine love I have sought to describe in these pages. Thank you. To my children, Charis, Eli, and Rosie, your love softens my heart when the pressures of this life threaten to turn it to stone; for that I am grateful.

List of Abbreviations

DP	Aquinas, Thomas. *Quaestiones Disputatae de Potentia*. Edited by P. M. Pession. Rome: Marietti, 1949.
DV	Aquinas, Thomas. *Disputed Questions on Truth*. Translated by Robert W. Mulligan, James V. McGlynn, and Robert William Schmidt. Chicago: Regnery, 1952.
HA	Ulrich, Ferdinand. *Homo Abyssus: The Drama of the Question of Being*. Translated by D. C. Schindler. Washington, DC: Humanum Academic, 2018.
LSI	Aquinas, Thomas. *Commentary on the Gospel of John*. Edited by The Aquinas Institute. Translated by Fabian R. Larcher. 2 vols. Latin-English Opera Omnia. Steubenville, OH: Emmaus Academic, 2018.
Sent	Aquinas, Thomas. *Scriptum Super Sententiis Magistri Petri Lombardi*. Edited by Marie Fabien Moos. Paris: P. Lethielleux, 1956.
SCG	Aquinas, Thomas. *Summa Contra Gentiles*. Translated by Laurence Shapcote. Latin-English Opera Omnia. Steubenville, OH: Emmaus Academic, 2018.
ST	Aquinas, Thomas. *Summa Theologiæ*. Edited by The Aquinas Institute. Translated by Fathers of the English Dominican Province. 10 vols. Latin-English Opera Omnia. Steubenville, OH: Emmaus Academic, 2018.
TD5	Balthasar, Hans Urs von. *The Last Act*. Translated by Graham Harrison. Theo-Drama: Theological Dramatic Theory, vol. 5. San Francisco: Ignatius, 1998.
Theses	Hemmerle, Klaus. *Theses Towards a Trinitarian Ontology*. Translated by Stephen Churchyard. New York: Angelico, 2020.
TL1	Balthasar, Hans Urs von. *Truth of the World*. Translated by Adrian J. Walker. Theo-Logic: Theological Logical Theory, vol. 1. San Francisco: Ignatius, 2000.
TL2	Balthasar, Hans Urs von. *Truth of God*. Translated by Adrian J. Walker. Theo-Logic: Theological Logical Theory, vol. 2. San Francisco: Ignatius, 2004.
TL3	Balthasar, Hans Urs von. *The Spirit of Truth*. Translated by Graham Harrison. Theo-Logic: Theological Logical Theory, vol. 3. San Francisco: Ignatius, 2005.

Introduction

THIS BOOK PRESENTS A constructive theology of retrieval that develops a metaphysical account of the trinitarian life *in se* grounded in the apostolic confession that "God is Love" (1 John 4:8, 16) through conversation with various theologians, primarily Thomas Aquinas (1225–1274) and Hans Urs von Balthasar (1905–1988).[1] I will argue that the perennial tension between oneness and threeness in trinitarian thought can be fittingly resolved by developing the image of triune love revealed in Jesus Christ.

Throughout Holy Scripture, and often at crucial points, God's self-revealing acts are presented through the lens of love. In the Old Covenant, the name that God gives to his people is not exhausted in his reply to Moses's fearful question before the burning bush—"I AM WHO I AM"—but is expanded in God's proclamation of the divine name, undertaken at his own initiative—"The Lord, the Lord, a God merciful and gracious, slow to anger, and abounding in steadfast love and faithfulness."[2] This full name of steadfast love is repeated throughout the texts of the Old Covenant,[3] offering love as a description both of God's action toward Israel[4] and of the kind of life he has called his people to live.[5] In the New Testament, love is not only a forthright description of God ("God is Love"),[6] but also the fundamental motivation identified for God's redemption of the world[7] and a common way to describe the relations between the Father, Son, and Holy Spirit.[8]

1. For an explanation of the task and methodology of theological retrieval, see Webster, "Theologies of Retrieval," 583–99, and Sarisky, "Tradition II," 193–209.

2. Exod 3:14; 34:6.

3. E.g., Num 14:18; 2 Chr 30:9; Neh 9:17; Pss 86:15; 103:8; 111:4; 112:4; 116:5; 145:8; Joel 2:1.

4. E.g., Deut 4:37; 7:7–8; 2 Sam 2:6; 1 Chr 16:34; Isa 54:8; Lam 3:22; Hos 11:1.

5. E.g., Deut 6:5; 30:6; Josh 23:11; Ps 18:1; Isa 56:6; Hos 6:6. See Fortman, *Triune God*, 3–8.

6. 1 John 4:8, 16.

7. See John 3:16.

8. E.g., John 3:35; 5:20; 10:17; 17:24, 26; see Fortman, *Triune God*, 11, 17, 20.

Yet this scriptural emphasis on love did not feature prominently in the developing trinitarian theology of the church's first three centuries.[9] Instead, because the trinitarian conversation primarily developed within the context of dialogue with (or defense against) the surrounding culture, it was the symbols of the surrounding Greek philosophy that shaped early efforts to confess the mystery of the one God who is Father, Son, and Holy Spirit in a way both consistent with Scripture and coherent to their culture.[10] Since many early theologians made recourse to some level of subordinationism, the images used to demonstrate the coherence of the Christian confession often presented the common divinity as being shared by the three persons in different degrees.[11] Though Tertullian was the first to use a clearly defined set of terms to describe the one God as a *trinitas* of three *personae*, it was Athanasius who is commonly credited with taking the critical leap of establishing relationality as a necessary mode of trinitarian discourse.[12] For him, the Father and Son are "correlational," such that there cannot be a Father without the Son, and vice versa.[13] The introduction of relation into trinitarian discourse and the convention of using the term *hypostasis* to refer specifically to the Father, Son, and Spirit rather than to the divine essence allowed the Cappadocian fathers to describe the three persons using an analogy to three human persons without clearly veering into tritheism, which is one of the great accomplishments of the Niceno-Constantinopolitan period.[14]

9. Love was not entirely absent in trinitarian grammar. For instance, see Clement of Alexandria's *Quis Dives Salveteur* §37, where he identifies the Father's love as "the origin of the generation of the Son" (*Clement of Alexandria*, 345–46); see also Fortman, *Triune God*, 53.

10. See Russell, *Source of All Love*, 82–87, who overviews Justin Martyr, Irenaeus of Lyons, and Tertullian as examples of the first three centuries of trinitarian development; see also Barnes, "Latin Trinitarian Theology," 70–84; Lingua, "Trinity, Number, Image," 1300–1301. Alongside the cultural element, the trinitarian theology of the church was primarily developed within its pastoral context, in which the liturgy and nascent canon took center stage; see Anatolios, "Canonization of Scripture," 15–26; McGuckin, "Trinity in the Greek Fathers," 49–69.

Though it did not often enter materially into trinitarian theology itself, reflection on love as a Christian virtue or as a characteristic of divine action was not absent in the patristics. For a detailed overview of patristic reflections on love as both a divine and created reality, see Vincelette, "Introduction," 32–75. See also Sarah Coakley's discussion of desire, particularly in Origen, Augustine, Gregory of Nyssa, and Dionysius, in *God, Sexuality and the Self*.

11. See Russell, *Source of All Love*, 89–90.

12. See Lingua, "Trinity, Number, Image," 1304; Anatolios, "Personhood, Communion, Trinity," 152–54.

13. Russell, *Source of All Love*, 90–91.

14. See Gregory Nazianzen, *Oration* 39.11; Fortman, *Triune God*, 798; Lingua, "Trinity, Number, Image," 1306–9; Russell, *Source of All Love*, 96; Zizioulas, *Being as*

This created a pressing need for new concepts appropriate to the relations among *hypostases* that could also be consubstantial. Though the Cappadocians did not regularly emphasize the concept of love, Khaled Anatolios observes that the Cappadocian concept of the "Trinity as a communion of persons" depended upon their "appropriation of biblical categories, such as delight and mutual glorification," which involve or invoke the notion of love.[15] Augustine took up this concept of trinitarian relationality, likewise arguing that the divine persons could only be identified by the relations between them. The difference, however, was that while the Cappadocians conceived of the relations communally, Augustine structured them according to the psychological categories internal to the rational soul, by which he clearly emphasized the connection between love and the Holy Spirit in his role as the bond of love between the Father and Son.[16]

Augustine's theology opened the door in the West for love to play a more central role in trinitarian formulations. This took various forms: the essentially Augustinian position found in both the scholasticism of Peter Lombard and the mysticism of William of Saint Thierry and Bernard of Clairvaux; the social emphasis found in Richard of St. Victor, which shared the Cappadocian emphasis on interpersonality lacking in Augustine's psychological analogy; the emphasis on goodness as a transcendental in Bonaventure, which expressed itself within the Trinity in a social framework similar to that of Richard; and that of Thomas Aquinas, who took up Augustine's psychological analogy and love's role therein, elevating his emphasis on relations to a rarefied metaphysical state.[17] This Augustinian influence remained consistent in the trinitarian role of love in Western theology through late medieval scholasticism and the traditions of the Reformation.[18]

Communion, 33–41; Anatolios, "Personhood, Communion, Trinity," 148–49. See also Eduard Fiedler's genealogy, following Theo Kobusch, of the influence of personalism in trinitarian theology as it came through Origen ("Klaus Hemmerle on the Trinitarian Ontology," 66–67).

15. Anatolios, "Personhood, Communion, Trinity," 162.

16. See Ayres, "Augustine on the Trinity," 131–34; see also Fortman, *Triune God*, 139–50. It is the interiority of the rational person that leads Augustine to move on from his initial analogy—that of a lover, beloved, and the love itself—to the mind by which a person who loves herself also knows herself, providing clearer distinction within the person herself; see Augustine, "On the Trinity," especially 9.1–3.

17. This list of positions is helpfully catalogued in Poirel, "Scholastic Reasons," 166–68, and Wawrykow, "Franciscan and Dominican Trinitarian," 182–96. See also the discussion of developments within the Franciscan and Dominican traditions from Aquinas to Ockham in Friedman, *Medieval Trinitarian Thought*, as well as Van Nieuwenhove, *Introduction*, 141–46, 150–55, 186–91, 212–22.

18. See Slotemaker, *Trinitarian Theology*, especially 57–75.

Nearly a century ago, the Swedish theologian Anders Nygren identified this influence and mounted a full-scale assault against it.[19] In his book, Nygren neatly divided all of Western theology occurring between Augustine and Luther into two camps: those who understand love as Agape, "self-giving and self-spending love," and those who allow Eros, which traffics in "desire [and] sense of need," to infiltrate the Christian definition of love, and therefore, of God.[20] For Nygren, these two are mutually exclusive, and only Agape truly expresses the Christian concept. Augustine is singled out as the culprit of the intermixture of these two opposing loves in Christian thought, resulting "in the emergence of a new conception of love, summed up in the word '*caritas*.'"[21] According to Nygren, this *caritas*-synthesis was continually maintained in the medieval—principally Thomist—attempt to understand the connection between self-love (*amor sui*, or *amor concupiscentiae*) and friendship (*amor amicitia*), and ultimately, between self-love and divine love itself. The alliance between the two opposing views of love, Nygren believed, was destined to dissolve from the beginning.[22]

Even while rightly questioning the accuracy of Nygren's simplistic reading of Augustine, and Thomas, Oliver O'Donovan agrees that the latter is the foremost medieval custodian of Nygren's Eros.[23] Using the more nuanced categories found in Pierre Rousselot's *The Problem of Love in the Middle Ages*, O'Donovan draws parallels between Nygren's Eros and Agape and Rousselot's physical and ecstatic conceptions of love.[24] The physical account prioritizes "unity . . . as the raison d'être, measure, and ideal of love," such that self-love and love for God are united within the concept of each nature seeking its own final good. Alternatively, the ecstatic account seeks to sever the connection between self-love and love for God completely, such that love for the other serves no "egoistic inclinations" but seeks only the lover's "absorption" into the beloved.[25] For Rousselot, Thomas is the great systematizer of the unitive inclination in Greek thought (Nygren's Eros),

19. See Nygren, *Agape and Eros*.

20. Nygren, *Agape and Eros*, 159; see also 23–40, 164–65.

21. Nygren, *Agape and Eros*, 39.

22. Nygren, *Agape and Eros*, 141, 147.

23. See O'Donovan, *Problem of Self-Love*, 146–59.

24. See Rousselot, *Problem of Love*; referenced throughout O'Donovan, *Problem of Self-Love*, 145–52. O'Donovan claims Nygren was familiar with this volume, though there are no references to it in *Agape and Eros*. Vincelette mentions that Nygren's work has shaped American discussions of the nature of love, and while Rousselot's played a comparable role in France, Rousselot's thought has not been as thoroughly received in English-language scholarship due to the lack of a translation ("Introduction," 11–12).

25. See Rousselot, *Problem of Love*, 77–79.

while both Richard of St. Victor and Bonaventure are aligned with the "ecstatic" camp (Nygren's Agape).[26]

It is important to note the danger of reductionism inherent in any scheme as tidy as Nygren's and, to some extent, Rousselot's. For instance, Bonaventure's theology represents a mediating position between Richard and Thomas on many counts. However, these dichotomies present a helpful pattern: on the one hand, the alignment between love understood as seeking one's own good and a theology which heavily emphasizes essential descriptions; on the other, the tendency for a theology that emphasizes the person as the first and most important element of experience and identity to describe love as the act of seeking the good of the Other. Stated concisely, more essentialist theologies tend toward Eros, while more personalist theologies tend toward Agape. To focus on the essential often leads to a focus on the possession of the good desired in Eros, while a focus on the personal often emphasizes a logic of reciprocity, thus implying the concept of gift-giving indicative of Agape.

This pattern of preferential tendencies can also be observed in much of the trinitarian thought produced in the past half century as a part of what has been called the Trinitarian Revival. This trend in theology has its roots in the landmark works of Karl Barth and Karl Rahner, who sought to revive the function of the Trinity for all of Christian doctrine, which to many at that time seemed to have been consigned to the status of a *prolegomenon*, a scholastic curiosity, or worse, a footnote to theology.[27] Hans Urs von Balthasar, a contemporary and interlocutor of both Barth and Rahner, also contributed to the establishment of this new era of trinitarian thought. His wide-ranging influence on Roman Catholic thought in the period around Vatican II is illustrated in the cadre of those who joined him in founding the journal *Communio*: Joseph Ratzinger, Henri de Lubac, Louis Bouyer, Walter Kasper. The initial contributions of Barth, Rahner, and von Balthasar bore fruit in the following decades through the work of theologians such

26. See Rousselot, *Problem of Love*, 78, 82–104, 164–67; Vincelette, "Introduction," 12–23. For an excellent presentation and defense of Thomas's thought placed within the context of his Greek and Latin predecessors and contemporaries, see Malet, *Personne et Amour*.

27. See Sonderegger, *Doctrine of God*, xxiii; see also S. Holmes, *Quest for the Trinity*, 199. Schleiermacher provides an excellent example of the historical complexities involved in emergence of the Trinitarian Revival. Though many have critiqued Schleiermacher's relegation of the Trinity to the very end of his *Glaubenslehre*, there has been in recent scholarship a growing awareness that the attitude toward this work in much English scholarship suffers from interpretive myopia, not taking into account Schleiermacher's greater project in the *Glaubenslehre* itself or in his wider corpus; for instance, see Walter, "Trinity as Circumscription of Divine Love," 62–74.

as Robert Jenson, Colin Gunton, Christoph Schwöbel, and John Zizioulas. Central to the work of all of these theologians was, as Fiedler has recently put it, "a critical reconsideration of the modern philosophy of the subject," with special regard to how the trinitarian persons ought to be understood in relation to the human person.[28] Some, like Barth and Rahner, eschewed the term "person" in favor of terminology that downplayed the similarities between the two realms of predication, instead referring to the divine hypostases as "modes of being."[29] Others, however, leaned the opposite way, attempting to speak of divine personhood in a concrete sense that included reciprocal action between the distinct subjectivities of the Father, Son, and Holy Spirit.[30] The central claims of both sides revolved around the nature of personhood and subjectivity, divine and created, all of which raised numerous metaphysical and theological questions.

Unsurprisingly, there has also been a "counter revival" to this tendency as well, questioning the wisdom and even the orthodoxy of "reviving" the doctrine of the Trinity in this fashion.[31] The concerns have taken on many guises: an overconfidence in theological language; a loss or weakening of traditional doctrines such as simplicity; categorical misinterpretations of sources from past eras of theology; and concerning many of the second generation of authors above, the possibility of lapsing into tritheism from an overly acute focus on the divine person as such.[32] Common to these concerns is a reticence to leave the "traditional" structure and language of trinitarian thought behind, or to continue to use it in a modern register too far removed from its original context, lest the functions of doctrines like divine simplicity and unity lose their regulative power over concepts such as relation and person, allowing unity to be overcome by multiplicity.

28. Fiedler, "Klaus Hemmerle on the Trinitarian Ontology," 60. In addition, see the excellent chapter "The Trinity from Schleiermacher to the End of the Twentieth Century" in Marmion and Van Nieuwenhove, *Introduction to the Trinity*, 142–200, as well as the brief but useful biographical note concerning twentieth-century developments in trinitarian thought in Coakley, *God, Sexuality and the Self*, 27–28.

29. See Heltzel and Winn, "Barth, Reconciliation, Triune God," 176–77.

30. For example, see the brief discussion of Moltmann in Van Nieuwenhove, "Trinitarian Indwelling," 388–91.

31. Sherrard, "Review," 337.

32. For examples, see S. Holmes, *Quest for the Trinity*, 199–200; Kilby, *Balthasar*, 109–22; Kilby, "Hans Urs von Balthasar and the Trinity," 212–17; Van Nieuwenhove, "Trinitarian Indwelling," 391; Sonderegger, *Doctrine of the Holy Trinity*, 351–52; Webster, "Perfection and Participation," 379–94; see also Russell, *Source of All Love*, 37–38. Some, such as Holmes and Webster, were involved to some degree with the Trinitarian Revival but grew uneasy with the developments in the theology of the group, offering critiques from Thomas Aquinas and Reformed Scholasticism.

Significant for this present thesis is the common focus in the revival of trinitarian thought on the way in which love ought to articulate the trinitarian life and identity of God.[33] Hans Urs von Balthasar forcefully argued for this approach from the beginning of this period, foregrounding the Johannine confession that "God is love" and adding to it an adapted notion of kenosis from Philippians 2 as the central description of what the divine life of love is. John Betz is correct to say that one of the great achievements of von Balthasar's theology is "to have thought the meaning of being anew in view of the kenotic form of God's self-revelation."[34] For this, von Balthasar has been charged with "destroying the Trinitarian faith of the Christian Church," a criticism that has been repeated, albeit with less intensity, by many for whom Thomas provides a more dogmatically suitable concept of divine love.[35]

In order to clearly lay out the conceptual terrain, I have organized the subtleties involved in describing trinitarian love into an architectonic with five layers. Each layer contains a conceptual pair that highlights a different aspect of the tension inherent in reflection on divine love *in se*:

1. Essential vs. Personal
2. Enstatic vs. Ecstatic
3. Seeking vs. Giving
4. Possessive vs. Dispossessive
5. Beatitude vs. Fecundity

None of these pairs represent two mutually exclusive options, but instead two ends of a spectrum within which reflection on love has taken place. Furthermore, each respective side of the spectrum holds together synthetically. While simplistic, the left side could be summarized under the heading of Essentialism, and the right, Personalism. As I will describe below, the preferred choice on any one layer inclines a theologian toward the same side of the next layer. Throughout this present thesis, the concepts in this architectonic will be used to frame the analysis of the thought of various theologians, as well as my own constructive aims.

33. For example, see Zizioulas, *Being as Communion*, 46; Schwöbel, "God Is Love," 307–28; Gunton, *Father, Son, Holy Spirit*, 17–18; Jenson, *Triune God*, 156–58.

34. Betz, "What's New," 131.

35. Mansini, "Hegel and Christian Theology," 999; see also Schwöbel, "Taking the Form"; Schwöbel, "Generosity," 267–88.

1. Essential vs. Personal

As Rousselot's category of physical love suggests, one of the great strands of reflection on love in the Middle Ages centered on the coincidence of self-love and the love of others that occurs as a rational nature fulfills itself by loving others. Vincelette summarizes Rousselot's position: "Thus in the physical conception of love the love of desire and the love of friendship are in perfect continuity; the love of others is in accordance with one's natural inclinations and tendencies. Indeed, the more one gives oneself to others, the more one finds and gains oneself."[36] When situated within the context of human persons, or between humans and God, the physical concept of love provides a synthesis between essence and person, where the essence of each person is fulfilled in their love for other persons. Rousselot contrasted physical love with the ecstatic concept of love, which is characterized "by the predominance of the idea of person over the idea of nature" to the extent that the Lover is ultimately lost in the Beloved.[37] The aim of ecstatic love is "in the complete sacrifice of the lover's personhood to the beloved's personhood."[38] While Rousselot's observation regarding the synthesis of the physical concept is compelling within the parameters of his own discussion of love involving human persons, when translated into a trinitarian grammar, the threeness of the divine hypostases within the one divine essence introduces a tension that led medieval theologians to lean toward one or the other, either the fulfillment of the one essence (Rousselot's egoist view) or the interpersonal love of the three persons (Rousselot's ecstatic view). Thus, the fundamental challenge of trinitarian thought—the oneness of God in three persons—reasserts itself at the beginning of any attempt to consistently apply the scriptural statement "God is Love" as a theological framework for the trinitarian life *in se*.

2. Enstatic vs. Ecstatic

Already present in the first dichotomy is the question of the primary geography of love, that is, the location within which the act of love is fulfilled: the essence of the Lover or the persons involved. While the ecstatic movement of love focuses on the outward, personal movement of the Lover toward the Beloved, who exists outside the bounds of their own personal circumscription, the physical concept of love maintains an emphasis on the fulfillment

36. Vincelette, "Introduction," 17.

37. Rousselot, *Problem of Love*, 152.

38. Rousselot, *Problem of Love*, 151.

of the Lover's own essence in the act of love. Though in ethical or salvific contexts this emphasis is held in tandem with an emphasis on the nature (and person) of the Beloved, in trinitarian grammar the unity of the divine essence raises the question of whether any ecstatic movement of love can be properly ascribed to the divine persons within the trinitarian life itself. This creates the possibility of an *en*-static yet physical form of divine love, aptly expressed by statements that use the term "God" for the subject and object, and even the medium, of the act of loving, such as "God loves Godself through Godself."[39] Such articulations tend to remove the relational semantic force of the ecstatic concept of love in favor of maintaining the intelligibility of the single divine essence that is hypostatized as Father, Son, and Holy Spirit.

3. Seeking vs. Giving

When the nature of love must be defined within these strictures, it tends either toward a seeking after one's own good or a giving of one's good to the Other. Once again, while Nygren's absolute juxtaposition between Eros and Agape does not hold up to scrutiny between human persons or between God and creation, when placed within a trinitarian context it expresses a common choice of emphases. Thus, for God to love himself is for God to love his own goodness, which is the divine essence, eternally possessed (and thus not sought), or, alternatively, for the divine persons to give themselves to one another ecstatically in a disinterested manner.[40] In this sense, Nygren's dichotomy maps an abiding tension between Eros and Agape as a function of one's inclination toward emphasizing either the divine essence or the divine persons.

4. Possession vs. Dispossession

The way in which the nature of divine love is characterized implies the goal of the Lover as it relates to that person, however conceived. If divine love is seen within the eternal Godhead primarily as an action oriented toward the good of the divine essence as such, the goal of love is the possession of one's own good. Alternatively, if it is depicted as an action oriented toward the good of the divine persons *qua* other persons, the goal of the act of love

39. For example, see R. Williams, "What Does Love Know," 265: "God is a movement towards God, God's wanting of God so that God may be fully and blissfully God, may enjoy the 'natural good' proper to divine nature."

40. See O'Donovan, *Problem of Self-Love*, 145–52.

is the dispossession of one's own good for the sake of the Other. Both ways of construing God's love *in se* form the basis for understanding God's gift to creation, but with different emphases. Love oriented toward the possession of good for oneself identifies God's action toward creation as a Gift of the divine plenitude, the "overflow" of God's eternal and replete possession of his own goodness.[41] Here, the gratuity of God's love for creation is underscored, providing a strong ground for the distinction between Creator and creature. On the other hand, love oriented toward the Other's possession of the good identifies it instead as the continuation of the gift-giving that is the nature of God's own life itself. In this view, creation is seen as a continuation of both the giving and receiving between the trinitarian persons, with creation being given by God and returning to God as reciprocal gift in the missions of the Son and Spirit.

5. Beatitude vs. Fecundity

The final conceptual pair that emerges in articulating the nature of divine love identifies the ultimate way in which the perfection of love is depicted within God's *actus purus*. Within an emphasis on the substantial unity of the divine nature, in which love seeks enstatic possession, the perfection of divine love is identified with beatitude, the state of knowing and rejoicing in the perfect and full possession of the Good of the divine essence. If the divine persons take conceptual priority as those between whom divine love is ecstatically enacted as the disinterested dispossession of gift-giving, love fulfills itself as a generative fecundity identified in the presence of the Other. Love is the act in which the Other is given to be *qua* Beloved and hence is inherently fecund.

Speech of God: Revelation, Reason, and Analogical Predication

This project is situated between the two major conceptualizations of love in the trinitarian life identified by this fivefold architectonic. Behind the inclinations of any theologian or school toward one end of the spectrum, however, lies the question of how it is that thought and speech about God are grounded and carried out. How is the category of divine revelation parsed in relation to creation, Scripture, reason, and spiritual authority? What is the relationship between philosophy more generally, and metaphysics more

41. For example, see Webster, "Love Is Also a Lover of Life," 156–71.

specifically, and the witness of Scripture to divine action and self-revelation? How these questions are answered is fundamental to how love—or any other concept—is attributed to God. Creaturely concepts cannot be uncritically and univocally attributed to God without violently constraining God's self-revelation within the finitude of creation, but neither can they be attributed in a solely negative fashion without becoming purely equivocal and losing all purchase on the revelation truly meant to be a communication from God to creatures. Both Thomas Aquinas and Hans Urs von Balthasar, the two theologians who will take up most of my attention in this book, sought to answer these epistemological questions in ways that rightly ordered divine revelation in Scripture and the philosophical systems that provided ontological and metaphysical explanations for the created world in which humanity lives. Though a full treatment and defense of this issue for Thomas and von Balthasar is out of the scope of this project, a short word is needed to establish some central similarities and differences that have shaped my own reading and use of these thinkers.

The concept of analogical predication, often (though not by Thomas himself) referred to as the *analogia entis*, was central to both thinkers. For Thomas, the *analogia entis* functioned first as an *analogia proportionalitatis* that enabled within it an *analogia attributionis.*[42] The first, the analogy of proper proportionality, identifies an indeterminate proportion of two proportions.[43] It is not a pure proportion, where two terms are related to one another by a determinate and often mathematical proportion.[44] Rather, the *analogia proportionalitatis* "involves a comparison of two proportions or relations."[45] For example, the relation between creaturely *essentia* and creaturely *esse* is similar (in an undefined but true relation) to the relation between the divine *essentia* and the divine *esse*. From what is known about the creaturely relation between essence and existence, a similarity to the divine relation between essence and existence is asserted through a third, middle relation between them that is undetermined yet apophatically present. The fact that the middle relation cannot be determined and positively described is what enables the *analogia proportionalitatis* to emphasize the

42. For an analysis of Thomas, see Tabaczek, "Trace of Similarity," 102–17; Long, "Thomas Aquinas, the Analogy of Being, and the Analogy of Transferred Proportion," 173–92; Long, "Doctrine of God and the Analogy of Being," 1101–18; Betz, "Humility of God," 789.

43. The label "proper" follows Cajetan's division of *proportionalitas* into improper and proper; see Tabaczek, "Trace of Similarity," 105–6.

44. Thomas gives the example of two's relation to unity as its double; see *DV* q.2, a.11 *resp*; see also Tabaczek, "Trace of Similarity," 104.

45. Tabaczek, "Trace of Similarity," 105.

divine transcendence even while asserting a true analogy between God and creation. Within this transcendental assumption, an analogy of intrinsic attribution functions such that terms related within an undetermined relation in the *analogia proportionalitatis* receive a more specific relation without falling into the mathematical specification necessary for a simple proportion between two univocal terms. Here, *esse* as an intrinsic perfection of creatures is attributed to God as the First Cause and infinite source of the creaturely perfection, emphasizing the causal dependency of creatures upon God for their perfection and, therefore, divine immanence in that relation. Through holding these two forms of analogy together, Thomas carefully demarcated what can be said about the divine in three ways: *per modum causalitatis*, in which all things that exist in creation are understood to preexist in God as their cause; *per modum negationis*, in which all limitations or defects in what exists in creation are denied of God's existence; and *per modum eminentiae*, in which whatever is attributed to God is understood to exist in him in a higher way than in creatures.[46] Taken together, these three modes of analogical predication stress the truly ontological nature of Thomas's *sacra doctrina*, which does not remain at the level of epistemology but situates theology's confession of who God is by means of who and what creation is in relation to him.

In large measure, von Balthasar maintained the form of Thomas's *analogia entis* he inherited from his teacher Erich Przywara, which can be seen in the abiding presence of one of Przywara's favorite dictums, taken from Lateran IV: "Between the Creator and the creature so great a likeness cannot be noted without the necessity of noting a greater dissimilarity between them."[47] While the concept of the *maior dissimilitudo* continued to exert its influence on von Balthasar's thought, the *similitudines* between Creator and creation that he asserted within the ever greater dissimilarity of the *analogia proportionalitatis* became increasingly Christological, and thus trinitarian.[48] Rather than focusing as Thomas did on the analogical relation of *analogata* such as the transcendentals of goodness, truth, oneness, and being

46. See Aquinas, *ST* Ia, q.12, a.1; q.13, a.8 *ad* 2. This latter category is especially linked to Thomas's use of an *analogia proportionalitatis*, well expressed by Mascall: "The word *eminentius* expresses this fact, but it does not tell us precisely what that mode is, for it must clearly exceed the capacities of our understanding. All we can really say is that God's goodness is related to his infinite Being in a similar way to the way in which our goodness is related to our finite being. This statement is an example of what is technically called an analogy of proportionality" (*He Who Is*, 117).

47. See the text in Denzinger, *Sources of Catholic Dogma*, 171.

48. See Johnson, *Christ and Analogy*, as well as the discussions of von Balthasar's interaction with both Przywara and Barth in Betz, "After Barth"; McCormack, "Karl Barth's Version"; Casarella, "Hans Urs von Balthasar."

apart from his description of the trinitarian persons, von Balthasar made the transcendentals beauty, goodness, and truth the overarching themes of each part of his triptych, respectively, in order to demonstrate the trinitarian foundations and Christological revelation of his *analogia trinitatis* for each one organically.[49] In his own words, the concrete *analogia entis* revealed in and as Christ, as the union of God and man, is ultimately trinitarian in a personalist sense, as "a *proportionalitas*, a 'proportional relation between proportional relations,' that is, between the relation of difference between God and creature and the relation of difference between Father, Son, and Spirit."[50]

Thus, though von Balthasar self-consciously relied upon a Thomistic *analogia entis*, the way in which he did so falls on a different side of the Essential vs. Personal spectrum above. One commentator has expressed the result quite strongly, though likely with respect more to certain Thomists rather than to Thomas himself: "Von Balthasar, by firmly basing the *analogia entis* in Christology and Trinitarian theology, has kept his metaphysics from becoming a static structure that encompasses and shackles God. Rather, analogy is a vibrant principle that expresses the relation of creature and Creator, based solely in the Creator's triune life."[51] In this sense, this present thesis is an exploration of consequences that flow from these differences between Thomas and von Balthasar for a theological rendering of the Johannine claim that God is Love, as well as a constructive account of how these two emphases might be further brought together in a fuller trinitarian ontology of love.

Argument

As the underlying structure of this constructive thesis is that of theological retrieval, the movement toward my constructive portrayal of the divine life as love is primarily driven by interaction with the thought of Thomas

49. See the topical division of Thomas's discussion in *ST* Ia, qq.2–16 and qq.27–42, whereas von Balthasar explored the whole of theology, especially demonstrating its coherence in the hypostatic union and its foundations in the Trinitarian life of unity and distinction, under the heading of each transcendental individually; beauty in *The Glory of the Lord*, goodness in the *Theo-drama*, and truth in the *Theo-logic*; see White, "Introduction," 18; Bieler, "*Analogia Entis*," 317. See also Fiedler's discussion of the emergence of the *analogia trinitatis* in Haecker's work in the early twentieth century, which occasioned the rise of what has become trinitarian ontology ("Klaus Hemmerle on the Trinitarian Ontology," 62–64).

50. *TL2*, 316.

51. A. Franks, "Trinitarian *Analogia Entis*," 558.

Aquinas and Hans Urs von Balthasar. These two thinkers have been selected for three reasons. First, Thomas and von Balthasar shared an emphasis on retrieving and revising the metaphysics of early theologians, making them both productive conversation partners for a constructive thesis that aims to remain tethered to the theology of the universal church. While both were attentive to the past, they also sought to push their inherited concepts forward both theologically and philosophically. For instance, while Thomas used the language of substance metaphysics from an Aristotelian framework, he sought to develop this toward a metaphysics of being as act or event without leaving the language of essence behind.[52] Second, both Thomas and von Balthasar wrote prolifically and widely, leaving behind a theology that is not only systematic (though this is especially true in Thomas's case) but total in its attention to doctrinal *loci*. This creates the possibility of developing this project into different topics of theology while remaining in conversation with Thomas and von Balthasar. Third, Thomas was one of von Balthasar's most important interlocutors for his trinitarian metaphysics, especially regarding the relation of the divine persons to the divine essence, yet their systems differ significantly on how love is to be situated within the divine life *in se*. Because of this, the consequences of the decisions on which they differ are more easily traced through their treatments of the trinitarian life. In addition to Thomas and von Balthasar, I explore the thought of Ferdinand Ulrich and Klaus Hemmerle. As a speculative Thomist whom von Balthasar relied upon often, Ferdinand Ulrich provides a helpful and understudied conceptual link from Thomas to von Balthasar. Klaus Hemmerle then indicates a way to go further down the road indicated by Ulrich and von Balthasar.

By interacting with these four primary resources, I offer a reconfiguration of the notion of the divine *esse* according to the concept of *amor* so that what is common to the three divine persons is the eternally plerotic movement of mutually kenotic love. In doing so, I propose a concept of divine love that integrates both sides of my architectonic of love. Seeking to unify the essential and personal emphases, I develop a notion of divine love that conforms to the way in which the Father, Son, and Spirit reveal the divine life concretely, rather than define what is common to the divine persons in a way that is formally abstracted from the relations that distinguish and identify them. The act of love takes place both ecstatically and enstatically because the whole—the divine *esse*—is depicted as an event of love constituted as such by the dynamic participation of the persons in giving and

52. See Gilson, *Thomism*, 153–74. For a discussion of "event" as it might be understood in Thomas (as opposed to modern thinkers such as Heidegger, Barth, and Jenson), see Kerr, *After Aquinas*, 189–206.

receiving their very selves. In this movement of love, the divine persons are oriented to the Others, and each seeks the Good of the Beloved rather than their own, but in the perfect fecundity of mutual and absolute love, the self-gift of the Father and Son is not only returned but exceeded by the Spirit who infinitely enlivens the Father and Son as the free continuation and intensification of their love. Thus, self-emptying love is paradoxically also self-fulfilling, uniting Eros and Agape in a more dynamic and relational manner than Rousselot's physical love.

While this book provides a concept of trinitarian love particularly with respect to trinitarian inseity (that is, the inner, self-referential vantage point of the life of the three divine persons), this narrow focus supports two further goals: a renewed understanding of trinitarian promeity (that is, the relation of God toward creatures), and a trinitarian ontology of created being itself that revises the metaphysical categories often used by Christian theology while challenging the assumptions that have accompanied those categories in the past. In the latter, I specifically have in mind the assumption that oneness—even as a transcendental without measure—is best expressed in categories consistent with a unity derived from individual substances in creation. Instead, the revelation of the one God as three divine persons in relation to each Other demands that the concepts of unity, substance, and relation—the latter of which is normally classified as an accident—be reconsidered in light of a trinitarian *analogia proportionalitatis*. The manner of God's self-revelation also suggests that the concept of identity, tied by Thomas to the individuating principles of a substance, and thus to a relatively static concept of being as *essentia*, ought to be revised according to a dynamic event of becoming in which relations are constitutive of identity. When this alternative view of identity derived from relational act is brought into the realm of the creature, it does not necessarily need to lapse into infinite becoming or dissolve into flux if the horizontal relational acts between creatures are consistently contextualized with the fundamental, vertical relation of every creature to its Creator, as it is within this relation to the trinitarian God that the relational self-enactment of all creation finds its ultimate ground and fulfillment.

The sheer amount of writing linked to the thought of both Thomas and von Balthasar—both from their own pens and from their respective hordes of commentators—as well as the boundless complexities involved in metaphysical and trinitarian discourse of this kind demand a severe delimitation concerning what will be dealt with in a treatise of this size. Regarding corpus, I have focused primarily on Thomas's *Summa Theologiae*, though at times I mention relevant claims or sections from other works, especially his *Lectura Super Ioannem*. Attending to Thomas's commentary on John's Gospel provides a helpful foil to how von Balthasar integrates the Johannine portrayal of the trinitarian persons into his theology. As for von Balthasar, the *Theo-logic*, and especially the two final volumes, *The Truth of God* and *The Spirit of Truth*, receive the bulk of my attention. These have received much less attention than the other two panels of the triptych (*The Glory of the Lord* and *Theo-drama*), even though they are written later and constitute one of the final occasions for von Balthasar to respond to criticisms of his theology stemming from earlier writings. Furthermore, the two final volumes of the *Theo-logic* are the only volumes of the triptych explicitly dedicated to the Son and the Holy Spirit, marking them as one of the most concentrated places to discover the heart and integrative power of his trinitarian theology.[53] As with Thomas, I signal where other writings are relevant to my argument, though no part of my argument depends upon them. With respect to Thomas's commentators, at times I identify a certain line of interpretation that I am going to follow (such as the Gilsonian line of Existential Thomism); along the way, I maintain conversation with leading contemporary Thomists such as Gilles Emery and Thomas Joseph White. For von Balthasar, I have attempted to engage a wide array of scholarship on his thought, including works specifically on the triptych, both critical and appreciative. The two additional figures that loom large in chapters 3 and 4, Ferdinand Ulrich and Klaus Hemmerle, help to interpret and magnify von Balthasar's own thinking.

Outline

Chapter 1 contains my reading of Thomas's treatment of the divine essence and persons in the *Prima Pars* of the *ST*, beginning with an exploration of Thomas's understanding of *esse* as the *actus essendi* of every concretely existing being (*ens*). *Esse* is fundamentally an act, and, as *esse* and *essentia* are identical in God, Thomas provided us with a decidedly verbal conception of God's being, a divine motion that is ultimately oriented toward its own fullness as the absolute good. From this, I overview the way in which Thomas structured the intentional motion of the divine act by attributing the rational operations of knowing and willing to the divine *esse*, which provides a foundation in God's life for the procession of the Son and Spirit. To read Thomas rightly, his sections *de Deo uno* and *de Deo trino* must be understood as mutually informative formalities under which the same topic—the trinitarian God—is treated. However, I argue that this does not

53. Ide provides a helpful "state of affairs" in the reception and study of von Balthasar's ideas in his essay "L'Amour Est l'Acte Suprême."

ultimately exonerate Thomas from the charge of confining the unity of the divine life to a concept of *unio substantialis* derived from a single rational hypostasis. Though this effectively safeguards against any threat of tritheism and does not necessitate modalism, it does lead to a deferral of central aspects of love, such as the ecstatic movement toward the Beloved and the centrality of gift-giving, to the Spirit's mission in the economy rather than seeing these aspects of love within God's own life. The tensions between the scriptural naming of the Son and Spirit and Thomas's analogical attribution of the perfections of a rational hypostasis to the divine *esse* are clearly illustrated in his interpretation of a key trinitarian passage, John 3:34–35.

Chapter 2 presents a reading of Thomas's anthropology that comes later in the *ST*, arguing that love (*amor*) ought to be understood as a correlative of *esse*, being the fundamental movement of all *esse* toward *bonum* that is modified and shaped by the *essentia* of the *substantia* in which *esse* subsists. If all *esse* is the movement of *amor*, then in what way can beatitude, as the perfection of the intellect, be understood as the *finem* of rational natures? From the assumption of the convertibility of *esse* and *amor*, I argue that the rational operations ought to be understood not only as interdependent but as reaching to God *in finem* in a different way than Thomas suggested, with the union of love mediating the union of intellect that constitutes the beatific vision. This presents significant parallels to the love of friendship (*amor amicitiae*) and our external end of friendship with God, which establishes a *unio realis* within which the *unio substantialis* of creaturely beatitude might be obtained. Thomas did not pursue this line of thought in *de Deo*, I argue, because of his prioritization of a form of a *unio substantialis* which precludes the relational categories necessary for its coincidence with a *unio realis* within the *unio amoris*.

Chapter 3 turns to von Balthasar to continue developing a trinitarian concept of the divine life that begins and ends with love. In answer to the difficulties encountered at the end of the previous chapter, von Balthasar countered that we must define the divine essence in concert with the divine processions. For von Balthasar, there could be no gap between essence, procession, relation, and person, even in the formalities under which they are conceived. Building off of Lateran IV, von Balthasar presented the Father and Son as their own personal enactments of the divine *esse* as love in their kenotic self-giving to the Other. His concept of kenosis must be understood not as a diminution of any divine quality but as a manifestation of the selfless nature of the divine love itself. Von Balthasar's trinitarian pneumatology differs significantly from his presentation of the Father and Son, though this does not mean that the Spirit plays an ancillary part in his trinitarian concept. The Spirit's roles as Bond, Gift, and Fruit have been well documented in Balthasarian scholarship, but the influence of Ferdinand Ulrich's concept of *bonitas* has scarcely been registered in the English language. Drawing on trends in recent French scholarship, I argue that understanding the Spirit as the bonitic *finis* of the trinitarian life allows the identity of poverty and wealth that von Balthasar identified in the giving and receiving of love to flower into a fecundity of life rather than a static, reciprocated transaction. Kenosis remains as the heart of this vision of divine love, but this absolute and mutual kenosis of love surges forth in the infinite freedom of the Spirit who manifests the plerotic fulfillment of mutual kenotic love. As this stretches beyond what von Balthasar himself said about divine love, chapter 3 ends by echoing the concluding call of chapter 2 for further metaphysical revision.

Chapter 4 brings the arguments of the previous chapters to a close, drawing Thomas, von Balthasar, and Ulrich together through the categories of Klaus Hemmerle's trinitarian ontology, in which the "whole" is conceived as a "process" or "event" in which all the particulars are understood as "poles" identified and constituted by their participation in the action that is the "flow" of the "process" of love. The distinction between common and particular, or the one and the many, is not that of composition but participation, and not of participation by degrees but in and as the act of love itself. Ontology is verbalized, the subject is expanded into an identity from plural origins, and the whole and all particulars are understood within a widened concept of love. Read through an *analogia proportionalitatis*, this ontology provides an image of the relation between the divine persons as the particulars and the divine *esse* as the whole which leans on a perichoretic concept of unity without making that unity the result of a previously conceived act. Elevating *relatio* to the level of *esse* in this way builds upon Thomas's notion of subsistent relations but identifies the person more thoroughly with the act associated with that relation, which for von Balthasar and Hemmerle simply is that relation. The identity of the persons is not that of a previously constituted Subject only subsequently identified by relations but rather is constituted by and as the relational act that locates each in the Others. The Spirit attains to his unique role at this point, expressing both a Thou in relation to Father, to Son, and to both, and a We that includes yet exceeds them. This builds upon statements by Thomas, Ulrich, and von Balthasar concerning the Spirit's relation to the divine *esse* in his unique *modus existendi* as Love. Understood in its trinitarian fullness, the act of love can be characterized as *amicitia*, in which the essential *unio substantialis* and personal *unio realis* coincide in the relational simplicity of the one absolute life of God, who is Love.

After summarizing my constructive proposal, I end by following the *analogia proportionalitatis trinitatis* to suggest the implications for the relation between God and creation and the relations within creation itself. The divine act of creation becomes a continuation of the divine self-giving in the Spirit, affirming and expanding Thomas's position in the *ST*. Finally, the sacrament of baptism serves as an example of all aspects of the *analogia*, as it is the God who is fecund, self-giving love who acts in baptism to recreate creatures by bringing them into unity with his Son in the Spirit.

1

Amor Procedens

The Convergence of Love and Interiority in Thomas Aquinas's Trinitarian Theology

Introduction

As is often the case with theologians whose influence has endured for centuries, Thomas's trinitarian thought exhibits a genius that eludes easy categorization, giving rise to various schools of interpretation and continuing to prove generative for the task of constructive theology today. Drawing upon a wide range of theological and philosophical resources, Thomas presents a systematic and comprehensive vision of "God, and all things in God," the final version of this being found in his unfinished *Summa Theologiae*.[1] The crowning jewel of his trinitarian theology was undoubtedly his conceptualization of the divine persons as subsistent relations, which enabled Thomas to coherently maintain the substantial unity of the divine essence while positing three really distinct subsisting hypostases.

In this chapter, I will argue that though he is consistent philosophically, the way Thomas attributes the perfection of rational natures to God leads to a subtle priority of the essence over the persons, the concomitant subordination of threeness to oneness, and a related priority given to his treatment of the Son over that of the Spirit, despite Thomas's sophisticated attempts to defend against all these dangers. To substantiate these claims, I will provide an overview of Thomas's account of the divine essence,

1. See Webster's discussion of the nature of theology, which draws heavily from Thomas's *ST*, in "Principles of Systematic Theology." On the history of the *ST*, see McGinn, *Thomas Aquinas's Summa Theologiae*.

operations, and persons in the *ST* before engaging more critically with this material to argue that the above issues in Thomas's account of the divine life must be addressed by revising his starting assumptions, both metaphysical and methodological.

The first treatise after the introductory question on the nature of theology is *de Deo*, which is organized into three parts: the first concerns the divine substance and its operations; the second the procession of the divine persons; the third the emanation of the world from God, which I will leave to the side in this present study. One of Thomas's most significant metaphysical contributions, the real distinction between *essentia* and *esse* in creatures, is immediately present. The interpretation of this claim has been contested among various schools of philosophical and historical theologians, but the compelling interpretation of Étienne Gilson and the school surrounding him in the twentieth century identified this distinction as the cornerstone of Thomistic philosophy. *Esse* is not simply a modal or factual state of a created *essentia*, Gilson and company argued, but an act added to an essence to bring it to subsistence, and therefore, reality. As the distinction between essence and existence does not apply to God's simple being, I will argue that this means that God's being is most rightly understood in verbal terms. This means that to describe the divine *essentia* is to speak of the divine *esse*, which is spoken of in terms of *quomodo* rather than *quid*.

God's "verbal" *esse*, however, is not formless and void, but like the order brought to the primordial sea through God's divine act of creation, the *actus purus* of the divine nature displays an intentional ordering, which Thomas describes according to the rational operations identified in his Aristotelian anthropology: knowing (*intelligere*) and willing (*velle*). Unlike creatures, however, for God both operations are perfected without reference to anything outside of the divine nature. This does not mean that God does not know or will anything outside of himself, but that he knows and wills all things other than the divine essence only by knowing and willing the divine essence. These rational operations provide the basis for the procession of the Son and Spirit, who are identified by their relation to the origin of their procession. As everything in God is identical to the divine *esse*, these relations must subsist, rendering all the divine persons equally consubstantial. In this way, Thomas arrives at subsistent relations.

The restriction of the operations to the "internal respect" of God's being limits their object, properly speaking, to the divine essence itself rather than a specific divine person. God knows God, and the subsistent persons know God (essentially), but the persons do not know one another (personally). Instead, Thomas identifies notional acts by which these essential operations manifest themselves between the persons without introducing any multiplicity into the essence. While the Son and the Spirit process from the Father by virtue of the essential intellective and volitional operations, Thomas only speaks of the persons relating to one another through the notional acts. This results in a clear doubling of language throughout *de Deo*, and so Thomas must constantly clarify what language can be used essentially and what can be used personally to prevent any multiplicity from being attributed to the essence. Though the two aspects of the treatise on God are meant to be read in light of one another, in the end the balance of influence between the two sides tips in favor of the divine essence. Especially due to the way that the concepts of unity, intellect, and will are attributed to the divine essence, I argue that Thomas's treatment of the three divine persons is constrained within the image of the interiority of a single rational hypostasis by his previous treatment of the essence.

To maintain his system, Thomas severely restricts the operations that he attributes to the divine essence. This is especially true for the will, with the consequence that his descriptive account of love and of the Spirit, who proceeds by and as love, pales in comparison to the conceptual depth and systematic necessity of the intellect and the Son. To demonstrate that following Thomas's program in *de Deo* creates problems for the execution of the very task of theology, which is the explication of the knowledge of God as revealed in creation and especially in Scripture, I will analyze an instance of Thomas's exegesis from his *Lectura Super Ioannem* that illustrates the contorting effect of his metaphysical decisions upon his understanding of Scripture.

Aquinas on Divine Being: *Esse* as the Motion of Life

Within the first three questions of the *Summa Theologiae*, Thomas introduces a distinction between essence (*essentia*), the quiddity or "whatness" of a substance, and existence (*esse*), the actuality of a substance. This second category can be interpreted in at least two distinct ways. The first remains more faithful to Aristotelian categories by emphasizing that formal act is the fundamental reason for the existence of a substance, insofar as a substance is prime matter in potential to which formal act is added. In this sense, "act" refers simply to the actuality of an essence, the form of the being (*ens*) that is actual because it exists.[2] This interpretation identifies the static reality of the essence as the basic description of reality, a position that can be identified

2. This interpretation seems plausible from Thomas's early comment in *ST* Ia, q.3, a.4 *resp*: "Therefore existence must be compared to essence, if the latter is a distinct reality, as actuality to potentiality."

as essentialism, and by doing so relativizes (or denies) the philosophical significance of the distinction.[3] An alternative interpretation, which emerged in force in the early twentieth century among Existentialist Thomists such as Étienne Gilson, emphasizes that Thomas intended to make a *distinctio realis* between the two concepts in composite substances, and that *esse* is not to be understood only as the fact of existence but rather as "interior act . . . in virtue of which an essence [*essentia*] is a 'being' [*ens*]."[4] According to these interpreters, Thomas pushed beyond an Aristotelian essentialism to offer an "existential ontology" which identifies *esse* as an *actus essendi*, the act by which all *entia* subsist "*in rerum natura*," as Thomas puts it.[5] This act

3. See Knasas, *Being and Some Twentieth-Century Thomists*, 4–14, for an overview of various Aristotelian Neo-Thomists and their core ideas. Benedict Ashley, OP also provides a helpful categorization of the various schools of Thomism after *Aeterni Patris* in 1879, outlining eight differing camps of interpretation focused mainly on the task and access of metaphysics; see *Way Toward Wisdom*, 44–54. While he terms his own camp "Aristotelian" and that of Garrigou-Lagrange "Essentialist," there is continuity between the two in emphasizing the satisfactory nature of Aristotle's own metaphysical system. For an accessible history of Thomism as it has developed since Thomas's own time, see Cessario, *Short History of Thomism*.

4. Gilson, *Elements of Christian Philosophy*, 131. *Ens* can either refer to a specific "being" or the reality of existence in general that depends upon the presence of *esse*, or the *actus essendi*. This is related to Thomas's *esse*/*ens commune*; see *ST* Ia, q.3, a.4, as well as Thomas's comments in chapter 4 of "On Being and Essence," in *Opuscula I: Treatises*.

As with the Essentialist Thomists identified in Ashley, *Way Toward Wisdom*, 44–54, the "Existential" Thomists possess a similar continuity with the "Platonizing" Thomists in their emphasis on formal causality in God's act of creation, which undergirds the doctrine of participation present in both groups. The defining difference, as suggested here, is the Existential Thomist emphasis on *esse* as *actus essendi*. On this point, Fergus Kerr helpfully shows how this emphasis not only divides Existential Thomists from Analytics (such as Anthony Kenny) but also how it provides a clear link to the theology of Hans Urs von Balthasar, who self-consciously upheld this Thomistic insight as what enables his own theological project to stand; see Kerr, *After Aquinas*, 73–96.

5. Aquinas, "On Being and Essence," 4.8. See Gilson, *Thomism*, 153–74; Gilson, *God and Philosophy*, 63–75; Gilson, *Être et l'Essence*, 75–78, 81–123, 130, 135; Owens, *St Thomas and the Future of Metaphysics*; Kerr, *After Aquinas*, 181–206; Knasas, *Being and Some Twentieth-Century Thomists*, 173–212; González, Actus Essendi *and the Habit*, 1–175; Maryniarczyk, "*Parvus Error*," 32–33; Maurer, "Introduction," 14–19; White, "Divine Simplicity and Trinity," 77–79. A selection of references to *actus essendi* in Thomas's own work can be found in *Sent* I, d.8, q.1, a.1; d.8, q.4, a.2 *ad* 2; d.8, q.5, a.2; d.25, q.1, a.4; *DV* q.1, a.1 *ad* 3; "On Being and Essence," 1.18.

It is also important to note here that by "existential ontology," Gilson did not intend to do away with the category of essence entirely. The term "existential ontology" does not mean that creatures are *only* their *actus essendi*, nor the more modern option of only their existential experience or life. Essence still obtains as a creaturely category because creatures are limited and therefore can be defined over against other creatures that are like or unlike them. As Gilson says, "Insofar as a substance can be conceived as one and defined, it is given the name 'essence.' Essence then is only substance insofar

displaces form or essence as the "heart, or . . . very root of reality," a gift not included in any creature's essential definition but added to that *essentia* by its Creator.[6]

Thomas mentions this point of ontology in the very beginning of the *ST* to draw attention to the fact that the distinction between *esse* and *essentia* does not apply to God: the divine essence (*essentia*) is nothing else other than God's own existence (*esse*, or *actus essendi*). Unlike creatures, God's *esse* is necessary, not a contingent addition to his *essentia*: his *essentia* and *esse* are identical.[7] For Thomas, God is *ipsum esse per se subsistens*, being itself subsisting in itself.[8] As William Hoye puts it: "God does not *have* his being; he *is* his being."[9] However, if this being is conceived of as an *actus essendi*, the way in which God is described becomes decidedly more verbal than substantival. Fergus Kerr expresses this aspect in Thomas's thought well, saying, "In short, the risk for Thomas is not to reify God as a static or motionless entity, but rather, just the opposite, to make so much of the divine essence as activity . . . that God becomes sheer process, perpetuum

as it can be defined" (*Thomism*, 155). Instead, the *actus essendi* is that which allows for the *essentia* to truly exist within the concrete particular of the *ens*, not the other way around. This is mirrored in Hans Urs von Balthasar's later insistence on the continued importance and even interdependence of both concepts of *essentia* and *esse*; see *TL*1, 219; *TL*2, 182.

6. Gilson, *Thomism*, 159; see also Phelan, "Existentialism of St Thomas," 73; *ST* Ia, q.6, a.3 *resp*. This means that God is not properly a *substantia* (*ST* Ia, q.3, a.5 *ad* 1). As Gilson puts it, "there is no essence, or quiddity, to stand under (*sub-stare*, *sub-stantia*) his *esse*. The name 'substance' does not befit the pure actuality of God"; see "*Quasi Definition Substantiae*," 120. Nevertheless, Thomas does utilize both *essentia* and *substantia* in addition to *esse* to denote what is common to the three persons.

7. *ST* Ia, q.2, a.3; q.3, a.4. Francis Klauder calls this God's "basic perfection . . . the perfection from which our intellect understands all his other perfections to flow," which fits with the fact that Aquinas's discussion of God's "perfections" (including simplicity, perfection, eternity, etc.) come after this point is made (*Philosophy Rooted in Love*, 275). For an example of a strongly dissenting opinion, held by many analytic Thomists, see Kenny, *Aquinas*, 52–60; Kenny, *Aquinas on Being*, 139–58. Kenny calls this doctrine, as well as its creaturely inverse, Aquinas's "most overrated" and "least admirable contribution to philosophy" because he was unable to accept Aquinas's Neoplatonic belief that there can be degrees to *esse*, which is seen in his response to the Fourth Way in *ST* Ia, q.2, a.3 that *esse* cannot mean existence (see especially *Aquinas on Being*, 139, 148). Kenny seems to take existence as only a fact or state rather than an act that can therefore be carried out with different degrees of potentiality or actuality. For a summary of responses against Kenny, see Feser, *Scholastic Metaphysics*, 277–82. See also Knasas, *Thomistic Existentialism and Cosmological Reasoning*, 106–30, for responses to objections voiced against Thomas's doctrine by multiple analytic Thomists.

8. *ST* Ia, q.4, a.2 *resp*; see Owens, *St Thomas Aquinas on the Existence of God*; Oliver, *Creation*, 72.

9. Hoye, *Divine Being and Its Relevance*, 1.

mobile. Thomas's God . . . is more like an event than an entity."[10] Later, Kerr brings together the various concepts: "Thomas redescribes the God of Christian revelation in terms of *actus purus*: meaning both actuality and activity. Being is act."[11] God is "the act of sheer 'isness'" subsisting in itself and only described as itself.[12]

This has important consequences for how Thomas speaks of God. As perfectly simple, God's essence is, in Malet's words, "to not have an essence."[13] Rather, God's quiddity is pure act, the perfect and infinite actuality of every perfection that cannot be described in essential terms, as essence is a limiting concept linked to the finitude of creatures, who are distinct from one another by their differences.[14] Though Thomas continues to use the term *essentia* (as well as *substantia* and *natura*) to refer to what is common to the persons of the Godhead, this ought not to obscure the fact that God's "essence" must be conceived of as *ipsum esse per se subsistens*, or as Kerr puts it, pure "activity—though activity with a certain subsistency."[15] This dynamic concept requires that God be described in terms of how (*quomodo*) he is rather than what (*quid*) he is, as to speak of the divine *essentia* is to describe his *actus essendi*.

Thomas begins his discussion of the divine *modus existendi* in *de Deo uno* by attending to God under the formality of Creator, that is, in the relation between the divine *esse* and created *esse*.[16] To begin here is not to begin

10. Kerr, *After Aquinas*, 190.

11. Kerr, *After Aquinas*, 200. See also Burrell, *Aquinas*, 118. For the link between Aristotle and Thomas's shared insight that act is at the heart of being because "actuality is activity," see Kosman, "Substance, Being and Energeia."

12. Hill, *Three-Personed God*, 72; see also Clarke, *Creative Retrieval*, 120–22.

13. Malet, *Personne et Amour*, 101, my translation.

14. See Clarke's discussion of "thick" vs. "thin" concepts of essence as limits upon *esse* in *Creative Retrieval*, 129–31.

15. Kerr, *After Aquinas*, 190. Clarke, though unfortunately falling into indeterminate subject language, concurs: "The 'is' is deeper than the 'what.' And a sign of this is that Saint Thomas himself chooses a verb form, *esse* (to be), to express the subject in God, and not vice versa" (*Creative Retrieval*, 122).

In the present study, I follow the approach shared by both Thomas and von Balthasar by using essence (and *essentia*) and nature (and *natura*) to speak of God's *esse*, with which they are truly identical, to signify more accurately what is being asserted about God in a particular statement according to our way of understanding. For example, I will say that God knows the divine essence rather than that he knows the divine *esse* because the concept of essence implies the ability to be defined, which is possible for God of the divine essence, if only of God.

16. By using the term *modus essendi*, I intend to differentiate the discussion of the *quomodo* of the divine *actus essendi*, wherein the manner and pattern of the movement of the divine *esse* is considered, from discussion of the relative *modi existendi* of the

at a place irrespective of the divine persons, but rather to begin with the *principium quo*, that which is hypostatized and through which the persons act indivisibly.[17] Thus, God is one Creator and three persons creating, and the one *principium quo* relates to creation as transcendent cause. For Thomas the cause is revealed in its effects. The circular motion inherent to creaturely existence as it proceeds from God and returns to him, famously expressed by M.-D. Chenu in the phrase *exitus et reditus*, reveals both the movement of creation and, though negatively and transcendentally, the pattern of the *opus essentia divinae.*[18] As Hankey argues, the pattern of the *Quinque Viae* expresses this circular motion clearly at the beginning of the *Prima Pars*:

> This motionless motion structures the five ways of the proof, which allows us some understanding of God's being . . . Thomas starts with the source of motion and concludes with the final cause, so that there is a return to the motionless beginning. Between these two opposed causes are placed, first the material cause, and then the formal. The reduction of the material cause to God shows that there is no barrier to his efficacy. The formal

divine persons; see *DP* q.2, a.1 *ad* 13; Emery, "Personal Mode," 54.

17. See Malet, *Personne et Amour*, 85.

18. See Chenu, *Towards Understanding St. Thomas*, 304–5. Indeed, this is not far from what Thomas himself says about the course of the Summa, which will teach the knowledge of God "*non solum secundum quod in se est, sed etiam secundum quod est principium rerum, et finis earum*" (*ST* Ia, q.2 *intro*). See also Torrell, *Saint Thomas Aquinas*, 55; Hankey, *God in Himself*, 43–45; Lombardo, *Logic of Desire*, 29.

On this circular movement within *de Deo*, see Hankey, *God in Himself*, 116. After he establishes God's existence in Q. 2 of the *Prima Pars*, Thomas proceeds in Qq. 3–13 to qualify the manner of God's *actus* utilizing categories such as simplicity, perfection, infinity, immutability, eternity, and so on. The focus remains, throughout *De deo uno* and indeed through *De deo trino*, upon describing the existence of God as to the manner of this act or activity, rather than the quiddity of an essence.

Furthermore, it is important to note that Qq. 3–13 must be taken as an exercise in negative theology, as Thomas notes in the intro to Q. 3: "*Sed quia de Deo scire non possumus quid sit, sed quid non sit, non possumus considerare de Deo quomodo sit, sed potius quomodo non sit.*" Torrell, *Saint Thomas Aquinas*, 32–33, 38–39, helpfully distinguishes between different ways in which God's essence can be said to be unknown. For instance, for Dionysius God's essence remains "completely unknown," whereas for Thomas we "attain to him as unknown," giving a sense of positive knowledge of something that cannot be defined; at this point in the *ST*, God is "known as the unknown," an affirmation that is "true" if not "positive." See Owens, *St Thomas Aquinas on the Existence of God*, 159, for a discussion of the way that we might know God from his "effects" in the world. For a helpful account of the relationship between negative and positive statements about God in this section of the ST, see Velde, *Aquinas on God*, 66–79; Burrell, *God and Action*, 116; Davies, "Summa Theologiae on What God Is Not." On the role of divine names in Aquinas, instead of speaking of divine attributes, which suggest a quiddative description, see Soskice, "Being and Love," 483–85.

> is linked to the final, since the moving end is the good as known and perfected in form, here the divine essence itself. Thus, the being which God is may be said to return to itself.[19]

What Hankey terms "motionless motion" is the *actus purus* of God's *esse*, eternally full (motionless) yet eternally acting (motion).[20] One way to understand this "motion" is to start with how Thomas, drawing upon Aristotle's *Metaphysics*, delineates between two various kinds of action (*actio*) that exist in different relations to the actor (*agens*) and therefore to actuality (*actus*).[21] On one hand, *actio* that "passes out to external matter" is the perfection of the thing that is moved (*ipsius moti*) from potentiality into actuality, not of the actor who moves (*agens quod movet*). Here, the *actus* of the thing being acted upon is "movement" (*motus*). On the other hand, however, *actio* that remains in the *agens*, such as knowing (*intelligere*), sensing (*sentire*), and willing (*velle*), is the perfection of the actor itself because it is an *actus* that moves its *agens* rather than another object. So, while movement in the first category is the *actio* of something in potentiality being

19. Hankey, *God in Himself*, 55. See the famous *Quinque Viae* in *ST* Ia, q.2, a.3 *resp.* For a conceptual expansion of this text, see Davison, *Participation in God*, 11–130.

The only modification I would make to Hankey's reading is to distinguish more clearly between the First Way and the following four. The First Way gives God the famous epithet of First Mover, but this is distinct from the way that God relates to the four Aristotelian causes in the remaining ways. For example, God as First Mover is not identical with God as first efficient cause (*secunda via*), though there is a close relationship. The *prima via* establishes that the relation between God and creation is one of dependence, establishing a sort of theological method for speaking about the divine life based on the structures of created being. As Hankey says elsewhere, "The motion and multiplicity within the divine spiritual life is the intelligible pattern and basis of the motion and multiplicity at the lower levels" (*God in Himself*, 56). The motion of the world, both in its movement and the way in which it moves, is oriented and driven by the motionless-motion of God's *esse*, which the remaining four ways illustrate. The subject in all these demonstrations is "the unmoved source of the motion, existence, goodness, and perfection of all else" (Hankey, *God in Himself*, 41). For an account of the *Quinque Viae* which most closely follows my adaptation of Hankey, see the essays "The Starting Point of the Prima via" and "The Conclusion of the Prima via" in Owens, *St Thomas Aquinas on the Existence of God*. For an alternative account based on a different conceptualization of actuality, both created and as attributed to God, see Kenny, *Aquinas on Being*, 135–41; Kenny, *Five Ways*, 46–95.

20. Gilson convincingly argues that it is created *esse* rather than *essentia* that is in view in the *Quinque Viae* (*Spirit of Mediaeval Philosophy*, 73). Gilson's argument provides sufficient ground on which to understand Hankey's argument of analogy from the *Quinque Viae* to the *opus divinae* as God's *actus essendi* (Hankey, *God in Himself*, 54). See also "Aquinas and the Five Ways" in Owens, *St Thomas Aquinas on the Existence of God*, especially p. 134; cf. the critique of Chenu's interpretation of the Five Ways in Smith, *Thomas Aquinas' Trinitarian Theology*, 13–17, 22.

21. See *ST* Ia, q.18, a.3 *ad* 1; I–II, q.31, a.2 *ad* 1.

moved into actuality (*actus*), in the second the *actio* is the movement of the actor itself *in actu*. The latter *actio* is the movement of life (*vita*) itself, which Thomas attributes to God in the "most perfect degree."[22] While the movement of change from potentiality into actuality is denied in God,[23] there is nonetheless a motion of the divine *vivere* closer to the Aristotelian *energeia* ("actuality") than *kinesis* ("movement").[24] God is not static but moves perpetually in a perfect action (*actio*) that is eternally replete in itself.[25]

Expressed within the Aristotelian framework of causality found in the *Quinque Viae*, the perpetually perfect motion of the divine life is itself the constant attainment of its final cause. The category of final causality implies the concept of goodness, as, in Hankey's words, "the moving end (*ratio finis*) is the good as known and perfected in form."[26] Said differently, goodness is the end which all acts desire. Thomas lays out a conceptual chain linking *bonum*, *perfectus*, *actus*, and *esse*, where *bonum* signifies the notion of desirability inherent in *perfectus*, which is the measure of *actus*, which is the measure of *esse*. *Esse* is *primus actus*, the first act of existing possessed by all substances, while *bonum* is *ultimus actus*, the ultimate perfection of the form.[27] Thus, to be fully in act is to be fully Good. By this logic, for God to be *esse per suam essentiam* is for God to be *actus purus*, which is for God to be *perfectissimum*, and therefore *bonum per suam essentiam* as the "ultimate perfection" of the divine *esse* simply considered.[28] By providing a rationale of the tendency of the act of *esse*, the concept of desirability gives

22. *ST* Ia, q.18, a.1 *obj/ad* 1; see Hankey, *God in Himself*, 103–4.

23. *ST* Ia, q.9, a.1 *ad* 1; see also q.18, a.4 *ad* 1, where Thomas's citation of Acts 17:28 makes it clear that the movement denied to God is that of the change seen in the created order.

24. See Oliver, "Trinity, Motion, and Creation Ex Nihilo," 181–82.

25. See Oliver, *Philosophy, God and Motion*, 85–137; Oliver, "Trinity, Motion, and Creation Ex Nihilo," 136–39. It is for this reason that I prefer Hankey's paradoxical phrase over other options that attempt to render First Mover in more descriptive terms, such Thomas Gilby's "immobile principle" whose "stillness is that of pure activity" ("First Way," 191–95). While this phrase gestures toward the concurrence of opposites in God's *actus purus*, I prefer the term "motionless-motion" because it avoids the negative connotations of an enclosed, unrelatable entity while including the paradoxical fullness of God's simple perfection. Similarly, Joseph Owens offers a reading of the *Summa contra Gentiles* in which he argues for an "immobile movent." However, his concept of *actus purus* in many ways mirrors the reading given above, and the link that he draws between motion and existence is particularly helpful in connecting the two interpretations; see *Aquinas on the Existence of God*, 208–27.

26. Hankey, *God in Himself*, 55.

27. *ST* Ia, q.5, a.1.

28. *ST* Ia, q.5, a.1 *ad* 1; q.4, a.1; q.6, a.3 *resp*. See Kwasniewski, *Ecstasy of Love*, 169–70; Velde, *Aquinas on God*, 88.

further detail to the divine act as the perpetually fulfilled *motus ad intra* of the absolute living Good.[29] The divine *actio* is not an immobile rest but the "unchanging activity" of a perfect spiritual nature enjoying the dynamic and eternal fulfillment of the divine *esse* as ultimate *finis*. Therefore, the attainment of *bonum* is not the static ending point of God's *esse* but signifies that very motion in its continuing fullness as *vita* and *actus*.[30]

The Operations of the Divine Life

Thomas's identification of the divine *esse* as *bonum per suam essentiam* signals that the movement of the divine life has, in Hill's words, "intentionality"; it is a "pure dynamism . . . [that] cannot be chaotic, unintelligible, utterly without meaning."[31] In order to provide an account of how this intentionality obtains in the divine *modus vivendi*, Thomas moves from considering the *quomodo* of the divine *actus essendi* to the *operationes vitae* he considers most fittingly attributed to God through the *via eminentiae*, *intellectus* and *voluntas*.[32] Though these two powers relate to the same object under two

29. Thomas avoids specifying a *causa finalis* or the related concept of self-diffusivity with respect to the divine *esse* itself because of the tendency of causal language to imply the very kind of motion of change that he was concerned to exclude from the divine simplicity. While this language can be found in some Victorine theologies to differentiate the trinitarian persons, Joseph Wawrykow is correct that Thomas instead opts to rely on his theory of subsistent relations to demonstrate the necessary distinction ("Franciscan and Dominican," 194). However, others suggest that some form of causal thinking is evident within Thomas's doctrine of God, seen principally in the convertibility of *bonum* and *esse* within the divine life; see Hill, *Three-Personed God*, 79; Kwasniewski, *Ecstasy of Love*, 117n38. Garrigou-Lagrange comes close to this suggestion in a slightly different register, claiming that although God's operations (meaning acts in relation to creation) are uncreated and therefore "have no cause, not even a final cause . . . . Still, in a sense, divine goodness is the purpose of God's free acts . . . God, says St Thomas, though He is not moved by purpose, still acts for a purpose. God is not his own cause, but He is His own reason" (*Beatitude*, 41). Similarities can be traced between God being "His own reason" and Thomas's interpretation of the self-diffusivity of the Good, which moves as the end or fulfillment of all motion rather than as an efficient or formal cause; see *ST* Ia, q.5, a.4 *ad* 2; *DV* q.21, a.1 *ad* 4; Hill, *Three-Personed God*, 79; Wippel, *Metaphysical Themes II*, 226–27; Kwasniewski, *Ecstasy of Love*, 60.

For an overview and analysis of Thomas's adoption and adaptation of Aristotle's category of final causality, see Follon, "Finalisme."

30. See *ST* Ia, q.6, a.1 *ad* 2. See also C. Franks, "Simplicity of the Living God," 280; Oliver, "Trinity, Motion, and Creation Ex Nihilo," 136–39.

31. Hill, *Three-Personed God*, 261.

32. *ST* Ia, q.10, a.1 *ad* 2; q.2 *intro*; q.14 *intro*. See Phelan, "Existentialism of St Thomas," 81, for his attempt to orient the concept of *actus essendi* as the "living source of dynamic power" for all specific operations, whether immanent or transient; contra Elders, *Metaphysics of Being*, 204–5.

different yet transcendentally convertible formalities—truth (*verum*) and good (*bonum*), respectively—Thomas's intellectualism is displayed in his insistence upon a clear order of these two operations, with the appetitive following the apprehensive.[33] In this way, the "latent intentionality" of the divine *actus essendi* "achieves explicit articulation in the concepts of knowing and willing as these activities give form and structure to the being of spirit."[34] In this section, I will present the intellect and will as Thomas does in *de Deo uno* by first describing the created analogue and then how they are attributed to the divine life, noting several places where Thomas restricts the created analogue by the *via negativa*.[35]

The basic act of the intellect is to reproduce internally "the form of some other thing" apart from itself through apprehending the intelligible form (which is the *essentia*) of the distinct object and reproducing that form enstatically (or, within itself) as an idea, such that "the thing known is in the knower."[36] As Schindler puts it, for Thomas knowing is "quite literally 'internalizing' [the] intelligible form."[37] Following this, in the final moment of judgment (*iudicatio*), or "composition and division," the intellect recognizes the correspondence between its intelligible form and the intelligible object

---

According to Aquinas, a rational nature is more perfect than a sensible (or non-sensible) nature due to their ability to abstract and relate to the forms of external objects. Because all perfections can be attributed to God according to his mode of existing (*ST* Ia, q.4, a.1), God can be understood by way of analogy as a rational nature; see also *ST* Ia, q.14, a.1; Klauder, *Philosophy Rooted in Love*, 301–2. For the link between being, living, and these "psychological" categories, see Bourassa, "Esprit Saint, 'Communion,'" 257; Hill, *Three-Personed God*, 261; Gilson, *Thomism*, 114; Hankey, *God in Himself*, 103.

33. *ST* Ia, q.19, a.1 *resp*; Emery, *Trinitarian Theology of Aquinas*, 58–59.
On the relation between the objects of the rational operations and the transcendentals, see *ST* Ia, q.5, a.1; q.14, a.6; q.16, a.1, 4; q.20, a.1. See also Gilson, *Thomism*, 155; Schindler, "Towards a Non-Possessive Concept of Knowledge," 582, later republished in condensed form as Schindler, "Does Love Trump Reason."

34. Hill, *Three-Personed God*, 261; *ST* Ia, q.18, a.3, *resp*. Thomas makes clear that the operations to which he turns express in new terms the same motion of life attributed to God in the earlier questions. See *ST* Ia, q.19, a.1 *ad* 3; Torrell, *Saint Thomas Aquinas*, 162–63.

35. As I will explore in the next chapter, Thomas's account of the rational operations differs in large measure in *de Deo uno* from later sections on the scope of the rational operations. It is noteworthy, though, that what Schindler calls "conventional" presentations of Thomas's epistemology tend to share the limitations present in *de Deo uno* rather than expressing the full scope of Thomas's actual epistemology; see Schindler's helpful example of one of these "conventional" presentations in Maritain, *Three Reformers*; cited as an example in Schindler, "Towards a Non-Possessive Concept of Knowledge," 580–89.

36. *ST* Ia, q.14, a.1; q.16, a.1 *resp*.

37. Schindler, "Towards a Non-Possessive Concept of Knowledge," 581.

itself as well as the enduring difference between the *essentia* that is reproduced in understanding and the *actus essendi* of the object that is known.[38] The will follows upon the intellect because the object apprehended by the intellect is then presented to the will, which is the appetitive faculty by which a rational nature "tends" toward the presented object, seeking union with it insofar as it is desirable as *bonum*.[39] It is possible to organize the act of the will into three moments: first, love (*amor*) is "the first movement of the will and of every appetitive faculty" that "regards good universally"; second, desire (*desiderium*) or hope (*spes*) "regard[s] good not as yet possessed"; third, joy (*gaudium*) or delight (*delectatio*) "regard[s] good present and possessed."[40]

Through these two powers, rational natures apprehend the truth of reality and navigate their way toward union with the Good. The end (*finem*) of a rational nature is twofold: considered as the end itself (*finis cuius*, or the "objective" end), it is God; as the end by which the objective end is obtained (*finis quo*, or the "subjective" end), it is the perfection of the intellect, which is itself the highest operation of a rational nature by which the objective end is enjoyed by the subjective end.[41] This latter end is what Thomas identifies as beatitude (*beatitudo*, or happiness), which is when a rational nature possesses by its intellect a "sufficiency of the good" that its will desires.[42] Beatitude is, therefore, specifically the perfection of the intellect, the full actuality of the intellect knowing and possessing the object of its highest good within itself.[43] While *in via* the object known by the intellect and desired by the will remains outside of the knower in reality due to its materiality, for Thomas, the beatitude of a rational nature is not in possession of any created object but rather the intellect's perfect possession of God through its vision of the divine essence.[44] As immaterial, God is not constrained to remain outside the intellect, but when the created intellect beholds God directly in the vision of glory, "the essence of God itself becomes the intelligible form of the intellect."[45] While God is not comprehended by creatures in the sense

38. *ST* Ia, q.16, a.2. See Gilson, *Elements of Christian Philosophy*, 226–32.

39. See Gallagher, "Thomas Aquinas on the Will as Rational Appetite"; Mitchell, "Free to Be Human," 31–32.

40. *ST* Ia, q.20, a.1 *resp*; I–II, q.26, a.2. For a more detailed account of the structure of the will and the relation between love, desire, and delight, see Lombardo, *Logic of Desire*, 49–74; Kwasniewski, *Ecstasy of Love*, 178.

41. See *ST* Ia, q.26, a.3 *ad* 2; I–II, q.2, a.8 *resp*.

42. *ST* Ia, q.26, a.1 *resp*.

43. See *ST* Ia, q.26, a.2 *resp*.

44. See *ST* Ia, q.12, a.1, 4; q.14 *intro*, *ad* 3; q.16, a.1; q.26; a.1; q.82, a.1; I–II, q.3, a.8.

45. *ST* Ia, q.12, a.5 *resp*.

of knowing God insofar as he is knowable, as his infinity exceeds all finite capacity, they do comprehend God in that "in seeing him, they possess him as present, having the power to see him always."[46] This allows the creature to understand God according to its finite mode of knowing, thereby attaining to a perfect enstatic union of knowledge with God.[47] Delight, as the operation of the will resting in the good that is possessed, is concomitant to this intellectual perfection, a "proper accident" rather than belonging to the essence of *beatitudo*.[48]

When Thomas discusses in what ways these operations can be properly attributed to the divine life in *de Deo uno*, his justification is based solely on the intellect. As knowledge is based upon the possession of intelligible forms, and a form is more infinite and perfect inasmuch as it is immaterial—that is, uncontracted by its instantiation by matter—a knower's "mode of knowledge" is dependent upon the "mode of immateriality."[49] But God is not uncontracted, created *esse*, which is perfect in one way while still needing the limitation of matter to subsist.[50] Instead, God is *esse per se subsistens*, completely immaterial, infinite, perfect, and subsisting in itself without the need for the limitation of materiality. As such, God occupies "the highest degree of immateriality," and thus, "it follows that He occupies the highest place in knowledge."[51] God's immateriality is not univocal with the immateriality of created forms, though, as the divine *esse* is *per se subsistens*; thus, the intellectual act in which knowledge is found is attributed to the divine life *secundum eminentiorem modum*. It is because intellect is attributed to God that both the will and beatitude are likewise attributed, as they are implied by the intellect itself as the correlated *appetitus* and the perfection of the intellect itself, respectively.[52]

A controlling concern for Thomas when attributing operations to God is that they must both remain and possess their full actuality *in ipso Deo*.[53]

46. *ST* Ia, q.12, a.7 *ad* 1.

47. See *ST* Ia, q.12, aa.1, 5–6; I–II, q.3, a.8; Schindler, "Towards a Non-Possessive Concept of Knowledge," 584.

48. *ST* I–II, q.2, a.6; see also q.3, a.4; q.4, a.1; Ia, q.26, a.2.

49. *ST* Ia, q.14, a.1.

50. See *ST* Ia, q.45, a.4.

51. *ST* Ia, q.14, a.1 *resp*.

52. See *ST* Ia, q.19, a.1 *resp* for his comments on the will, and q.26, a.2 *resp* for his comments on beatitude.

53. See *ST* Ia, q.14 *intro*, aa.2–4; q.37, a.1; Hankey, *God in Himself*, 103. This does not exclude God's knowledge of or love for creation, as q.25, a.1 *ad* 4 makes clear. Rather, Thomas defines two "terms," or "points of termination," for the divine operations, and both intellect and will find their commensurable object in the divine essence alone, by

While for rational creatures the intellect is oriented outward toward intelligible species that are not their own forms and the will is oriented outward to goods that are not already possessed, for God both operations find their fundamental termination point in the divine essence itself. Thus, the divine intellect is perfect in its identity with the divine act, such that God's "intellect, and the object understood, and the intelligible species, and His act of understanding are entirely one and the same."[54] God's understanding of the divine essence and of everything created through his understanding of himself is the perfection of the divine intellect, so that "when God is said to be understanding, no kind of multiplicity is attached to His substance."[55] Because of this, *iudicatio* does not apply to God's knowledge of the divine essence itself, and only to his knowledge of all things through the divine essence by virtue of the "simple act of intelligence [in which He] judges of all things and knows all things complex."[56] Since *iudicatio* is properly correlated with the imperfection of finite intellectual acts and objects, it is only attributed to the divine intellect because God is truth by virtue of the identity of his being and act of intellect.[57]

The will, too, is shorn of "everything that savors of imperfection" when applied to the divine *esse*.[58] Just as with the divine intellect, the *appetitus intellectivus* is identical to God's *esse*.[59] Because this operation also has the divine essence as its object, the will is limited for Thomas to the third phase of loving and rejoicing in the Good that God possesses, which is the divine *esse* itself.[60] Thomas rejects the notion of *desiderium* in the divine life *ad intra* because the divine will is identical to the Good that it always possesses, restricting the ecstatic aspect of the divine will to God's relation to creation.[61] As God always knows that he perfectly possesses the Good of the divine *esse* "in a most excellent manner," beatitude, "the perfect good an intellectual nature . . . which is capable of knowing that it has a sufficiency of

---

which they are perfected internally. Nonetheless, these two "terms" do not describe two acts of knowing or willing but only two different relations of the one single act of God's life; see Levering, "Christ, Trinity, and Predestination"; Emery, *Trinitarian Theology of Aquinas*, 36–50.

54. *ST* Ia, q.14, a.4.

55. *ST* Ia, q.14, a.4; see also a.5.

56. *ST* Ia, q.16, a.5 *ad* 1.

57. See *ST* Ia, q.16, a.5 *resp*.

58. *ST* Ia, q.14, a.1 *ad* 2.

59. See *ST* Ia, q.19, a.1.

60. See *ST* Ia, q.19, a.1 *ad* 2.

61. For example, see *ST* Ia, q.20, a.2 *ad* 1, and the related restriction of the Holy Spirit's name, Gift, to his actually being given in creation in q.38, a.1 *ad* 4.

the good which it possesses," also "belongs to God in the highest degree."[62] Thus, divine beatitude is, as for creatures, the perfection of the divine intellect rather than the divine will, as the intellectual operation is that by which the rational nature "grasps everything."[63] Thus, to be happy (*esse beata*) is related to the intellectual operation as its perfection, or full actuality, just as in creatures.

The Trinitarian Persons

In the course of his discussion on the *operationes vitae* in God, it is clear that Thomas is setting up a form of the psychological analogy introduced to Western theology by Augustine in the fourth century, though in a more scholastic manner.[64] While Thomas also adopts Augustine's emphasis on *relatio* to understand the divine persons, Thomas begins *de Deo trino* by focusing on the concept of procession in God because the relations which allow him to identify and distinguish the persons are established by distinct processions, motions from a principle toward an end that establish a relation between the two.[65] As Thomas holds that "*omnis processio sit secundum aliquam actionem*," he must identify two acts by which the processions are put into motion but, importantly, which also remain *in ipso Deo*.[66] If not already suspected, the reader realizes that there is an additional reason for identifying and describing *intellectus* and *voluntas* in God in the way that Thomas does. By identifying them as the only immanent operations that remained internal to the agent and by establishing the perfection of their operation in God on their identity with their object, Thomas perfectly sets up the transition from a discussion of their fittingness to be analogically predicated of God to their fittingness as *actiones* to establish the *processiones*, and therefore connection between the divine *esse* and the relations of

62. *ST* Ia, q.26, a.1 *resp*. See also *LSI* 14.1853.

63. *ST* Ia, q.26, a.2; see Wittman, "Logic of Divine Blessedness," 135. This notion depends upon Thomas's theory of the internalization of what is known through the operation of the intellect discussed above.

64. See Emery, "Dignity of Being a Substance."

65. *ST* Ia, q.27 *intro*; q.28, a.1.

66. *ST* Ia, q.27, a.1 *resp*. Thomas rejects the use of cause and effect language here because an effect is generally understood to be external to the cause. This is more transparent in the case of the Arian emphasis on the createdness of the Son, as this was necessarily extrinsic to the divine essence. Thomas applies this same logic to Sabellianism, suggesting that God is only called Son "in assuming flesh" and the Holy Spirit "in sanctifying the rational creature," both of which are effects extrinsic to the divine act itself, which is identified as the Father.

the persons. To put it simply, it is his careful analogical attribution of his anthropological categories to the divine *esse* that allows Thomas to identify and differentiate the divine processions (and thus relations and persons) while remaining within the divine essence so conceived.[67] He makes his method clear, stating:

> The divine processions can be derived only from the actions which remain within the agent. *In a nature which is intellectual, and in the divine nature, these actions are two, the acts of intelligence and of will.* The act of sensation, which also appears to be an operation within the agent, takes place outside the intellectual nature, nor can it be reckoned as wholly removed from the sphere of external actions; for the act of sensation is perfected by the action of the sensible object upon sense. *It follows that no other procession is possible in God but the procession of the Word, and of Love.*[68]

These processions, one of the intellect and one of the will, establish a relation of origin between that which proceeds and the principle of the procession.[69] But because these divine operations are only logically distinct *in re*, they themselves do not provide a ground for the real relation (and thus distinction) between Son and Spirit. Rather, it is only in that they proceed by "dint," to use Emery's expression, of these operations, as the fruit of a particular "action of knowledge and love," that they are distinct.[70] Thus, to identify the divine persons, the essential operations must be understood within the personal nexus of the notional acts.

This transition is one of the most difficult to grasp in Thomistic thought, as its coherency is not easily adaptable to modern sensibilities. As Gilson puts it, in the essential act of divine knowing, "God is known in God knowing," but this only "finds its full sense in the affirmation 'the

67. However, it should not be said that Thomas has only considered the philosophical utility of this structure, for Thomas identifies multiple scriptural, traditional, and theological grounds for following this particular path; see *ST* Ia, q.27, a.1 *sed contra, resp*; q.27, a.3 *sed contra*; q.28, a.4; see also Thomas's comments in *LSI* 1.24–33, 221; 13.1845; 14.1909, 1911, 1941, 1959; 17.2214.

68. *ST* Ia, q.27, a.5 *resp*, emphasis added.

69. The Holy Spirit does not proceed from the will conceived as a free, contingent decision, such as the decision to create is often conceived. Rather, the Holy Spirit proceeds as Love, as shall be seen, a metaphysically necessary ecstatic movement toward the Good that is nonetheless carried out in true freedom; see Malet, *Personne et Amour*, 120–21.

70. Emery, *Trinitarian Theology of Aquinas*, 70. This expresses that the processions proceed in certain modes, proceeding "by" (*par*) intelligence or will; see also Malet, *Personne et Amour*, 121.

Father speaks the Word,' where it manifests its intelligibility."[71] Malet goes further than this, arguing that Thomas has "personalized" the divine essence because it is the essence through which the divine persons act, and therefore it must be understood in personal categories from the beginning in order to "play its part" in the notional acts.[72] In either case, whether as its manifestation or intended purpose, the language of *de Deo uno* is ordered toward *de Deo trino*. In his notional act, the Father speaks only what he knows, and as a hypostasis of the divine essence, that means that the Father speaks the divine essence, indeed, the "whole Trinity" itself.[73] The Word that proceeds from the Father's act of speaking signifies what the Father knows, which is the whole of the divine essence itself. Because the Word is a perfect "likeness of the object [intellectually] conceived," the speaking of the Word is simultaneously the generating of the Son.[74] Both names, Son and Word, simultaneously point to the consubstantiality of the Son, or Word, with the Father, or Speaker, and to the distinction inherent in his procession from an origin. The content of the Word is identical to the nature of the Speaker, and they remain distinct in this relation only.[75] Thomas is careful to define the Word as the "concept of the intellect," as opposed to a "vocal sound" or that which is signified by that sound, in order to maintain the inward terminus of his procession.[76] For the Son to be generated "by way of an intelligible operation" is for the Son to exist within the Godhead as the personal hypostatization of God-spoken.[77]

Likewise, the essential act of divine willing is ultimately manifested in the notional acts of the Father and Son loving one another, by dint of which the Spirit proceeds as the Love between the Father and Son. While the Father and Son can be said to love one another "by their essence," the Father and Son can also be said to love one another notionally, just as the Father's speaking is his personal manifestation of his essential knowing.[78] The Father and Son loving each other notionally "means nothing else than *to spirate love*; just as to speak is to produce a word."[79] The Love that is spirated is the Holy Spirit as the Love proceeding between Father and Son, distinct as a

71. Emery, "Essentialism or Personalism," 545.

72. Malet, *Personne et Amour*, 78–79, 86, 138–39.

73. *ST* Ia, q.34, a.1 *ad* 3.

74. *ST* Ia, q.27, a.2 *resp.*

75. See *ST* Ia, q.27, a.1 *resp*; Emery, *Trinitarian Theology of Aquinas*, 70; *LSI* 5.750.

76. *ST* Ia, q.34, a.1 *resp.*

77. *ST* Ia, q.27, a.3 *resp.*

78. *ST* Ia, q.37, a.2 *resp.*

79. *ST* Ia, q.37, a.2 *resp.*

procession from his origin. As the love that proceeds between the Father and Son, the Spirit is the "*habitudo amoris ad rem amatam*," the "*nexus patris et filii*."[80] The Spirit is not reduced to only a *nexus* between the Father and Son but is himself a divine person, a relation (of origin) subsisting in the divine *esse*.[81] However, like the Word, the *amor procedens* is likewise restricted by deriving the interiority of love from the interiority of the *verbum mentis*: "so when anyone loves an object, a certain impression results, so to speak, of the thing loved in the affection of the lover; by reason of which the object loved is said to be in the lover."[82] Thomas takes advantage of a similarity between *spiritus* and *amor* to tie these two names for the Spirit together, explaining that *spiritus* signifies an "a certain vital movement and impulse, accordingly as anyone is described as moved or impelled by love to perform an action."[83]

Thus, the divine processions are defined in relation to the essential operations as they exist in a rational hypostasis. The Son and Spirit proceed not from the essential operations as such, but from the notional acts that manifest those essential acts relationally. As these two processions each imply their origin, they establish double relations, paternity-filiation and spiration-procession.[84] The Father relates to the Son through paternity and to the Spirit through spiration; the Son relates to the Father through filiation and to the Spirit through spiration; the Spirit relates to the Father and to the Son through procession.[85] While "relation in its own proper meaning signifies only what refers to another" as "purely outward-bound," it is important that they are real relations, truly existing in God himself.[86]

Here, Thomas's theory of the divine persons as subsistent relations comes into focus.[87] Having identified two operations of the divine *esse* to notionally establish two distinct processions that establish real relations

80. *ST* Ia, q.37, a.1 *ad* 2–3; see also Torrell, *Saint Thomas Aquinas*, 186. It is this understanding of the Holy Spirit as bond that leads Thomas to clearly see the implied presence of the Holy Spirit in the Scriptures where the Father and Son are mentioned, "especially in matters pertaining to the grandeur of the divinity," because the Holy Spirit is "the bond of the Father and Son"; see *LSI* 6.1004; 17.2187.

81. See *ST* Ia, 1.37, a.1 *ad* 3.

82. *ST* Ia, 1.37, a.1 *resp*.

83. *ST* Ia, q.27, a.4; see also q.36, a.1; *LSI* 15.2062.

84. See *ST* Ia, q.27, a.1 *resp*; q.28, a.4 *resp*.

85. *ST* Ia, q.28, a.4.

86. Emery, *Trinitarian Theology of Aquinas*, 93. For a succinct overview of these different types of relations, see Oliver, *Creation*, 48–50.

87. For the following concept of subsistent divine relations, see especially *ST* Ia, qq.27–29, 39–40; Malet, *Personne et Amour*, 90–105; Emery, *Trinitarian Theology of Aquinas*, 84–103; Emery, "Dignity of Being a Substance," 994–97; Levering, *Scripture and Metaphysics*, 220.

between the divine persons, Thomas points out that though relations have an accidental existence in creatures, anything "considered as transferred to God" is identical to his essence, as the divine essence is perfectly simple.[88] The term *persona* is not equated with *relatio*, however, but includes *relatio* in its signification along with the *essentia* in which the relation subsists. *Persona* signifies what is distinct in each nature—that is, the individual—the individuating principles of each nature belong to the definition of any particular person: "thus in human nature it signifies this flesh, these bones, and this soul."[89] In God, the only individuating principles of the persons are the relations, which in the simplicity of the divine life are identical with the essence, thus providing "subsistent relations" as the only possible definition of a divine person.[90] However, *persona* and *relatio* reserve their respective significations. While *relatio* considered *per se* signals only a reference to another, its "capacity to be referred to hypostatically" is derived from its identification with the simple divine essence.[91] *Persona*, therefore, does not signify a *relatio* directly according to its definition or formality qua relation but only by virtue of its subsistence in the divine essence.[92] Thus, God the Father is the divine paternity subsisting, God the Son is the divine filiation subsisting, and God the Spirit is the divine spiration subsisting. Though divine personhood refers to a relation, it does not depend upon the structure of that relation itself to be a subsistent person. In its distinguishing aspect, relation enters "into the notion of the person indirectly"; on the other hand, *persona* directly signifies both the essence that is identical to the hypostasis and the relation insofar as it hypostatically subsists.[93] The emphasis of *persona* is not the relation qua relation, but the relation as subsisting in the divine essence. In this way, Thomas attempts to maintain the absolute simplicity and unity of the divine essence alongside the multiplicity of the

88. *ST* Ia, q.28, a.2 *resp*; see q.3, a.6 for Thomas's discussion of the impossibility of accidents in God per divine simplicity. See Emery, *Trinitarian Theology of Aquinas*, 117; White, "Divine Simplicity and the Holy Trinity"; *DP* q.9, a.4 *ad* 1.

89. *ST* Ia, q.29, a.4 *resp*.

90. White, "Divine Simplicity and the Holy Trinity," 86, notes that there is no "pure analogue in our ordinary human experience of created realities" to Thomas's notion of subsistent relation, underscoring the creative and bold character of Thomas's claim. See also Emery, "Dignity of Being a Substance," 998, who says, "The constitution of a person by a relation remains the exclusive prerogative of the Trinity, because only in God does a relation subsist."

91. Emery, *Trinitarian Theology of Aquinas*, 117; see *ST* Ia, q.29, a.4, and the extended comments on Thomas's analysis of person, relation, and essence in Emery, *Trinitarian Theology of Aquinas*, 114–18.

92. *ST* Ia, q.29, a.4 *ad* 1; Emery, "Dignity of Being a Substance," 1001.

93. *ST* Ia, q.29, a.4 *resp*.

divine persons without the concept of relation losing its fundamental "formality of 'relation to another.'"[94]

The Unity of the Essence and the Distinctions of the Persons

Although the metaphysical sophistication of Thomas's doctrine of subsistent relations has allowed his account of the Trinity to remain dominant in many theological circles, a central criticism over the past century and a half has been that beginning with *de Deo uno*, with its focus on what is common to the divine persons—consistently referred to as the divine *essentia*—rather than with *de Deo trino* strips the "personal traits in the creative and redemptive action of God" from the trinitarian persons in favor of defending the unity of the divine being.[95] Gilles Emery has argued that this criticism stems from a failure to read *de Deo uno* and *de Deo trino* together through the principle of *redoublement* that he adopts from Lafont.[96] Correctly understood, Emery explains, these two first parts of Thomas's treatise on God introduce no "question of a 'one God' or of a 'tri-God,' but of God considered *under the aspect* of the essence and *under the aspect* of the distinction" of the persons.[97] The essence is treated first because it provides the very substance or nature in which the persons are said to subsist, and therefore the essential operations are only truly—that is, concretely—manifested in the relational context of the divine persons.[98] "In virtue of his doctrine of relation," Emery says, "Thomas does not think of God as the subject of a notional act without posing immediately and simultaneously two persons from the fact of the relations that constitute them."[99] This reinforces the

94. Emery, "Personal Mode," 118.

95. Emery, "Essentialism or Personalism," 524. See Emery, "Essentialism or Personalism," 521–27, for a survey of various analyses of this aspect of Thomas's work since the Leonine revival; see also the critiques mentioned in Malet, *Personne et Amour*, 71–72; Kerr, *After Aquinas*, 181–85, 201–6; Smith, *Thomas Aquinas' Trinitarian Theology*, 1–8; Kilby, "Aquinas, the Trinity, and the Limits of Understanding," 415–17.

96. See Lafont, *Peut-on Connaître Dieu*, 130; quoted in Emery, "Essentialism or Personalism," 534.

97. Emery, "Essentialism or Personalism," 532. Smith echoes this claim, also pointing out that the identification of the first and second sections of the *Prima Pars* as *de Deo uno* and *de Deo trino* was a late-nineteenth century innovation that has exerted significant *a priori* influence over how they are read; see Smith, *Thomas Aquinas' Trinitarian Theology*, 23.

98. See Emery, "Essentialism or Personalism," 535–36; Hill, *Three-Personed God*, 63.

99. Emery, "Essentialism or Personalism," 545.

claim that there is no "monopersonal God" in *de Deo uno* lurking behind the treatise on the Trinity, in the sense of an additional and separate agent.[100] The notional acts of *de Deo trino* rely upon the operations established in *de Deo uno*, as they are "unthinkable without this essential activity common to the three persons."[101]

Malet made a very similar argument, published thirteen years before Lafont's volume, in which he adopts the term "*monopersonnel*" as a positive way to describe the aspect under which Thomas treats the divine essence in *de Deo uno*.[102] This does not mean, for Malet, that the essence is considered as a person itself, nor that the persons are derived from the essential activity itself. Rather, Malet uses the very term that Gilson avoids in order to underscore that the way Thomas describes what is common to the Persons is itself determined by his understanding of a person—an individual subsistence of a rational nature. Because a person must possess a rational nature, to speak of the essence of the divine persons is to speak of God as an "'indeterminate' Person."[103] Gilson is correct to point out that the essence is considered first because of the conceptual ordering of what is common before what is particular, but Malet's insight identifies why the essence is considered in precisely the way it is.[104] Thomas's method is, as Penido summarizes, to "make clear the essential characteristics of the life of the spirit, confront them with the data of the Faith, and when, as a result of this rapprochement, one discovers some correspondences, to bring into play the ways of remotion and of excellence in order to obtain purified and proportional notions

100. Emery, "Essentialism or Personalism," 546.

101. Emery, "Essentialism or Personalism," 545; see also C. Holmes, "Architectonics Matter," 135. Thomas maintains "the double perspective of the common nature and the Trinitarian relations" largely to avoid the ditches of Sabellianism or Arianism; see Emery, "Essentialism or Personalism," 528.

102. See Malet, *Personne et Amour*, 78–79, 86, 138–39. The term "monopersonal" has been used pejoratively in recent decades in evaluations of Thomas's trinitarian thought that Malet and Emery both would critique as mistaken and oversimplified; see also Van Nieuwenhove, "Trinitarian Indwelling," 392–93.

103. Malet, *Personne et Amour*, 138, my translation.

104. See Emery, "Essentialism or Personalism," 535. Smith, *Thomas Aquinas' Trinitarian Theology*, 59, objects to this sort of characterization of the progression within qq.2–43, arguing that it is a progression from "unity to distinction, not from essence to supposita." His concern is that by considering *de Deo uno* to be a discussion of what is common, that which is proper to the persons, which is also that which concretizes that very essence, will be excluded. In my view, Smith overstates the "presence of Persons in what is billed as 'common,'" and his way of stating the situation does not seem substantially different in the end from either Emery or Malet. His point that what is established in the first section is that in which the divine unity can be discerned is surely true, although it supports my point that substantial unity looms large in the *Prima Pars*.

of the divine Persons."[105] The essence is considered in the particular way that it is because it assumes the trinitarian persons as those in whom the essence acts.

Both Emery and Malet emphasize the interdependence of the two different formalities and argue that *de Deo uno* only comes to its full intelligibility in the notional acts of *de Deo trino*. Both argue in different ways that Thomas's trinitarian system cannot be either essentialist or personalist and seek to establish that Thomas achieves an integration of these two perspectives. In short, because the essence of each person *qua* subsistent relation is the divine essence, the *ratio* of each person and the unity among the persons are established by and included within the *operationes* of that *esse*, which lead to the *processiones* that establish the *rationes* themselves. In fact, the order of material present in the *ST* adapted that of Lombard's *Sentences* by moving the operations from their original position between the Trinity and the procession of creatures to their position in the *ST* between the treatment of the divine substance and the divine persons.[106] This emphasized the connection between the essential operations and the persons, as well as the close integration between the procession of the persons *ad intra* and divine causality in creation *ad extra*.[107] However, the way in which unity and rational nature are correlated *ad intra* raises a question concerning how essential unity is integrated with personal unity, and whether, as Hill suggests, Thomas is able to move in the *Prima Pars* from "*essential* unity to *interpersonal* unity."[108]

Unity and the Concept of Hypostatic Rationality

The unity attributed to God in Q. 11 is that of an "undivided being [*ens*]": God is "supremely one" because God's "substance" is both "supremely being" and "supremely undivided."[109] Because Thomas has identified rational nature as the highest form of created being, it is this structure that is attributed to his concept of divine unity as well. In created rational nature, a rational essence is individuated in a singular hypostasis having one intellect and one will and possessing itself in *unio substantialis*. It is primarily this

105. Penido, "*Cur Non Spiritus Genitus*," 522, 524, my translation.

106. See Hankey, *God in Himself*, 28.

107. See Emery, "Essentialism or Personalism," 528–31.

108. Hill, *Three-Personed God*, 63; cf. Smith, *Thomas Aquinas' Trinitarian Theology*, 21–22, referencing *ST* Ia, q.26, *pro*, q.26, a.4, *ad* 2, and q.27, *pro*, to argue that Thomas explicitly parcels out unity to *de Deo uno* and distinction to *de Deo trino*.

109. *ST* Ia, q.11, a.4 *resp* and *ad* 3.

kind of union that can truly be called "unity" and function as the proper correlative to the transcendental *unitas* attributed to God as *unum*.[110] Therefore, since there is one divine *esse*, there is only one divine act of knowing and willing, all of which are identical to the perfect divine *esse* in reality, and the substantial unity is then described under the aspect of the operations as beatitude, which is God's knowledge that he perfectly possesses the good of the divine essence through his intellect.[111] Because these operations must remain *in ipso Deo*, Thomas's discussion of the operations of God's *esse* is restricted to the limits of the rational operations as they remain and are perfected within the *unio substantialis* of a single rational hypostasis.[112]

In his essay "What Does Love Know?" Rowan Williams warns that it is a mischaracterization to say that Thomas thinks that "the Father's self-knowledge is what the Son is and the Father's self-love is what the Spirit is, as if the Trinity were essentially the inner relations of a single self."[113] Thomas, Williams avers, knows quite well that the trinitarian confession is a mystery irreducible to any created structure. The *analogia entis* remains an analogy for Thomas, a way in which creaturely language can signify the divine life according to our mode of understanding while not attributing the imperfections of finitude to the infinite and simple divine being. Furthermore, Williams points out that to hold back from speaking of knowing and willing in God would obscure the meaning of the Christian confession

110. See *ST* Ia, q.11, a.4 *ad* 3; q.28, a.3 *sed contra*; Flood, *Metaphysical Foundations of Love*, 11–13.

111. See *ST* Ia, q.26, aa.1–2.

112. See Najeeb Awad's reading in "Thomas Aquinas' Metaphysics of 'Relation' and 'Participation,'" 659–60, in which the ambiguity that exists between the personhood of the essence and of the persons due to Thomas's emphasis on the substantial perseity of personhood is displayed: "'Persons as relations' does not threaten the oneness of God's substance, since the various real relations in God are all founded on one, single, and simple substance. They are not relations for individual persons, but relations for one, single divine person"; cf. Emery, "Dignity of Being a Substance," 994–97.

Rik van Nieuwenhove argues that Thomas's model has the distinct advantage over "interpersonal" models of being able to account for the "intimate link between the intra-divine life and the understanding of the human being as made in the image of God" ("Trinitarian Indwelling," 393; see also 394–96). This assumes, however, that the image of God in humanity can refer only (or at least primarily) to a one-to-one correspondence between individual humans and the entirety of the "intra-divine life." This fits with Thomas's understanding of beatitude as the perfection of the individual's intellectual act. But if the image of God in humans includes—constitutively and not accidentally—relations with other persons, the advantage of Thomas's model as Van Nieuwenhove presents it fades significantly.

113. R. Williams, "What Does Love Know," 266.

of God as Creator of creatures who know and will as the *imago Dei*, and of the Scriptures that speak of God's knowledge of and love for the world.[114]

Williams is correct in these cautionary claims. The Son and the Spirit are not reduced to the inner faculties of the Father as a divine Uber-person in either a Sabellian or Anselmian fashion.[115] Nor is the attribution of the faculties of knowing and willing *per se* to God an issue, and Thomas is careful to neither make the essence a person nor allow them to so divide the persons that the essence itself is split. However, Thomas's identification of rational nature in its individually hypostatized form as the most proper finite mode of being to attribute to the tri-hypostatic divinity leads him to consider the ecstatic and interpersonal aspects of the rational operations, through which hypostases normally relate to one another, as unfit to attribute to the trinitarian God. Ultimately, this allows a concept of a single divine "self" to exert significant influence on Thomas's language concerning how the persons relate to one another and therefore can be spoken of as unified.

To illustrate this, I briefly turn again to the structure of knowing and willing in creatures. Understood generally, they both involve an ecstatic element relating the knower or lover to the essence of the object that is known or loved, between which is a real relation which implies distinction.[116] While knowing an object brings it into the knower through its immaterial intelligible form, the intellectual act remains oriented externally insofar as its object remains outside of the knower in reality, as is acknowledged in the final moment of judgment. The will desires the object according to its appetibility, but the will also wishes for this good to be possessed by someone, either by the lover herself (which remains *amor concupiscentiae*, or more specifically as *amor sui*) or by another (*amor amicitiae*).[117] In either case, the will is an ecstatic "stimulus of motion away" from the subject toward the object, the opposite of the movement of the intellect above.[118] The outward movement of desire seeks a real unity with the really distinct Beloved, the unity being a kind of possession modulated by whether the appetitive object is a good

114. See R. Williams, "What Does Love Know," 266–67.

115. See Emery, "Essentialism or Personalism," 540–41; Smith, *Thomas Aquinas' Trinitarian Theology*, 2–4.

116. For an extended discussion of *extasis* regarding both knowledge and love, see Kwasniewski, *Ecstasy of Love*, 229–49.

117. See *ST* I–II, q.28, a.1 *resp*.

118. R. Williams, "What Does Love Know," 264–65; see also Hankey, *God in Himself*, 106; Kwasniewski, *Ecstasy of Love*, 108. For a more detailed discussion of the unitive power of love and the relation between concupiscence, friendship, and self-love, see Flood, *Metaphysical Foundations of Love*, 1–24.

or a person. Between persons, this union is a *unio realis*, which "in keeping with the demands of love" does not lead to the subsumption of either Lover into the other. Both remain distinct while enjoying a "suitable and becoming union" that approximates as much as possible the *unio substantialis* that each individual enjoys with themselves.[119] *In via*, therefore, this *unio realis* sought with other persons and caused ecstatically by love is "closer than that which is caused by knowledge."[120] This is true even in relation to God as our *summum bonum*, as "to love God is something greater than to know Him, especially in this state of life."[121]

If, however, these operations are restricted to the relation of a rational hypostasis to itself, the object of the intellect and will remains internal to the essence of a rational creature while not being identical to the essence itself, by which only logical relations between oneself as subject and as object are constituted.[122] As there is no other substantially distinct person to desire, there is no *unio realis* with the beloved to seek. Instead, the individual possesses itself in a *unio substantialis*, which causes "the love with which one loves oneself," that is, *amor sui*.[123] When Thomas applies the operations to God in *de Deo uno* in this hypostatically restricted manner, there is no ecstasy permitted to the divine operations. However, as both operations are spoken of only under the aspect of what is common, with God's essence as the subject and object of the divine knowing and willing, this threatens to only establish logical relations between the persons, leaning toward the "Sabellian heresy."[124] Thomas thus appeals to divine simplicity to transform the logical relations of self-speaking and self-loving within a singular person

119. *ST* I–II, q.28, a.1 *ad* 2. See Flood, *Metaphysical Foundations of Love*, 7–8, 38–39, 55–57.

120. *ST* I–II, q.28, a.1 *ad* 2–3.

121. *ST* II–II, q.27, a.4 *ad* 2; Schindler, "Towards a Non-Possessive Concept of Knowledge," 585.

122. See *ST* Ia, q.27, a.2 *ad* 2; q.28, a.1 *resp* and *ad* 1.

123. *ST* I–II, q.28, a.1 *ad* 2. In one's own substantial unity, the good of one's nature that is loved for its own sake is possessed by the person subsisting in it, and so self-love ought to be understood first as a metaphysical love for the Good considered in itself and only second as a hypostatic love for oneself, by which the Good that is loved in itself is then referred to a person. As Malet argued, this means that self-love is not necessarily "*egoïste*," since it is ecstatically related to the Good as its formal (abstract) object and only then related to the self as its concrete object (*Personne et Amour*, 130–32). See also Flood's explanation of the connection between *amor sui* and *amor amicitiae*, which derives from the underlying connection between *unio substantialis* and *unio similitudines*, as this explains why the *unio affectum* seeks a *unio realis* with the Beloved that approximates a *unio substantialis* as far as possible (*Metaphysical Foundations of Love*, 7–8, 11–14, 39).

124. *ST* Ia, q.28, a.1 *sed contra*.

into real relations that can therefore subsist in the divine essence and form the basis for speaking of three divine hypostases.[125] Though there are real relations between the divine persons, only a *unio substantialis* (evocative of an individual rational hypostasis) obtains between them because the interrelationality that intellect and will normally involve between rational hypostases and that lead to a *unio realis* has been precluded by Thomas's "personalization" of the divine essence according to the categories of rational creatures. Thomas expresses this succinctly by quoting Boethius: "The substance contains the unity; and relation multiplies the trinity."[126] In this sense, it is difficult to see how the unity attributed to God in the *ST* includes or is fully manifest in the notional acts as a unity of persons, which is the *unio realis* sought by the *amor amicitiae*.[127] Instead, because of the separation between essential and notional language, the only unity that can be attributed to the trinitarian persons is the *unio substantialis* of the essence, even though the one-to-one correspondence of essence and hypostasis does not hold true in God.

Unio Substantialis and the Procession of the Son and the Spirit

Many Thomists and other theologians who have adopted Thomas's psychological analogy and concept of subsistent relations defend these concepts because they effectively safeguard against the threat of tritheism perceived in modern (and medieval) personalist ontologies while maintaining the consubstantiality and distinction of the divine persons grounded in Nicene theology.[128] Thomas is clear that this form of essential unity does not "ex-

125. See *ST* Ia, q.28, a.2 *resp*; q.37, a.2 *resp*. Kilby notes that by doing so, Thomas removes the ground on which the processions were able to establish the relations in the first place, that is, that there is a distinction between that which processes and that from which it processes ("Aquinas, the Trinity and the Limits of Understanding," 419–20). Kilby does not mean this as a criticism, as it serves her overall argument that we ought not to assume that Thomas believed that formulations such as this truly gave us insight, functioning rather to touch the limits of theological language and rest there in contemplation. However, her observation illustrates perfectly how the way notions such as simplicity or unity are derived from created reality, or more precisely, what we consider to be imperfections of created reality, end up restricting our ability to say clearly other things that Scripture says, which Kilby notes is Thomas's motivation in discussing the processions. The other two examples that Kilby provides in her article demonstrate the same pattern.

126. *ST* Ia, q.28, a.3 *sed contra*; quoting Boethius, *De Trinitate*, 6.1.

127. See Flood, *Metaphysical Foundations of Love*, xi, 39.

128. Katherine Sonderegger is a prime example of a modern theologian who has

clude . . . the plurality of relations," as they do not "import composition in that of which they are predicated," even if they are real relations considered as relations of identity.[129] Though they are not excluded, there is a significant shift in Thomas's language between the "absolute" register of the operations of God's rational ("personalized") essence and the "relative" register of the notional acts of the subsistent persons themselves.[130] Within this shift, an imbalance emerges in which both the Spirit and the concept of love are less developed and central to Thomas's Trinity than are the Son and the intellect.

Essentialiter, God knows and wills God, and each person likewise knows and wills by virtue of their common subsistence in the divine essence, but what they know and will is the divine essence. Therefore, Thomas says that "each Person understands and is understood," which can be expanded to include the will.[131] However, the Father cannot be said to "know" or "understand" the Son as the object of his knowledge, as the essential operations only reference the divine essence and therefore cannot import a relation to another as a person.[132] Instead, the Son is spoken in the sense of a *verbum mentis*, which by definition remains within an intelligent agent while still importing the relation of Speaker to Word.[133] Because the intellectual concept implies a "similitude" to the object understood, the intellectual procession can also be called *generatio*, a fact that Thomas utilizes to draw a connection between the names "Word" and "Son" through his concept of the intellect.[134] Thomas then attributes the third name of "Image" to the Son based upon the same principle, as the Son receives the likeness of the Father specifically through being born and proceeding as a word.[135] In speaking and begetting the Son, the Father does not "know" him personally but relates to him as another of the same essence, though in speaking the Word the "whole Trinity is *spoken*."[136] However, for the Father to know the Son in a way that identified their relational distinction would be to allow

---

aligned herself with this Thomist vision. In the first volume of her Systematic Theology, she prioritizes a monadic concept of unity overwhelmingly derived from the Shema (Deut 6:5), and in the second volume seeks to develop this vision according to a "doubled unity," following the lead of Gilles Emery; see *Doctrine of God*, 23–35; *Doctrine of the Holy Trinity*, xxi, 420–33.

129. *ST* Ia, q.28, a.1 *ad* 3; see also *resp* and *ad* 2.

130. See *ST* Ia, q.34, a.1 *resp*.

131. *ST* Ia, q.34, a.1 *ad* 3.

132. See *ST* Ia, q.37, a.1 *resp*; q.34, a.1 *ad* 3; q.37, a.1 *ad* 2; a.2 *ad* 3.

133. See *ST* Ia, q.34, a.1.

134. See *ST* Ia, q.27, aa.2, 4.

135. See *ST* Ia, q.35, a.2 *resp*.

136. *ST* Ia, q.34, a.1, *ad* 3.

the intellectual act to exceed the hypostasis of the Father in way that would, for Thomas, multiply the divine essence. Thus, while Thomas can say that the Father speaks the Word, or generates the Son, these notional acts are both based upon an undifferentiated act of knowing in which the essence references itself without being able to do so through the full personal range of its rational operations.

Thomas admits that the requirement for an operation that remains in the agent "applies most conspicuously" with the intellect.[137] Two reasons can be adduced for this. The first, which Thomas gives in Article 1 of Q. 27, is that as the intellect understands, the *verbum mentis* (or here, the *verbum cordis*) proceeds internally in the knower. The second, which must be derived from what has come before, is that the intellectual operation more easily coheres with his concept of divine unity than the will, since the intellect is conceived in less ecstatic terms. Thus, it is easier for Thomas to provide a robust account of the character of the Son's procession within the analogy of a hypostasis's self-reference. When turning to the Spirit, however, the character of this second procession in God undergoes much more severe restrictions by virtue of the same analogy. The analogy provides a tidy and coherent rationale for the presence and specific number of the divine processions—because the will follows the intellect in rational natures, there must be one, and only one, other procession *per modum voluntatis*.[138] However, the operations of the will do not fit as neatly into the single-hypostasis model to which Thomas is committed, and neither does the will support the emphasis on substantial unity as well as the intellect, because the will seeks to move outward toward the *bonum* it desires.

The difficulty involved in the will's ecstatic character is evident in the way Thomas discusses the Spirit's proper names. Though both *spiritus* and *amor* signify "a certain vital movement and impulse, accordingly as anyone is described as moved or impelled by love to perform an action," the Spirit must only express this movement *ad intra* as the love which proceeds internally by the essential act of love for that very same essence.[139] This leads to curious circumlocutions, such as Thomas's claim that for God to love

137. *ST* Ia, q.27, a.1 *resp*. Emery observes the same pattern in Thomas's *LSI*, which he attributes to the fact that the "fourth Gospel expressly mentions the Word and thus gives the textual opening for an exposition on the Word, whereas it is not the same for Love" ("Biblical Exegesis and the Speculative Doctrine," 32). See also Smith's helpful discussion on how Thomas's discussion of intellectual generation in God is primarily negative rather than positive in *Thomas Aquinas' Trinitarian Theology*, 79–81.

138. See *ST* Ia, q.27, a.5 *resp*; q.36, a.2 *resp*; q.41, a.2 *ad* 3.

139. *ST* Ia, q.27, a.4; see also q.36, a.1; *LSI* 15.2062. Flood, *Metaphysical Foundations of Love*, 13, also argues that God's love for himself is the highest example of appropriate *amor sui*.

essentially is for the Father and Son to love "each other not by the Holy Spirit, but by their essence," while taken notionally it does mean that the Father and Son love each other "by the Holy Spirit, or by Love proceeding."[140] This *amor procedens* that is the person of the Spirit is not the act of love itself but only the internal "impression . . . so to speak, of the thing loved in the affection of the lover."[141] Here, love is reconfigured according to the structure of the mental word (*verbum mentis*)—which Thomas claims is more fully understood than love[142]—in order to isolate it from its relational structure. Likewise, while Gift is also a proper name for the Spirit, as "love has the nature of a first gift, through which all free gifts are given," the ecstatic and interpersonal implications of this name vanish *ad intra*, as the Spirit does not signify a gift between Father and Son, but only the fact that he has an "aptitude for being given."[143] The Spirit's aptitude to be given is grounded in his procession from the Father and Son, but this aptitude is not enacted in eternity between the divine persons but only between God and creatures in time.[144] In eternity, Thomas is only comfortable allowing that the essence is given in the processions, allowing Hilary's comment that "the divine essence is the Gift which the Father gives to the Son" to stand with the clarification that the essence is the Father's ("*hoc esse huius*") by identity, or subsistence, alone.[145] The Spirit subsists as a gift not given *ad intra*.

These two ways in which Thomas restricts the ecstatic implications of both proper names of the Spirit are both rooted in the necessity that his procession remains internal to the divine essence construed as the interior *unio substantialis* of a single hypostatic nature. For the Spirit to be Love personally can only be "construed as importing the relation of a formal effect" of the substantial unity properly established by the intellect in the intellectual unity of the Father as Speaker and the Son as *verbum mentis*.[146]

140. *ST* Ia, q.37, a.2 *resp*.

141. *ST* Ia, q.37, a.1 *resp*. Torrell, *Saint Thomas Aquinas*, 184–85, points out that Thomas recognizes essential, notional, and personal acts in relation to loving, in which each person loves essentially and expresses that love personally in interrelated ways. However, the Spirit still fades back into a *nexus amantium* in this framework, not being loved or loving as a divine person other than as a subsistent relation in the divine essence.

142. See *ST* Ia, q.37, a.1 *resp*.

143. *ST* Ia, q.38, a.2 *resp*; a.1 *resp*.

144. See *ST* Ia, q.38, a.1 *ad* 4. See also Levering, "Holy Spirit in Trinitarian Communion," 139, for an account of how Augustine restricts the Spirit's agency as Gift to God's relation to the world, reducing Gift in the Trinity to an expression of the Father-Son relation just as Thomas does in *ST* Ia, q.38.

145. *ST* Ia, q.38, a.1 *obj*/*ad* 2.

146. Parallel to this is Thomas's restriction of the Spirit's role as *ratio finis* to the

This parallels Thomas's restriction of beatitude to the intellect, which renders joy and happiness a concomitant "proper accident" to the perfection of a rational nature.[147] For the Spirit to be given as a gift between the Father and Son would establish an interpersonal and relational *unio realis* by their mutual spiration in which each gives themself to the other in the Spirit, which would redefine the divine *unio substantialis* by the notional acts. This would problematize the Son's consubstantiality for Thomas, however, because it would signal a remaining ecstatic element between the Speaker and the Word that needed to be united.[148]

Thus, while Williams is right that Thomas attempts to maintain the distinction of the trinitarian persons so that they are not reduced to a single self, the fact that Thomas disallows the very portrait of the Spirit as the gift of love between Father and Son that Williams attributes to him demonstrates the powerful influence of his operative concept of unity, which is itself derived from a single self.[149] Thomas cannot allow the Spirit to be the gift between the Father and Son; what is given in his generation is only the divine *esse*. To say that the Spirit is the gift between them would be to confuse love with intellectual generation, which for Thomas would come too close to what Williams seems to want him to say: "The natural good of the divine life is, it seems, something like the state of wanting another's good. If we could imagine a condition of unbroken and unqualified commitment to the good of another, we should have imagined something like the divine life."[150] This suggests a unity too interpersonal for Thomas's framework in the *ST*. The Spirit's relation to the divine unity expressed in the *verbum mentis* is that of the *nexus* (bond) of common spiration that expresses their substantial unity as a proper accident of the intellectual procession of the Son, but not as that unity itself.[151] The procession of the Spirit must follow after that of the Son, and so Thomas must avoid any language that would suggest that the Spirit has anything to do with the intellectual generation of

relation to creation alone, not allowing the Spirit to exert any final diffusivity within the divine life as the fulfillment of the processions, a distinction that Malet elides in his discussion (see *Personne et Amour*, 123).

147. *ST* Ia, q.37, a.2 *resp*.

148. Though Kwasniewski, *Ecstasy of Love*, 279, notes that the ecstasy present in both knowing and loving might explain how the divine *esse* could be both given and received in God's life in a kind of *extasis* without meaning that God must "surpass or fall beneath or stand outside of Himself," significant modifications to Thomas's mode of attribution would be necessary for this to be explored more fully.

149. See R. Williams, "What Does Love Know," 265. The same interpretive issue is present in Hankey, *God in Himself*, 121–22.

150. R. Williams, "What Does Love Know," 265.

151. See *ST* Ia, q.37, a.1 *ad* 3.

the Son. In other words, the Spirit's procession is not logically necessary to the generation of the Son *per se*, nor to the relation of the Father and Son, as that is already established by virtue of the intellectual act alone.[152]

Love and Procession in Thomas's Exegesis of John 3:34–35

It seems, then, that Thomas's development of unity from the analogy of a nature normally hypostatized by one person inhibits his pneumatology much more than his account of the Son. Though Thomas might not see the Spirit's state being likened to a "proper accident" as inherently problematic, as it remains necessary to the divine act, when Thomas comments directly upon the relationship between love and the divine processions in Scripture, significant tensions arise.[153] One particularly pertinent example is in his exegesis of John 3:34–35,[154] in which the full and perfect presence of the Spirit explains the way in which Christ "bespeaks the Father," and the Father's love for the Son explains Christ's possession of "all things."[155] These can be expressed in two pairings, the Spirit and the Son's "bespeaking," and Love and the Father's "giving," both of which Thomas explains with respect to Christ's two natures.

First, Thomas explains that the fact that Christ "bespeaks the Father" means that he "spoke of nothing but the Father and the words of the Father, because he has been sent by the Father, and because he himself is the Word of the Father."[156] According to his divine nature, Christ has the Spirit "inasmuch as the Spirit proceeds from him."[157] In other words, God the Father gives the Son the ability to spirate the Spirit, and the Spirit is given to Christ in that he comes from Christ and is as much the Spirit of the Son as he is the

152. See *ST* Ia, q.27, aa.3–5. Malet confirms this reading, while warning that this does not meant that the procession of the Spirit is potentially unnecessary: "La procession du Saint-Esprit, tout comme celle du Fils, ne peut pas ne pas être" (*Personne et Amour*, 120). Furthermore, Malet draws attention to influence of the finality of both Love and Spirit in *Sent* I, where the procession of the Word "est ordonnée à la procession par amour et le Verbe à la Esprit" (*Personne et Amour*, 122; citing *Sent* I, d.10, q.1, a.1). Both observations demonstrate the complexity of Thomas's system, but neither indicates an expansion of the Love of the divine life *ad intra*.

153. See *LSI* 1.41, 3.545, 5.753; *ST*, Ia, q.37, a.2; q.41, a.2.

154. The exegesis of this section is largely reproduced in *LSI* 5.753, on John 5:20.

155. *LSI* 3.540, 545; see also 5.753. Aquinas also entertains the possibility that "God" in "God is true" can also refer to Christ, but this interpretation is not pushed forward.

156. *LSI* 3.540.

157. *LSI* 3.543.

Spirit of the Father.[158] As man, however, Christ receives and has the Spirit "as Sanctifier," or as the anointed giver of the Spirit.[159] This reception of the Spirit as man is a grace from God, in that he received the Spirit as an unmerited gift from the Father. The most pertinent aspect of this gift, among the three that Thomas mentions, is the grace of the hypostatic union, which is "given to Christ in order that in his human nature he be the true Son of God, not by participation [as we are], but by nature, insofar as the human nature of Christ is united to the Son of God in person."[160] This grace was given to Christ in the Spirit, and thus he did not receive the Spirit by measure, as the gift given was union to an infinite nature. It is the combination of these two, his reception of the divine nature from the Father and the attendant ability to spirate the Spirit, and the union of Christ's humanity to his divinity in the hypostatic union and his relation to the Father in the Spirit, that function as the support for John's assertion that Christ speaks the words of God.[161]

Second, Christ was able to speak "divine truth" because "the Father loves the Son, and he has given all things into his hand."[162] Taken in regard to his divinity, the Father's love ("*diligit*") for the Son cannot be the reason that the Father gives the Son all things, which is understood to be the eternal generation of the Son by which the Father gives the fullness of the divine *esse* to the Son. Rather, God's *dilectio* is only the sign of this action, a "formal effect" or "proper accident," for if it was understood as a principle, then it would mean that the "Father generated the Son by will, and not by nature," which would be "the Arian heresy."[163] In like manner, since "the love [*dilectio*] of the Father for the Son is the Holy Spirit," to say that love is

158. *LSI* 3.543. That Thomas is here primarily talking about intra-trinitarian processions and not John 20:22 is clear from his mention of the Spirit's procession from the Father and Son (*sicut ab eo procedit, ita et filio*) and the everlasting generation of the Son through which the Father gave the Son this ability (*dedit ei per aeternam generationem*); see Levering, *Scripture and Metaphysics*, 138. In relation to the next point, the Spirit is "la fleur ou le fruit de la communion de Père et du Fils" by which the Father has given him all things, "le terms et la perfection en acte" of the generation of the Son. In his study on the Spirit in Thomas's *LSI*, Denis-Dominique Le Pivain describes the Spirit as "le signe, non la cause . . . comme la fleur ou le fruit de la communion de Père et du Fils . . . le terme et la perfection en acte" (*Action du Saint-Esprit*, 83–84). See also Levering, *Scripture and Metaphysics*, 138; Emery, *Trinitarian Theology of St Thomas Aquinas*, 155.

159. *LSI* 3.543.

160. *LSI* 3.544; see also Levering, "Participation and Exegesis," 595.

161. This also highlights that the Spirit is a gift given to the Son, primarily in the self-gift of the Father, seen in the gift of all that the Father is to the Son in both his divine (eternal generation) and human natures (hypostatic union). See Levering, "Participation and Exegesis," 595.

162. *LSI* 3.545.

163. *LSI* 3.545. See Emery, "Biblical Exegesis and the Speculative Doctrine," 29.

the reason that the Father generated the Son would make the Spirit of God the principle of the Son's generation, which Thomas repudiates.[164] When it comes to the divine nature, the love of the Father for the Son is only a "sign" that the Father has communicated the fullness of the divine *esse* and as such is the perfect good which God loves: "For since likeness is a cause of love (for every animal loves its like), wherever a perfect likeness of God is found, there also is found a perfect love of God."[165] Taken in relation to Christ's humanity, however, the love of the Father for the Son does now imply a principle, in this case construing the simple connective (*καὶ/et*) to signify a parallel idea to the logical connective above in verse 34 (*γὰρ/enim*).[166] Not only is the Father's love the reason for giving Christ all things, but it is so because "the Father's love [*dilectio*] is the reason for creating each creature."[167] Thus, the *dilectio* of God is the reason for the creation of all things, which includes not only the initial creation but also the "[infusion] of goodness into [them]," but it is specifically related here to the creation of and bestowing of grace upon the Son's human nature.

Thus, in explaining how John commends the divine truth to which Christ testifies, Thomas identifies four ways that the Spirit and love relate Christ to God:

1. The Father gives his Spirit to his Son without measure as his own Spirit, which they both breathe out; this identifies Christ as God, and thus his words are God's words.
2. The Father gives his Spirit to his Son without measure through the grace of the hypostatic union, so that all things that Christ does as incarnate are the actions of God himself, and thus his words are God's words.
3. The Father loves (*diligit*) his Son, which is the sign of the eternal generation of the Only Begotten from the Father, through which Christ receives all things from the Father, namely the infinite divine nature.
4. The Father loves (*diligit*) his Son, and therefore he gives him all things in the creation and blessing in grace of Christ's humanity.

164. *LSI* 3.545; see also 5.753; *ST* Ia, q.37, a.2. See Bourassa, "Sur la Propriété de l'Esprit Saint"; Sabathé, "Originalité," 226; Waldstein, "Analogy of Mission and Obedience," 38.

165. *LSI* 5.753; see also 3.545.

166. Levering, "Participation and Exegesis," 596, notes that the level of intra-trinitarian gift described above "undergirds what Aquinas has to say . . . referring to the Son in his humanity."

167. *LSI* 3.545.

The restrictions of Thomas's *analogia* are clear by the opposite ways he applies the same texts to the relation between Christ, the Spirit, and the love of God. There are other aspects of Thomas's thought within the *LSI* itself that are in tension with the clear statements of love being only a "sign" of the Son's full deity, such as his comments on John 5:20, "*Pater enim diligit Filium*":

> For since the good alone is loveable, a good can be related to love [*ad amorem*] in two ways: as the cause of love, or as caused by love. Now in us, the good causes love [*amorem*]: for the cause of our loving something is its goodness, the goodness in it. Therefore, it is not good because we love [*diligimus*] it, but rather we love [*diligimus*] it because it is good. Accordingly, in us, love [*amor*] is caused by what is good. But it is different with God, because God's love [*amor*] itself is the cause of the goodness in the things that are loved [*dilectis*]. For it is because God loves [*diligit*] us that we are good, since to love is nothing else than to will a good to someone.[168]

Here, God's love, at least toward creation, functions in the opposite manner to creaturely love: God's love is the principle of good, in that his love for the Good as final end leads to his efficient act of power in granting to creatures to possess this Good in various degrees. But when Thomas turns the relation between God's love and the Son's procession, God's love for the Son cannot be the principle that it is for creatures simply because that would suggest that the will and the Spirit were involved in the Son's generation even though this forces Thomas to read the same connector (*et*) in 3:35 in two contradictory ways. This is a prime example of the sophistication of Thomas's metaphysical scheme leading to tension with the very scriptural witness it is trying to develop. And though Williams notes that Thomas comes "within a whisker of suggesting" that the Son and Spirit are perichoretically involved in the generation of the other (as John's Gospel seems to suggest), the fact remains that Thomas expressly rules this out, adverting to the difference between absolute and relative predication. The very ecstatic "impulse" of *spiritus*, *amor*, and *donum* that Williams says characterizes Thomas's understanding of the divine life is expressly excluded by Thomas from the Spirit *ad intra* due to the restrictions of hypostatic interiority.[169]

168. *LSI* 5.753.

169. See R. Williams, "What Does Love Know," 266; see also Weinandy, *Father's Spirit of Sonship*, which takes up this suggestion and develops it in conversation with both Eastern and Western theologies.

Conclusion

Though Thomas is successful metaphysically in threading the needle between the oneness of the divine *esse* and the threeness of the divine persons through his theory of subsistent relations, there is a cost to his method. While the essence is construed in terms very much like an infinite and perfect, yet singular, rational essence that each of the divine persons hypostatizes, the persons are unable to relate and act upon each other reciprocally through the very operations by which they are constituted as persons. The Father cannot be said to know the Son interpersonally, and though the Father speaks the Son notionally, he does so only as a word in the divine intellect, with which the Father is identical. Things are even worse for the Spirit, as the love which subsists in the divine essence is described in terms derived from the internal *verbum*. Thomas's distance from the language of Scripture, closely related to the proximity he maintains to his metaphysical system, is aptly illustrated in the ways he must interpret God's self-revelation in Christ in opposite ways depending upon which nature he has in view.

I have argued that the root of these shortcomings is Thomas's insufficiently critical attribution of the created perfections of substances. Thus, the divine *essentia* is already defined in terms of how created *essentiae* are individually hypostatized and relate to other, discretely hypostatized *essentiae*. The *unio substantialis* of a singular rational hypostasis forms the basis for the tri-hypostatic divine essence, precluding *a priori* true reciprocal relationality between the divine persons who are, ironically, subsisting relations. In terms of the architectonic of love developed in the introduction, Thomas ends up prioritizing the oneness of the essence to the detriment of his ability to speak of the divine persons as fully acting as the subsistent persons of the divine *esse* that he confesses them to be.

I am aware that this argument will not concern (let alone convince) someone who shares Thomas's substantialist ontology as it is attributed to God. In the next chapter, therefore, I will remain with Thomas to develop an account of created being from his own anthropology that raises further questions about the suitability of his own method of attributing the rational perfections to the divine nature. Rather than moving to von Balthasar too quickly, my aim is to allow Thomas and his commentators to continue demonstrating my case that a more nuanced and relational ontology is needed for theology's explication of God's self-revelation in Christ and the Spirit.

2

Amor Amicitiae

The Challenge of the Love of Friendship to the Concept of Divine Unity in Thomas Aquinas

Introduction

IN THE PREVIOUS CHAPTER, I argued that Thomas's choice to attribute the perfections of a rational nature, particularly the rational operations understood as remaining within the unity of an individual substance, leads to tensions in his theological language concerning God's triunity. To continue exploring this tension in Thomas's *analogia*, this chapter will take a closer look at Thomas's theological anthropology later in the *ST*, in which he presents a complex and nuanced vision of the interrelatedness of created natures and operations.[1] In these later sections, *amor* and its various forms take on a far greater importance than in *de Deo*. Whereas only one question is devoted to love in relation to God's essence and another question in relation to the Spirit's name as love, when Thomas turns to creation, *amor* plays a central role in his understanding of what it means for rational creatures—and indeed, all created being—to enact and fulfill their natures as dependent and relational beings. Furthermore, in the two questions in *de Deo*, love is attributed to God in basic and highly restrictive terms, while

1. By "theological," I indicate two ways in which his anthropology relates to his theology proper. First, as Thomas claims in *ST* Ia, q.13, a.13 *resp*, the perfections attributed to created beings—including knowing and willing—more properly belong to God and are only attributed to creatures by their participation in the divine perfections by the gift of creation. Second, these perfections are ultimately oriented toward God as their transcendental source and fulfillment, and so the form intellect and will take in rational creatures must be understood within this relation of final causality.

later in relation to humanity it is a highly developed concept that leads us through desire and relation to our fulfillment in God.

In this chapter, I will argue that Thomas elevates love to a place of prime importance in two ways.[2] The first is the fundamental priority Thomas gives to love as the expression of created nature's dependence upon God, which is seen in his nuanced account of the rational operations. Though Thomas maintains the intellectualist claim that the will is dependent upon the intellect for its object, it becomes clear that—at least for creatures—the intellect is also dependent upon the will for its very movement. When this circle of dependence is traced to the bottom of created nature, it is the will (*amor intellectivus*) that is its first act. In fact, as every kind of nature possesses *appetitus*, an orientation toward the particular expression of the Good determined by its form, this means that all created things regardless of kind possess *amor*, the first act toward the final end identified by the *appetitus*. The formal orientation of *appetitus* is received in *essentia*, suggesting that the basic act of *amor* is received in *esse*, and Thomas identifies these as the way in which God first orients and moves creatures, even those endowed with intellect, to act for their end.

Second, while beatitude is positioned as the end of God's perfection in *de Deo*, the primary position of *amor* in *esse* is complemented by its position at the end of creaturely perfection, which is friendship, or *amicitia*, with God. As *amicitia* is the fulfillment of *caritas*, the highest form of love, the intellectual and enstatic perfection of beatitude is in the last analysis contextualized with the ecstatic and amorous perfection of friendship with God.

These two forays into Thomas's anthropology set the stage for me to ask the question: Why not God? Building on the previous chapter, I argue that Thomas cannot have followed these trains of thought back into *de Deo* because of his early commitment to *unio substantialis*, itself based in the form and content of his *analogia entis*. Love inherently pushes toward the relational, and so even though the New Testament offers *Deus caritas est* (1 John 4:6) as a parallel to *Ego sum qui sum* (Exod 3:14), Thomas remains within his school's parameters by identifying the latter as the most proper name for God. Since much of the additional detail given to the rational operations is connected to the way in which created natures relate to one another, Thomas includes very little discussion of it when attributing the rational operations to God in *de Deo uno*. I argue that this absence is

2. Schindler identifies both ways, and though the solutions that I pursue here follow some of his suggestions, I will draw more directly upon Thomas in this chapter rather than turning to von Balthasar as he does ("Towards a Non-Possessive Concept of Knowledge," 582–86). I will then go on to apply my own suggestions to God's own life rather than remaining within the realm of anthropological epistemology.

unnecessary apart from the constraints by attributing to God only the perfections of *substantia* individually considered.

This raises issues concerning God's essential operations. If God's knowledge of the divine essence does not involve *iudicatio*, it seems like only the essence as such and not the Trinity and all its concomitant relations can be the object of divine knowledge. If, on the other hand, *iudicatio* is attributed to the divine self-knowledge, this would too easily lead to a consideration of *amicitia* between the divine persons. Thus, theological language is left with a severely restricted vocabulary to describe God's life that results in improbable if impressively nuanced statements where "God" consistently references himself but the trinitarian persons are not invoked. These complications lead me to the conclusion that if love and relation are fundamental to created *esse*, and not as a function of its limitation but as its perfection, then these concepts should be placed at the center of any theological inquiry into the nature of the trinitarian life.

Esse and *Amor*: An Alternative Reading

In the later anthropological sections of the *Summa Theologiae*, Thomas's account of the rational operations displays a greater interdependence than earlier on in *de Deo*. While the intellect still moves the will "after the manner of a formal principle . . . [by] presenting its object to it," the will also moves the intellect as an efficient cause, as it is in virtue of the desired end that the other powers of the soul are used.[3] D. C. Schindler identifies this relationship, explaining that "[their] relation is always *reciprocal* . . . . [T]hough it is true that the will can act only under a conception of its object, it is nevertheless true as well that the intellect can understand only because it is good to understand!—which is to say that . . . there is no act of the intellect that is not willed by the will."[4] Though the will cannot desire without an object supplied by the intellect, the intellect needs to be moved to understand because it is desirable to do so.

3. *ST* Ia, 1.82, a.4; I–II, q.9, a.1 *resp*; see also I, q.19, a.1; q.83, a.4 *ad* 3; I–II, q.6, a.4; q.26, a.1. See the relevant discussions in Brady, "Aquinas the Voluntarist," 862–67; Gallagher, "Thomas Aquinas on the Causes of Human Choice," 292–94; Levering, *Scripture and Metaphysics*, 96–98; Westberg, "Did Aquinas Change His Mind."

4. Schindler, "Towards a Non-Possessive Concept of Knowledge," 582. R. Williams expresses a similar interdependency between the intellect and will in God based upon the identity of their transcendental formalities, saying that love "always presupposes understanding of a sort; yet the intellectual act that produces the *verbum* is the apprehension of an act of primordial love" ("What Does Love Know," 266).

This introduces the risk of an infinite regress between the intellect and will, which Thomas addresses in a handful of places. The development seen in his solution between *De Veritate* and the *ST* is instructive.[5] In the earlier composition, this infinite regress is insufficiently resolved into the presence of a "natural appetite by which the intellect is inclined to its act."[6] As Jordan points out, natural appetite is "ill defined" here; it could either refer to the appetite of a rational nature (*appetitus intellectivus*), which is the will, thereby simply restating the problem, or it could refer to the appetite that is natural to the power of the intellect itself.[7] When the same question is asked in the *ST*, however, Thomas appeals to Aristotle to ground a more specific answer:

> There is no need to go on indefinitely, but we must stop at the intellect as preceding all the rest. For every movement of the will must be preceded by apprehension, whereas every apprehension is not preceded by an act of the will; but the principle of counselling and understanding is an intellectual principle higher than our intellect—namely, God—as also Aristotle says (*Eth. Eudemic.* vii, 14), and in this way he explains that there is no need to proceed indefinitely.[8]

Here, the necessity of apprehension for the movement of the will is upheld, but the apprehension is not found in the creature's own intellect but in God's. While it is possible to read the particular wording of this text as suggesting that God's intellect moves the creature's intellect directly, thereby moving the creature's will by its own intellect in the normal intellectualist fashion, this reading is not supported by Thomas's clarification in the *Prima Secundae*. There, he claims that the will is first moved by some "exterior mover," citing the exact same text as above.[9] Therefore, though apprehension remains necessary for the movement of the rational appetite, the will first moves based upon the act of the divine intellect rather than the

5. What follows depends upon the treatment of this issue through the *ST* and *DV* in Jordan, "Transcendentality of Goodness and the Human Will," 139–50. As Jordan finds no substantial difference between the section he treats from Thomas's treatise *De Malo* and the text in *ST* I–II, the former text will not be included here.

6. *DV* q.22, a.12 *ad* 2.

7. Jordan, "Transcendentality of Goodness and the Human Will," 139. See *DV* q.22, a.4 *resp*; *ST* Ia, q.78, a.1 *ad* 3.

8. *ST* Ia, q.82, a.4 *ad* 3; see Schindler, "Towards a Non-Possessive Concept of Knowledge," 582; Gilson, *Thomism*, 283–84.

9. *ST* I–II, q.9, a.4 *resp*; see Gallagher, "Thomas Aquinas on the Causes of Human Choice," 160; Jordan, "Transcendentality of Goodness and the Human Will," 139–40; Schindler, "Toward a Non-Possessive Concept of Knowledge," 583.

creature's own. This establishes an important parallel between the will (*appetitus intellectivus*) and the *appetitus naturalis*, which seeks what is "suitable" to a natural form based upon an apprehension found "not in them, but in the Author of their nature."[10] While Thomas juxtaposes the locations of apprehension for these two appetites under everyday circumstances, rational natures are fundamentally dependent upon divine apprehension for the principal orientation of their appetite, just like natural forms.[11]

The primal apprehension undergirding both natural and intellectual appetite (as well as the sensible appetite) is found in God's self-knowledge, which also contains the divine ideas.[12] In knowing himself perfectly, God also knows the way in which each finite creature imitates and participates in the divine goodness. These divine ideas serve as the exemplars by which God bestows form in giving each creature a particular *essentia* through which to act. In creation, the *causa finalis* is first in the order of causality because it reaches back from the end in the bestowal of the form that orients the *appetitus* of each creature to its respective participation in the Good known by God in the divine ideas.[13] Form points ahead to *finis*. God also moves the creatures whom he orients, granting them their own secondary efficient causality by which to seek their ends through their participation in God's own primary causality.[14] So, *appetitus* is the primordial orientation given in each form, even to forms without apprehensive powers, and *amor* is the first movement of any nature toward the end toward which it is oriented.[15] While for a non-sensible nature *amor naturalis* is the only kind of love present as its "connaturalness with the thing to which it tends," for rational natures *amor naturalis* exists virtually within *amor intellectivus*.[16]

10. *ST* I–II, q.26, a.1.

11. For a summary of Thomas's understanding of appetite as an "essential constituent of anything that exists," see Lombardo, *Logic of Desire*, 24–54. See also Diggs, *Love and Being*, 12–17.

12. See especially *ST* Ia, q.14, a.5; q.15, a.3; q.44, a.3. For an insightful explanation and defense of the Thomistic doctrine of divine ideas as a necessary mediation between the divine simplicity and God's knowledge of a multiplicity of created objects, see Geiger, "Idées Divines." See also Doolan, *Aquinas on the Divine Ideas.*

13. See *ST* Ia, q.44, a.4, *ad* 2. See also Thomas's comments on Aristotle's connection between formal and final causality in Aquinas, *Commentary on Aristotle's Physics*, II.11.242; Falcon, "Aristotle on Causality," §3.2.

14. See *ST* Ia, q.44, a.4 *ad* 4; see also q.105, a.5 *resp*; q.2, a.3 *resp*.

15. See *ST* I–II, q.26, a.1 *resp*; I, q.20, a.1; q.82, a.4 *ad* 3. See also Kwasniewski, *Ecstasy of Love*, 178; Lee, "Relation Between Intellect and Will," 331.

16. *ST* Ia, q.60, a.1; q.76, a.3. That the natural appetite is present not only in "vegetal souls" but in all created beings, even spiritual natures, is clear from *ST* I–II, q.26, a.1, *ad* 3: "Natural love is . . . universally in all things." This contradicts Flood's claim that

For intellectual natures, this means that *amor intellectivus* is the movement of the will given by God by which all the powers of the intellectual soul are moved for the sake of obtaining the Universal Good, removing any threat of infinite regression between *intelligere* and *velle*.[17] When viewed from within the rational operations, *amor intellectivus* is present as *dilectio*, which "implies, in addition to *amor*, a choice made beforehand."[18] Here, the initial movement of *amor* flowers into *dilectio*, love measured by knowledge. Apart from the rational faculty where intellectual apprehension lies, however, *dilectio* is not possible, but *amor* still exists as a natural movement toward that nature's good.[19] In this sense, *amor* exceeds the dichotomy of intellect and will, thus being more fundamentally a corollary of *esse* itself rather than of the rational operations.[20]

From this, I suggest the following way of organizing these concepts based on Thomas's real distinction: *appetitus* expresses the orientation of form given in *essentia*, and *amor* is the movement of *esse*. Both are attuned to *bonum*, but while *appetitus* expresses the connaturality between a nature

---

amor naturalis is only "love" by simile (*Root of Friendship*, 6). By this I understand him to mean that a stone cannot properly love because love is an act of a living entity at the least. Thomas seems to associate *amor* with *esse* itself, such that the presence of *amor naturalis* is rooted most basically in the underlying *actus essendi* of all created existence, so that the form, or essence, of all created things has at bottom a reference to *esse* as their Good, the most basic perfection of all *ens*. Thus, *amor* "is a being's most basic affective determination. It is that formal determination by which the being has the tendencies and strivings it has" (Gallagher, "Thomas Aquinas on the Causes of Human Choice," 54). Gilson also implies this same expansion of the universal natural appetite in the spiritual faculties (*Spirit of Mediaeval Philosophy*, 273–74); see also Schultz, "Love of Friendship," 210–11.

17. See *ST* I–II, q.26, a.1 *resp*; a.3 *resp*, *ad* 3; see also I, q.105, a.4, *resp*; *LSI* 21.2622. Jordan's discussion of the pertinent passages in the later *De Malo* solidifies this interpretation ("Transcendentality of Goodness and the Human Will," 144–45); see also Kwasniewski, *Ecstasy of Love*, 180; Diggs, *Love and Being*, 21–24.

18. *ST* I–II, q.26, a.3. Also see *LSI* 21.2622; Gallagher, "Thomas Aquinas on the Will as Rational Appetite," 559–84; Kwasniewski, *Ecstasy of Love*, 180.

19. See Diggs, *Love and Being*, 21–24.

20. Thus, Thomas: "Hence, natural appetite will be found, of necessity, in all created things directed to ends—even in the will itself, with respect to its ultimate end" (*Sent* III, d.27, q.1, a.2; translation from Aquinas, *On Love and Charity*, 130); see also Diggs, *Love and Being*, 35–36. This interpretation of Aquinas provides a clear parallel to von Balthasar's own theology of love, particularly to his claim that love is the "meaning of being," the inner mystery of all existence. In light of our interpretation of Aquinas here, it is maybe less surprising that von Balthasar adopted this way of speaking from speculative Thomists such as Gustav Siewerth and Ferdinand Ulrich; see *TL*2, 177; *TL*3, 227–28; Healy, "Christ's Eucharist," 5; Schindler, "Towards a Non-Possessive Concept of Knowledge," 589.

and its good, *amor* is the act of *esse* moving toward that end.[21] This corresponds to Thomas's own descriptions of love as a "kind of driving and moving force," which Torrell specifies as the movement that manifests life itself.[22] That is, though the specific form given as *essentia* expresses the way that that good as final cause diffuses itself by "eliciting desire or appetency (natural, sensible, or rational-voluntary) of itself," the motion of seeking and resting in that good (*amor*) is rooted not in a particular essence but in "the act whereby it is," that is, the *actus essendi*.[23] *Amor* is found in all natures, even those with no proper powers of their own; even a rock has an *appetitus* for its *ratio finis* derived from the divine goodness, and its *actus essendi* can be described as *amor naturalis*.[24] Thus, *amor* is a correlative of *esse* that is modified but not constituted by *essentia/forma*.[25]

If love can be identified as a fundamental aspect of being itself, then the operations of knowing and willing are the rational movement of *esse* as *amor* seeking its perfection in God as the *ratio finis* according to the orientation of *appetitus*. The rational operations of knowing and willing move toward a particular good identified in the *appetitus* of essence, but the movement itself is the universal movement of *amor* that is intrinsic to *esse*.[26] This is not to root the movement of the intellect in the operation of the will, creating a voluntarism of total freedom which becomes a-rational, if not irrational. At the bottom of knowing and willing is not a fully spontaneous

21. See Diggs, *Love and Being*, 29–31; Anderson, *Cause of Being*, 154. Diggs's suggestion that love is the "simple presence of the end" (*Love and Being*, 29) in created natures must be clarified in this way, in that *appetitus* and *amor* represent the end in different manners.

22. See *SCG* IV, 20.1; Torrell, *Saint Thomas Aquinas*, 162–63.

23. Anderson, *Cause of Being*, 152–53; see also Gilson, *Spirit of Mediaeval Philosophy*, 273–74.

24. See *ST* I–II, q.26, a.1 *resp* and *ad* 3. For a summary of Aquinas's understanding of appetite as an "essential constituent of anything that exists," see Lombardo, *Logic of Desire*, 24–54; see also Diggs, *Love and Being*, 12–17; Aertsen, *Nature and Creature*, 342–45, 356–60.

25. Diggs, *Love and Being*, 31; Anderson, *Cause of Being*, 154.

26. Interestingly, Gilson notes in his Gifford Lectures that for Aristotle, "[The First Mover] moves only by the love it excites—which is excites, observe, but does not breathe in . . . the love that moves the heavens and the stars in Aristotle is the love of the heavens and stars for god, but the love that moves them in St. Thomas and Dante is the love of God for the world; between these two motive causes there is all the difference between an efficient cause on the one hand and a final cause on the other" (*Spirit of Mediaeval Philosophy*, 76). This complements my suggestion that the ways in which rational natures move toward God are necessarily caught up in the fundamental movement of love received from God in creation. For Soskice, the fact that Love, like Being, is a participatory link between God and creation means that both names signal not attribution (like Omnipotence) but identity ("Being and Love," 489).

and unguided intellective act but the dependence of creatures upon God to orient the will and thereby move the intellect according to the formal/final order bestowed in creation. Love is at the beginning and end of the rational operations because love, the *actus amoris*, is a fundamental aspect of being itself, the *actus essendi* of *esse* as *amor*.[27] Returning to Thomas's terms from the *Prima Pars*, *amor* is a description of the *quomodo* of *esse* which is modulated by the *quiddity* of the *essentia*.

Beatitude and Rational Perfection

If *amor* is expanded into a descriptor of the *quomodo* of created *esse*, then Thomas's identification of *beatitudo* from the *Prima Pars* as the final end of a rational nature, where *amor* plays a secondary role and is constrained to the operation of the will, also needs to be re-evaluated. As a created perfection attributed analogically to God, beatitude is the *finis quo* of a rational nature, the end by which "the essence of God itself becomes the intelligible form of the intellect" in the "vision of the Divine Essence."[28] Thus, the *finis cuius* of the divine essence is "acquired" by the *finis quo* of beatitude, the perfection of the intellect that allows the creature to understand God according to the creature's finite mode of knowing, thereby attaining to a perfect enstatic union of knowledge with God.[29] In other words, in the *visio Dei*, creatures "possess [God] as present, having the power to see him always," and by this the created intellect is perfected and the will rests in delight, a "proper accident" to the intellectual perfection.[30] Thus, the threefold criteria for beatitude are met: seeing God in the *visio Dei*; possessing God by having the power to always see him; enjoying God as the greatest Good possessed.[31]

The well-known priority of the intellect in beatitude is in fact a reversal of the creature's relation to God. Considered absolutely, or *per se*, it is true

27. On this point, see Elders's presentation of the "collaboration between the intellect and the will in free-choice" in *Philosophy of Nature*, 327–32; Finnis, "Object and Intention," 129–34; Löwe, *Thomas Aquinas on the Metaphysics of Human Act*, 89–97.

28. *ST* Ia, q.12, a.5 *resp*; I–II, q.3, a.8; see also I, q.12, a.1, 4, 7; q.14, intro, a.1 *ad* 3; q.16, a.1; q.82, a.1.

29. *ST* I–II, q.2, a.8 *resp*; see also I, q.12, a.1, 5–6; I–II, q.3, a.8.

30. *ST* Ia, q.12, a.7 *ad* 1; I–II, q.3, a.4. Canty phrases it in this way: "Happiness is an end, therefore, not in the sense that God is an end, but in the sense that the enjoyment of God follows the attainment of God. God is an uncreated end, but enjoyment is something created in the soul when the soul attains what it has ultimately desired . . . the essence of happiness is attaining the end, whereas the *per se* accident is enjoyment" ("Aquinas and Scotus on God," 271).

31. *ST* Ia, q.12, a.7 *ad* 1. See Canty, "Aquinas and Scotus on God," 268–74.

that for Thomas the intellect is "intrinsically higher" than the will by virtue of its more universal object (being) and the fact that because it abstracts from the real order to the ideal, it is able to "internalize the perfection to which it is ordered."[32] Considered relatively to a particular object, however, the intellect is only higher in relation to lower goods, while the will is higher in relation to higher goods.[33] This is grounded in the complementary tendencies of the intellect and will; while the intellect's operation is enstatic, meaning that truth resides in the intellect through its acts of understanding and judging, the will's operation is ecstatic, meaning that it is "inclined to the thing as existing in itself," where the Good concretely exists.[34] Because of this, if the intellect knows an object that is lower than itself, the intelligible form in the intellect is sufficient to its object, for it raises its object up into itself through abstraction. On the other hand, when the intellect knows an object that is higher than itself, it is incapable of reaching its nobility because the intellect cannot reproduce its superior goodness within itself. In these cases, most clearly seen in the soul's relation to God *in via*, the will is higher than the intellect because in its ecstatic movement the soul is raised up to its object more perfectly than through the intellect. Hence, Thomas says that "the love of God is better than the knowledge of God" in being able to reach up to the Good that is infinitely higher than the soul.[35] Or as Gilson puts it, "Nothing can be loved unless it is known, but some objects can be loved better than they are known."[36]

In beatitude, however, this relation is reversed when Thomas claims that the intellect is higher *in fine* because God enables it by grace to receive the divine essence as its intelligible form in the beatific vision.[37] By an act of illumination, the intellect is elevated and enabled to know what exceeds its nature, and by seeing it comes to possess the divine essence in such a way that it is always available to be beheld and enjoyed. Though the created intellect in its current state is incapable of knowing the formal infinity of God's essence because of its "natural aptitude for material objects only," in glory this "defect of intellect" will be removed to allow the created intellect to see the divine essence.[38] In order for the will to rest in delight, however, it must have achieved the possession of the good it desired, which in beatitude

32. Schindler, "Towards a Non-Possessive Concept of Knowledge," 583–84.

33. Schindler, "Towards a Non-Possessive Concept of Knowledge," 584.

34. See *ST* Ia, q.82, a.3 *resp.*

35. *ST* Ia, q.82, a.3 *resp.*

36. Gilson, *Elements of Christian Philosophy*, 258.

37. See *ST* Ia, q.12, a.1, 5–6; q.26, a.1; I–II, q.3, a.8.

38. *ST* Ia, q.86, a.2 *ad* 1.

occurs when the intellect possesses of the divine essence. Thomas is clear that this does not imply that the created intellect comprehends the divine essence in such a way that the latter is "included" in or circumscribed by the former.[39] Rather, each "created intellect knows the Divine essence more or less perfectly in proportion as it receives a greater or lesser light of glory."[40] The understanding arrived at in the beatific vision, then, is comprehension in the sense of attainment, as the Latin *comprehendere* also means to "lay ahold of."[41] By this, the union that creatures attain with God is unmediated, meaning that it is a union with the divine essence itself through intellectual participation in it.[42] Thus, though Thomas maintains that the finite intellect never comprehends the divine essence in the sense of the latter being included in the former, he claims that this attainment of the created intellect to God is sufficient for the perfection of the intellectual power and therefore also for the fulfillment of the movement of desire in the rest of delight.

In his overview of Thomas's understanding of beatitude, Schindler questions whether this sort of intellectual attainment is sufficient such that there is no more need for "the soul's volitional movement above itself" toward God.[43] Only if this requirement is satisfied can it be true to say that the intellect is higher than the will in relation to God *in fine*, which, as Schindler points out, means that our "essential end," that is, union with God, "overturns our essential nature," in which we are ecstatically elevated to God by love.[44] Thus, the question is, does the gift of the divine essence as the intelligible form of the intellect in the *visio Dei* negate the need for any ecstatic relation to God, by the will or otherwise?

Schindler helpfully suggests that the answer to this question must begin by clarifying the role of judgment in the intellect attaining to truth. To know truth is not simply to possess an intelligible form but to know the conformity between that form and the object as it exists in reality. *In via*, seeing secures the "likeness of the visible thing" within the intellect, but only by knowing "its own conformity to the intelligible thing" in judgment itself does the intellect know truth.[45] Thus, the intellect remains ecstatically

39. *ST* Ia, q.12, a.7 *ad* 1–3; q.86, a.2 *ad* 1; see also Smith, *Thomas Aquinas' Trinitarian Theology*, 50–53.

40. *ST* Ia, q.12, a.7 *resp.*

41. *ST* Ia, q.12, a.7 *ad* 1; see also I–II, q.4, a.3 *ad* 1. If the term "apprehension" were not normally used for the basic function of the sensible and intellectual powers, this would be a more appropriate English word for this sense of *comprehendere.*

42. Townsend, "Deification in Aquinas," 231.

43. Schindler, "Towards a Non-Possessive Concept of Knowledge," 585.

44. Schindler, "Towards a Non-Possessive Concept of Knowledge," 585.

45. *ST* Ia, q.16, a.2 *resp.* The direction of the following discussion of judgment and

oriented within the created order because the *actus essendi* of an object in its subsistence always remains distinct from the intellect's understanding of that form.[46] As Schmitz puts it, there is an irreducible distinction between the *ens rationis* and *ens naturae*, and truth resides in the intellect by virtue of the understanding of this fact.[47] As Thomas conceived of it, the *visio Dei* differs from the scenario *in via* in two important ways. First, because God is not a material object, the intellect need not acknowledge the difference between intelligible form and material subsistence in God. This leads to the second, which is that the *ens rationis* and *ens naturae*, which exist respectively in the intentional and real orders, are not distinct in the *visio Dei* insofar as the divine essence is the intelligible form of the mind.

However, the basic fact of the distinction between the actual *modus essendi* of the divine essence, which is *ipsum esse per se subsistens*, and the mode in which creatures can *comprehendere* that essence remains. Even if the divine essence becomes the intelligible form of our intellect, it nevertheless infinitely exceeds the capacity of the finite intellect according to its *actus essendi*, which in creatures is that which undergirds separate subsistences and must be acknowledged in *iudicatio*. The identity of the divine form and the intelligible form in a beatified created intellect does not elide the relative insufficiency of the intellect to contain an infinite form. While the intellect may be perfected in the reception of the divine essence as intelligible form insofar as it can know it, it seems that to know it truly it must go on to maintain the excess of God's essence above its ability to possess it intellectually. Indeed, as Thomas insists that the intellect is perfected simply by knowing the quiddity of a thing, it must be allowed on his account of the intellect that the attainment of the *visio Dei* perfects the intellect according to its capacity.[48] This does not necessitate, however, that there is no more to know of God for any particular created intellect, as the knowledge bestowed in the *visio Dei* is proportionate to the "light of glory received into any created intellect," which in turn is proportionate to the charity of that creature

whether Thomas had truly integrated it into his concept of beatitude is suggested but not developed in Schindler, "Towards a Non-Possessive Concept of Knowledge," 585, endnotes 45–47. Similarly, as Schindler suggests, Thomas's notion of *esse* as the *actus essendi* does not seem to enter "centrally into his theory of knowledge" through judgment ("Towards a Non-Possessive Concept of Knowledge," 603, endnote 45). Rather than developing his theory primarily toward the singular unity of the universals, Thomas would have also had to account for the fact that by its necessary subsistence in distinct *essentia*, *esse* demands that knowledge consider the relational diversity of subsistent individuals alongside their universal commonality.

46. See *ST* Ia, q.16, a.2, 5; see also Gilson, *Elements of Christian Philosophy*, 226–32.

47. Schmitz, "Enriching the Copula," 500–503.

48. See *ST* I–II, q.3, a.8 *resp.*

for God.[49] The role of judgment in created beatitude is much the same as it is in knowledge of material things, though God as *actus purus* "ceases to be conceivable as any definable essence."[50] In beatified judgment, creaturely knowledge of God becomes true knowledge because it acknowledges the infinite excess of God's *esse* that remains above and beyond what the creature knows. The perfection of the intellect includes—if it knows truly—the acknowledgment that this intellectual attainment to the divine *esse* is only partial, even if it perfects the intellect itself.

Thus, the act of judgment suggests that the intellectual union of beatitude with the divine essence remains quasi-ecstatic in that the object cannot be fully brought into the intellect. However, the union of love rooted in the *appetitus* expressed rationally in the will remains capable of perfectly reaching God: "We know God only as man can know Him, but we can love God as God is in Himself."[51] The tension of the created intellect's inability to attain to a complete intellectual unity with God is seen early on in Thomas's tenuous language of the "quasi-contact" that the intellect accomplishes with the divine essence.[52] That the intellect can only attain to a "quasi-contact"—which is clarified as referring to the way in which "every object of knowledge is *in* the knower insofar as it is known"—reinforces the argument that the intellect cannot fully and enstatically possess the divine essence through the full operation of the intellect, for in its judgment the created intellect must forever affirm that God's essence exceeds the intellect's ability to contain it. Just as judgment identifies the reason that Thomas acknowledges the superiority of the union of love (especially the *unio realis*) *in via*, the ecstasy inherent in rightly judging an object, especially a higher and more noble one, is not eradicated even in the beatific bestowal of the divine essence as the intelligible form *in fine*.

There may be, as Schindler suggests, a hint of this later in the *ST* when Thomas says that "to love God is something greater than to know Him" and then adds the specifying phrase "especially in this state of life."[53] It may be that Thomas was then able to entertain the thought that the union of love is still closer, or more complete, *in fine* than the union of intellectual possession because the incompleteness of *comprehendere* as attainment

49. *ST* Ia, q.12, a.6–7.

50. Gilson, *Elements of Christian Philosophy*, 233.

51. Gilson, *Elements of Christian Philosophy*, 259.

52. *Sent* IV, d.49, q.1, a.1, qa.2.

53. *ST* II–II, q.27, a.4 *ad* 2; see the assessment in Schindler, "Towards a Non-Possessive Concept of Knowledge," 585, of the contradictory ways in which Thomas must speak of the operation and directionality of the intellect in order to solve this problem; see also *Sent* III, d.27, q.1, a.4.

leaves space for the creature to reach God more fully by desiring and loving the very *actus essendi* the intellect is unable to truly comprehend. In other words, the incompleteness of the intellect's immediate and internal union with the divine essence is nevertheless mediated and completed by the ecstatic impulse of love toward the divine *actus essendi*. The beatification of the intellect is thus a meeting in the middle, where the union of knowledge is suspended in the middle of the relation constituted in the union of love. Rather than the union of love passing away in favor of the more complete and perfect union of knowledge, then, it remains as the union that makes creaturely knowledge and vision of God possible.

Thomas does not speak this way about beatitude because it creates the risk that the will never truly attains its end, only desiring it and never delighting in its attainment. Beatitude is restricted to the intellect as the internal perfection of the creature because it is the intellect—rather than the will—that possesses the end of seeing God, whereas *delectatio* is the "completion and crown" of beatitude as the "consummation" of the love that moves one to the *visio Dei*.[54] However, attainment of an end can happen in multiple ways, as is clear from the various types of *unio*. Here, the intellectual end of beatitude corresponds to a *unio substantialis* as the perfection of an individual's own nature. By participating in the light of glory, the intellect knows that which is the source and end of all its own perfections, and the will rests in its enjoyment of the knowledge of that end. Based on my previous argument, though, the intellect is satisfied with this union only in terms of the divine essence becoming the intelligible form; the *modus essendi* of the divine life, recognized in judgment, exceeds the capacity of a *unio substantialis*. In this conceptualization, the will relates to the beatific perfection of the intellect in *delectatio*, but because the created intellect knows God in proportion to the light of glory given to it, this does not exclude the continued presence of *desiderium* in relation to the infinite excess of the divine *esse*.[55] The light of glory given to the created intellect can infinitely increase

54. *LSI* 17.2186; *ST* I–II, q.3, a.4. Garrigou-Lagrange is representative of mainstream Thomism on this point when he argues that although joy is necessary, it is less important than vision, i.e., the intellectual component. For Thomas, vision is the cause of joy, and Garrigou-Lagrange maintains that the cause is greater than the effect (*Beatitude*, 87–94).

55. *ST* Ia, q.12, a.7 *resp.* Canty notes that when Thomas discusses the will's enjoyment of the intellect's perfection, he "envisions enjoyment overflowing (*per redundantiam*)" into the body, though he has already made it clear that a "disembodied soul experiences perfect enjoyment of God" ("Aquinas and Scotus on God," 274; see *ST* I–II, q.4, a.5 *ad* 4). This means that even while enjoying the perfection of the intellect, the will "still desires its separated body to share in that perfect enjoyment," which provides a supportive parallel to my suggestion that the will can desire the excess of God's *esse*

without exhausting this ecstatic excess. The intellect remains perfected even as it can continue to be perfected to infinitely greater degrees as the union of knowledge grows asymptotically closer in the mediating union of love. What is required by this excess is a union of love that is analogous to a *unio realis* between multiple persons, in which neither is subsumed into the other while they enjoy a union commensurate with their mode of relating.[56]

It is striking to notice with Schmitz the similarity between this description of judgment and its mediation through love, and the perfection of charity that Thomas calls friendship (*amicitia*).[57] When the union of knowledge is accomplished in judgment through the mediation of love, the Other is allowed to remain distinct as one who is both united in mutual knowledge and exceeds the knower. Likewise, the love of friendship (*amor amicitiae*) loves and seeks the good of the Other, rather than the possession of good for the Lover herself.

The importance of this similarity can be demonstrated by Thomas's way of framing *amor concupiscentiae* and *amor amicitiae*. In its most basic sense, *amor concupiscentiae* is the love of an object due to its goodness.[58] A further determination regarding the person for whom this good is wished must be added to this, leading either to *amor sui* or *amor amicitiae*.[59] While self-love is still a form of *amor concupiscentiae*, *amor sui* has its proper place for Thomas as an orientation to one's own true good.[60] More importantly, it functions as the "form and root of friendship."[61] When one loves something as their own good, they do not only desire and delight in their own possession of the beloved good (*concupiscentia*) but also desire for that beloved good to be shared with others as far as possible (*amicitia*).[62] Love for others is the fulfillment of self-love in that it is as we are drawn to the Good that

even while delighting in the intellect's perfection.

56. See Wadell, *Primacy of Love*, 75–77.

57. Schmitz, "Enriching the Copula," 496; see *ST* I–II, q.65, a.5; q.26, a.1.

58. See *ST* I–II, q.26, a.4 *resp*, where one loves with *amor concupiscentiae* the object that one wills to another in *amor amicitiae*; see also I, q.82, a.5. David Gallagher provides an excellent and detailed explanation of the ways in which these forms of love relate to each other and to different forms of union in his essay "Desire for Beatitude and Love."

59. See *ST* I–II, q.26, a.4 *resp*.

60. See *ST* II–II, q.25, a.7 for Thomas's discussion of the various kinds of self-love; see also Flood, *Root of Friendship*, 1–24; Gallagher, "Thomas Aquinas on Self-Love." However, Janice Schultz points out that Thomas most often uses *amor sui* "without qualification to indicate disordered self-love as the ground of sin" ("Love of Friendship," 226).

61. *ST* II–II, q.25, a.4 *resp*; see also I–II, q.27, a.3 *resp*.

62. See *ST* Ia, q.19, a.2; see also I–II, q.27, a.3 *resp*; q.28, a.1 *resp*.

we can then desire that others share in the same Good. In this way, Thomas says that *amor* has "the nature of a first gift, through which all free gifts are given."[63] And, when the lover works to spread its own beloved good to others, the "lover is placed outside himself, and made to pass into the object of his love, inasmuch as he wills good to the beloved; and works for that good . . . even as he works for his own."[64] Only as concupiscible self-love flowers into the ecstatic love of seeking the good of someone else in friendship can creatures attain to charity, or *caritas*, which is the highest virtue only as our love of and friendship with God.[65]

The final end of rational creatures is not only found their own intellectual perfection, their *unio substantialis* through participation in the divine essence. This is only the internal end, the possessive perfection of the activity of the intellect.[66] The external end is God, to whom creatures relate not only in knowledge but ecstatically in the perfection of love, which in this relational context is *amor amicitiae*. As Wadell paraphrases Thomas's explanation of beatitude later in the *ST*, because humans are not made for themselves, "selfhood is a relationship" with that for which they were made: "To be is to be in love with it."[67] If put in terms of union, the *unio substantialis* of intellectual *beatitudo* is fulfilled in the *unio realis* of *amor amicitiae*. This is a mutual indwelling that involves both the apprehensive and appetitive powers. While the Beloved is in the apprehensive power of the Lover, by that same power the Lover is in the Beloved because the Lover seeks to continue to know the Beloved as much as possible. With respect to the appetitive power, the Beloved is in the Lover by way of complacency, that is, by the way that the Lover is oriented toward the good of the Beloved, and the Lover is ecstatically in the Beloved insofar as the Lover considers her Beloved to be her very self. By virtue of both powers, both Lover and Beloved are placed in one another, constituting a dynamic unity achieved by love.[68] In a similar

63. *ST* Ia, q.38, a.2.

64. *ST* Ia, q.20, a.2 *ad* 1. Thomas quotes approvingly from Dionysius's *The Divine Names*, IV.1 here: "On behalf of the truth we must make bold to say even this, that He Himself, the cause of all things, by His abounding love and goodness, is placed outside Himself by His providence for all existing things."

65. See *ST* I–II, q.65, a.5; II–II, q.23, a.1 *resp*. See Wadell, *Primacy of Love*, 62–78. For friendship as the fulfillment of self-love, see Gallagher, "Thomas Aquinas on Self-Love," Mansini, "*Duplex Amor*," 178–80; Miner, "Thomas Aquinas and Hans Urs von Balthasar," 508–10.

66. See *Sent* IV, d.49, q.1, a.1, qa.2.

67. Wadell, *Primacy of Love*, 54.

68. See *ST* Ia, q.28, a.2 *resp*; see also R. Williams, "What Does Love Know," 264–65; Kwasniewski, *Ecstasy of Love*, 108, 179, 229–49; Gallagher, "Desire for Beatitude and Love of Friendship," 25–26; Flood, *Root of Friendship*, 12–14.

way, the individual (i.e., internal) end of beatitude is only possessed within the relational context of friendship with God, in which there is a "certain mutual return of love, together with mutual communion."[69] In this reorientation of the conversation, *amor* may be elevated from the metaphysical desire of each nature for their own individual good to the orientation toward an Other to whom one desires to be ecstatically united through the mutual knowing and loving.[70] As a kind of unity that depends on both knowledge and love, *amor amicitiae* is neither solely possessive nor disinterested. It is a *unio realis* between relational natures that simultaneously identifies and enables the *unio substantialis* of each. True *beatitudo* is contextualized within *amicitia* with God.

Amor in the Divine Life

The later sections of the *ST* suggest that *amor* is the *quomodo* of *esse*, and I am suggesting that this reframing of *esse* as *amor* places the intellectual perfection of individual beatitude firmly within the relational context of *amicitia* with God. Furthermore, this reading involves each of the central concepts Thomas attributed to God in the *Prima Pars*. Indeed, *intelligere*, *velle*, and *beatitudo* are all identical with the divine *esse*. From this, it seems reasonable that some of the relational implications derived from this understanding of *amor* for both the operations and beatitude ought to obtain in some sense in God, a possibility underscored by the similarities between "*Ego sum qui sum*" (Exod 3:14) and "*Deus caritas est*" (1 John 4:16). Yet in the *ST*, Thomas systematically denies these features in the divine life *ad intra*, and especially between the trinitarian persons, almost entirely forgoing the Johannine expansion on the Tetragrammaton.[71]

The reason for this lies in Thomas's identification of *Qui est* as the most proper name for God by virtue of its universality in predication from created being, even in light of Dionysius's support for *Boni* as the most

69. *ST* Ia, q.65, a.5.

70. It is interesting that one of the objections Thomas raises against Love being a proper name for the Holy Spirit comes from Dionysius's claim that, as Thomas cites it, "love [*amor*] is . . . a unitive force" (*ST* Ia, q.37, a.1 *obj* 3). In a passage Thomas cites from *The Divine Names*, IV.15, however, the word that Dionysius uses for "love" is *eros*, which Dionysius explicitly equates with *agape* in IV.12; see Dionysius, "Divine Names," 105, 107–8. It is precisely this element of "yearning" or "desirous love" that Thomas disallows to divine love both essentially and personally, though Thomas does not address this in his response to the objection, instead carefully defining the Spirit's *nexum amantium* by virtue of the *filioque* (*ST* Ia, q.37, a.1 *ad* 3).

71. See *ST* Ia, q.6, a.4; q.19, a.1 *ad* 1.

excellent name for God.[72] Being (*esse*) is first in the order of knowing because it refers to a thing's substantial being, or *primus actus*, while *bonum* refers to a thing's ultimate perfection, or *ultimus actus*.[73] In this sense, *esse* is more universal for Thomas because it includes all things regardless of their attainment to *ultimus actus*, whereas *bonum* relates to things insofar as they attain to perfection. In the order of knowing, *esse* is apprehended by the mind first, which is then followed by *verum*, and only then completed in *bonum*, and each step becomes more determinate by adding relations to *ipsum esse*.[74] On the other hand, while *bonum* is last in the order of knowing as the *ratio finis*, it is first in the order of causation.[75] As the "cause of causes," *bonum* beckons the *primus actus* to its *ultimum actum* through fulfilling its form.[76] This means that *bonum* is only fully known in perfection, while *esse* is known simply and immediately in a thing's *primus actus*.[77]

Since the creature's attempt to name God always "falls short of the mode that God exists in himself" in this life, Thomas considers it more proper to opt for *Qui est* as a "less determinate" and "more universal and absolute" divine name. In short, the "act of sheer existing" is "Thomas's preferred description of God" because it says the least about God while standing on the solid ground of being the first and most universal perfection that flows from God to creatures.[78] This divine self-naming provides the "metaphysic

72. See *ST* Ia, q.13, a.11 *resp*, *ad* 2. Though Thomas cites a scriptural authority, the scriptural provenance of *Qui est* is ultimately secondary to Thomas's analogical theory. However, it is also true, as Soskice also notes, that Thomas is standing in a long line of reflection upon the divine names, and his choice of the *locus classicus* of Exod 3:14 reflects this heritage that extends at least back to Augustine ("Being and Love," 485; see also Soskice, "Aquinas"). That the importance of scripture is ultimately relativized by Thomas's philosophical and theological tradition and paradigm is clear from the fact that the Johannine expansion of Exod 3:14, where love (*caritas*) is added as a predicate of "*Deus est*," is not considered until Thomas cites it as the authoritative ground for attributing love (*amor*) to the divine being (I.20.1, *sed contra*). See the helpful chapter "Divine Names" in Velde, *Aquinas on God*, 95–121.

73. See *ST* Ia, q.5, a.1 *ad* 1.

74. See *ST* Ia, q.16, a.4 *ad* 2.

75. See *ST* Ia, q.5, a.2.

76. Gilson, *Thomism*, 74. See also the discussion of the four causes in Carpenter, "Analogy and Kenosis," 832.

77. As Diggs puts it, "there is more in goodness than what we call by the name of being, or by the name of unity" (*Love and Being*, 158). This is because goodness is the "fulfillment of potentiality," or, said differently, the fullness of actuality, which is itself perfection. Though this reverses Thomas's preference for the order of knowing, it reinforces the importance of considering the epistemological development that is signaled in the fact that being and truth themselves will only fully obtain where goodness is complete.

78. Kerr, *After Aquinas*, 196. See *ST* Ia, q.13, a.11 *ad* 3; Soskice, "Being and Love,"

of Exodus," which is "fundamental to Thomas's whole discussion of the divine nature" by determining the shape of his *analogia entis*.[79] Because *esse* is non-subsistent apart from being limited by *essentia* in a substance, the entry-point for Thomas's order of knowing is that of the perfection of the *primus actus* of a substance, its possession of itself.[80] In other words, just like the operations in the previous chapter, Thomas's method for organizing the divine names is based in the *unio substantialis*. Though God is not a substance, the unity that is attributed to God is fashioned after that of a substance, wherein the "being of anything consists in undivision; and hence it is that everything guards its unity as it guards its being."[81] He attributes this undividedness supremely to God in reference to the divine essence, and a concept of transcendental unity derived from created substances takes on a controlling role in the way in which the divine *esse* and everything attributed to it is described.[82]

This attribution of *unio substantialis* to God's *esse* closed off the possibility of considering the implications of the ontological correspondence between *amor* and *esse* in God. While love is attributed to God absolutely vis-à-vis the *analogia entis rationalis* and relationally as a personal name of the Holy Spirit, for *amor* to function as a fundamental description of the manner of God's *actus essendi* would create significant tension with the model of divine unity that Thomas has established. Most basically, *amor* implies relation, while *esse* only identifies a perfection in which we participate.[83] As *amor* is enacted in *caritas*, it always implies two subjects, the good and the one to whom the good is willed, even if that is the Lover herself. It is possible for *caritas* to be rightly ordered as *amor sui*, while only the love

---

485–89. C. Holmes, "Architectonics," 141, is incorrect to claim that "Goodness is the first name of God because all else participates in it." While he correctly identifies the order of causality as sketched out in *DV* 21.3 and *ST* I.5.2, Thomas is clear that *Qui Est* is the first name of God in the way theological language is most properly used. Milbank helpfully cautions against setting *esse* and *bonum* against one another absolutely, both because intellection for Thomas never happens apart from the movement of the will and because *esse* is the place of the "transcendental coincidence of truth, beauty, and goodness, *including* the self-diffusing character of the latter" ("Can a Gift Be Given," 143).

79. Mascall, *He Who Is*, 13.

80. See Velde, *Participation and Substantiality*, 42–43, 270.

81. *ST* Ia, q.11, a.1 *resp*. As Gilson points out, Thomas does not apply *substantia* to God, as in God "there is no essence, or quiddity, to stand under (sub-stare, sub-stantia) his *esse*. The name 'substance' does not befit the pure actuality of God" ("*Quasi Definition Substantiae*," 120).

82. See *ST* Ia, q.11, a.4; see Merriell, "Trinitarian Anthropology," 123–27, 133–34.

83. *ST* Ia, q.13, a.11 *ad* 3.

of friendship (*amor amicitiae*) "consists in sharing with another."[84] In either case, the fact remains that love is a transitive act—ecstatic toward both the beloved Good and the Beloved subject, whether that is oneself or an Other. On the other hand, if considered separately from *amor*, God's *esse* is not transitive in this way; on the contrary, the divine *esse* is self-subsistent and requires no external relation, creating the conceptual bounds within which the operations must remain. Thomas expresses this rationale clearly: "For when we say that God exists, no relation to any other object is implied, as we do imply when we say that God wills. Therefore, although He is not anything apart from Himself, yet He does will things apart from Himself."[85]

By rejecting Richard of St. Victor's view that all self-love is bad, Thomas attempts to conceptualize self-love as both "pure disinterestedness" and "absolute ecstasy."[86] Love (*amor*) *per se* is considered in pure referentiality to the Good, which allows God's self-love not to be "egotistical" while paradoxically self-referential.[87] Nonetheless, for Thomas self-love remains imperfect, in comparison to friendship, which is perfect and to which self-love is ultimately ordered as its fulfillment.[88] For this reason, Malet tries to argue that because *caritas* "can also exist from subject to subject" as *amicitia*, this "already tells us that the love of the divine Persons will be a love of friendship."[89] The plurality of the persons requires this move from self-love to friendship for Malet, as the essence was intentionally discussed in such a way that it could be concretized in the relations of the divine persons: "The plurality of Persons introduces the love of friendship into God, which we know is the most perfect of all loves."[90] Furthermore, he identifies the Spirit

84. See a.7, *ad* 11–12 in Thomas's *De Caritate*, where he clarifies that the *ratio* of *caritas* does not include two subjects, which means that Gregory's famous dictum that love requires at least two subjects references only applies to charity "as it includes the aspect of friendship" (*On Charity*, 64).

85. Thomas expresses this rationale clearly: "For when we say that God exists, no relation to any other object is implied, as we do imply when we say that God wills. Therefore, although He is not anything apart from Himself, yet He does will things apart from Himself" (*ST* Ia, q.19, a.2 *ad* 1).

86. Malet, *Personne et Amour*, 129, my translation.

87. Malet, *Personne et Amour*, 129–32, my translation; see *ST* II–II, q.25, a.7. Holmes's claim, following Emery's understanding of plurality, relation, and essence, that speech of God's goodness is essential and distinct from relational talk of God is complicated by the fundamental ecstasy attributed to the divine goodness—rightly, in my judgment—by Malet; see C. Holmes, "Architectonics," 134; see also Emery, "Essentialism or Personalism," 191.

88. See Malet, *Personne et Amour*, 113–14; *ST* II–II, q.17, a.8, *resp.*

89. Malet, *Personne et Amour*, 134, my translation; see 134–59 for his full argument.

90. Malet, *Personne et Amour*, 139–40, my translation.

as "the fruit . . . of the love of friendship of two subjects," a possibility he grounds in the psychological analogy itself, as the Spirit proceeds as Love from both Father and Son.[91]

However, because divine unity has been carefully defined according to self-subsistence, love in God remains within the bounds of *unio substantialis*, which means that Thomas cannot use fully relational language for the love of the trinitarian persons. Despite Malet's insistence, nowhere in the *ST* is *amor amicitiae* attributed to the divine persons.[92] Instead, the love that is identified in God is simply his love for the divine essence by which God is Good. Likewise, though Spirit proceeds as the "mutual Love" of the Father and Son, it is framed essentially as the internal impression of the Beloved in the Lover rather than the ecstatic movement of love toward the Other.[93] Thomas illustrates this line of reasoning in his assertion that a man cannot properly be "a friend to himself, but something more than a friend, since friendship implies union . . . whereas a man is one with himself which is more than being united to another."[94] Thus, if a rational creature cannot be a friend to himself, neither could it be proper to attribute *amor amicitiae* to the persons of the divine life, as they are one substantially, that is, subsisting in the "same individual nature."[95] Even when Thomas describes a *duplex unitas* in God, while commenting on the High Priestly Prayer in John 17, a high point of St. John's proto-trinitarian grammar, the *unitas amoris*, which here is also a *unitas spiritus*, is subordinated to the *unio substantialis*.[96] While God's *unio substantialis* is mirrored in a *unio similitudinis* among creatures, the *unitas amoris* that flowers into *amicitia* with God and others is only understandable in God by removing relationality: the trinitarian persons *ad intra* are only "one by a love that is not participated and *a gift*

91. Malet, *Personne et Amour*, 159, my translation.

92. Commenting on *communio* views of divine perfection, such as Richard of St. Victor's, Thomas Joseph White argues that arguments of communion in God from interpersonal communion in creatures "implicitly denies the reality of biblical monotheism" because "perfection for persons is attained only through mutual communion of persons, *for all created persons*, precisely because they are composed of act and potency in the order of being and specifically in their spiritual operations of intellect and will" ("Divine Simplicity and the Holy Trinity," 84). The implication here is that *amicitia* only constitutes the perfection of creatures because they cannot be perfect in themselves, unlike the divine persons.

93. *ST* Ia, q.37, a.1 *ad* 3.

94. *ST* II–II, q.25, a.4 *resp*.

95. *LSI* 17.2214.

96. For the concept of proto-trinitarian grammars, or "depth-structures," in Scripture, see Schwöbel, "God Is Love," 312; see also Schwöbel, "Trinity Between Athens and Jerusalem," 30; Schwöbel, "Christology and Trinitarian Thought."

from another."[97] Based upon Thomas's own taxonomy of love and unity, a *unitas amoris* based within a *unio substantialis* is constituted by *amor concupiscentiae*, one's love of what belongs to one's self.[98] Thus, the *unitas amoris et spiritus* within the trinitarian life is still restricted to the weaker *nexus patris et filii* attributed to the Spirit in the *ST*, in which the Spirit is not a gift of love between the Father and Son but only the sign of their mutual love based on consubstantiality.

Other Thomistic commentators have tried to press toward the integration of the essential and personal unity of God around the language of love. For example, Bourassa says:

> The unity of love . . . does not contradict or exclude the unity of essence, but to the contrary, demonstrates it according to this other passage: "The Father loves the Son and has given him all things" ([John] 3:35). To love, to give—these are the acts of persons. In this way, it is possible to see first of all the unity of essence from the personal action by which the Father gives all to the Son.[99]

Bourassa presents two interpretations of Thomas's trinitarian thought in the *ST* that roughly correspond to my reading of Thomas in the last chapter and the direction toward which this chapter presses. The first explanation divides the essential and personal into different registers—ontological and phenomenological, respectively—which, though complementary, must be kept distinct.[100] Alternatively, the second, though acknowledging that our way of thinking "obliges us to distinguish between nature and person" and thus to distinguish the interpersonal communion of the divine persons from the communication of the divine nature along the lines of the relations, presses on toward a further synthesis of the two registers. Thus, Bourassa says that the Father can only communicate the divine *esse* to the Son by "giving his very self, in an act of total complaisance 'in the Holy Spirit.'"[101] Though Thomas gestures toward the identity of these two registers—"it is clear that in God relation and essence do not differ from each other, but are one and the same"—he is not able to commit himself to the interpersonal

97. *LSI* 17.2214, emphasis mine; see 13.1838; 15.2012; 17.2247.

98. See *ST* I–II, q.28, a.1; *LSI* 15.2036.

99. Bourassa, "Esprit Saint, 'Communion,'" 254, my translation.

100. Bourassa, "Esprit Saint, 'Communion,'" 279, my translation.

101. Bourassa, "Esprit Saint, 'Communion,'" 279, my translation; see also Malet, *Personne et Amour*, 148.

language of giving toward which Bourassa and Malet, as well as Williams, press.[102]

Yet the framework for further development in this direction is present in Thomas. As *amor amicitiae* requires both *benevolentia* and *communicatio* between persons, Thomas's language of both giving and communication between Father and Son is of particular importance.[103] However, to try to realize Malet's suggestion of something analogous to *amor amicitiae* in the trinitarian life requires a reconsideration of the scope of the divine operations, which in turn will affect the nature of divine unity.

For example, in the case of the divine intellect, while the process of composition and division is absent, God still "judges of all things and knows of all things complex" in his "simple act of intelligence."[104] That this includes the Trinity is made clear once, in a text that Williams points to: "the Father, by understanding Himself, the Son, and the Holy Spirit, and all other things comprised in this knowledge, conceives the Word; so that thus the whole Trinity is spoken in the Word."[105] While only the Father speaks, his speaking is the notional manifestation of the essential act of understanding common to each person. Thomas's intent here is to protect the distinction between "knowing" and "speaking" in God, thereby maintaining the ability of "speaking" to designate relation between the Father and Son. Thus, only the Father speaks, only the Son is the Word that is spoken, but in that Word each Person is signified, and in the divine essence, "each Person understands and is understood."[106] From this, Williams argues that what is known by God is "neither the divine essence as some abstraction from the divine life, nor 'himself' as a divine individual" but rather "what is involved in the divine life," that is, the fact that "he (the Father) is already actively giving what he is to another . . . he knows himself in generative relation to another."[107]

102. *ST* Ia, q.28, a.2 *resp*.

103. *ST* II–II, q.23, a.1 *resp*. See Mansini, "*Similitudo*, *Communicatio*, and Friendship."

In a rare example, Thomas allows Hilary of Poitiers's claim that the Father "gives" (*dare*) the divine essence as a "Gift" to the Son in his generation to stand insofar as the divine *esse* is the Father's by identity (*hoc esse huius*); *ST* Ia, q.38, a.1 *obj* 2, *ad* 2. More prevalent is his language of *communicatio* in God: *ST* Ia, q.27, a.3 *ad* 3; q.27, a.4 *ad* 3; q.30, a.2 *ad* 4; q.39, a.5 *ad* 6; q.41, a.3 *resp*; q.42, a.5 *resp*; q.42, a.6 *ad* 2.

104. See *ST* Ia, q.16, a.5 *ad* 1, where Thomas says that God "*iudicat de omnibus, et cognoscit omnia complexa*" without either "*composition et divisio*."

105. *ST* Ia, q.34, a.1 *ad* 3; see also R. Williams, "What Does Love Know," 263.

106. *ST* Ia, q.34, a.1 *ad* 3. Other than this text, Thomas almost always identifies the essence as the object of the essential operations, as in *ST* Ia, q.37, a.3, where the Spirit proceeds as the love of the "primal goodness whereby the Father loves himself."

107. R. Williams, "What Does Love Know," 263.

Williams is pushing for a reading of Thomas that follows Emery's *redoublement* by not pitting *de Deo uno* and *de Deo trino* against one another. However, this calls for a kind of *iudicatio* to obtain within the divine knowing for each person to "understand" and be "understood" not only according to their common essence but according to their relative mode of subsisting.[108] The Father's knowledge would then be a self-knowledge mediated through knowledge of an Other, occurring relationally in a divine "motion [of] self-differentiation" in which, as Williams puts it, the Father "knows himself in generative relation to another . . . [by] recognizing his own action of self-giving, bestowal of what he is."[109] In this kind of divine knowing, the divine persons would apprehend the others each as an "other self," to which each "wills good to him as to himself" and communicates this good to that Other—the two elements of Thomas's later definition of *amicitia*—precisely in the act of self-giving that is their relative subsistence in the divine *esse*.[110]

This is fitting, for if the essential act of knowing includes the distinctions inherent to the trinitarian relations, then the *unio substantialis* must also be capable of being understood in terms like a *unio realis* established in the love of friendship. Here, the circle of unions established by Thomas is closed in the infinite simplicity of the divine of love. For creatures, the *unio substantialis* of each is the ground of any *unio similitudinis* with other creatures, which in turn is the ground of the *unio affectum* by which the Beloved is considered to be the Lover's very self. Because of this identification in love (which Thomas likens to *unio substantialis*), the Lover seeks a *unio realis* with the Lover in order to arrive as close to a *unio substantialis* as possible, though this is precluded by their substantial distinction.[111] In God, however, there is no substantial distinction, and thus the *unio realis* sought

108. If it is not the case that the distinct *modi existendi* of the persons are essentially known by each person in the divine intellect, then it seems that *via negativa* simply leaves us with a bare and undifferentiated divine *esse* that as itself cannot be known in any distinct or relative terms. It is better, as Schindler argues, to retain both poles of created being (*essentia* and *esse*) and integrate them in the divine being rather than denying one or the other, as both participate in God ("What's the Difference," 25). This allows us to emphasize both *ipsum esse* and *subsistens*, God's being as both unrestricted yet subsisting in this particular way of threefold personal relation.

109. R. Williams, "What Does Love Know," 263.

110. *ST* I–II, q.28, a.1 *resp.* It is this transfer of self, in which a Lover is placed outside of himself in the Beloved, that drives the Lover to share their own good with the Beloved, which Thomas limits to God's relation to creation in q.20, a.2 *ad* 1. See the discussion of *extasis* in God and its limitation by Thomas's concept of divine unity and simplicity in Kwasniewski, *Ecstasy of Love*, 279–83.

111. *ST* I–II, q.28, a.1 *ad* 2; see Flood, *Metaphysical Foundations of Love*, 38–39.

between the persons in love may truly be the personal mode of their *unio substantialis*, while still admitting of the relation excess between them identified in *iudicatio*. The *unio amoris* thus may eternally mediate and include the intellectual perfection of *beatitudo*, opening the door to the possibility of describing a true unity-in-distinction that does not separate the essential and personal but unifies them in the coincidence of the *unio substantialis* and *unio realis*, where the concurrence of desire and attainment seen in created beatitude is fully expressed in the divine *amicitia* of the Trinity.[112]

A sentence found in Williams's essay aptly illustrates the need for this kind of move by the startling juxtaposition of interpersonal expressions with a single, repeated referent: "God is a movement towards God, God's wanting of God so that God may be fully and blissfully God, may enjoy the 'natural good' proper to the divine nature."[113] There is an echo here of Thomas's choice of *Qui est* without a consideration of *Deus caritas est* in the identification of God in terms that do not at all conform to the divine self-identification in the New Testament, where "God" overwhelmingly refers to the Father in distinction from (and often in relation to) the Son and the Spirit. The subordination of personal union to essential unity in Thomas's *ST* prevents trinitarian revelation from revising the ontology used to speak of God. Though carried out powerfully and coherently, speaking and reading doubly do not sufficiently account for the disparity between Thomas's description of the trinitarian life and that of the Scriptures. What is necessary is a true revision of what is meant by *essentia*, *esse*, and *unio* that considers the content and form of the revelation of the Trinity's personal interrelatedness. In the end, this is in keeping with Thomas's own foundational premise that we do not know what God is but only that he is, and so we can only describe God according to the manner of this act, which has

112. Thus, although Lombardo is correct to say that *appetitus* only applies to God as "an inclination toward a good already possessed," the movement of appetite moves through desire and continues in its perfection in the actuality of a completion, as above (*Logic of Desire*, 28). This movement that is linked to desire is necessary to attribute life, as Jean-Pierre Torrell argues from *SCG*, IV.20: "Love is provided with a certain force of impulsion or movement. . . . It is movement above all that manifest life" (*Saint Thomas Aquinas*, 162–63). Hankey, quoting this time the *ST* (Ia, q.19, a.1, *ad* 3), puts it this way: "Treating God as object of himself in will, Thomas is required once again to speak of him as moving upon himself. 'And this is what Plato meant when he said that the first mover moves himself'" (*God in Himself*, 101). All of these locutions become more cogent when God is spoken of in interrelational terms rather than as a single referent.

113. R. Williams, "What Does Love Know," 265. Tourpe expresses something of the sort in his own reading of Thomas's ontology of love but with operational language even closer to what I am proposing here, saying, "*Dieu a en propre, et au plus haut point, une telle extase connaissante de son, qu'achève l'enstase amoureuse en soi avec soi*" ("Thomas d'Aquin Est le Penseur de l'être Comme Amour," 552).

been revealed as trinitarian love, requiring a reconfiguration of both *esse* and person in the divine life.

Conclusion

Thomas's more robust emphasis on love in his account of created natures provides resources for its further development, but this fact underscores the tension between the essential and personal aspects of *de Deo* earlier in the *ST*, as a fuller consideration of love would have lessened the demand to keep the language of these two perspectives separate. Exploring the possibility of identifying something analogous to *amicitia* within the Godhead would enable the divine persons to relate to one another through the full ecstatic range of the rational operations Thomas has attributed to the divine *esse*. But it would also raise further questions concerning the nature of *esse* itself and of the kind of unity that is most fundamental to our existence and to the life of God. Soskice is surely right to see the danger of tritheism in simply saying that "the three 'Persons' are friends of each other," but she also recognizes the possibility of saying that "'the Trinity is friendship' much as one says 'God is love.'"[114] In other words, the concept of *amicitia* may express the combination of unity and diversity found in the Godhead better than the internal self-relations of a singular hypostasis.

If Thomas's concept of *amicitia* is to provide direction, though, it is important to note that Thomas develops this notion even further in his commentaries on Scripture. While in the *ST* friendship is the extension of self-love in sharing what you love with those you love, in the *LSI* it is the fulfillment of love itself, standing on its own as superior to self-love. It is no longer only a sharing of one's own good but a self-denial or self-sacrifice where self-love transcends its restriction to the lover.[115] This is particularly clear in Thomas's comment on John 15:13: "It is clear that the sign of the greatest love is to lay down one's life for one's friends."[116] This theme runs throughout his commentary on the Passion in St. John's Gospel, where it is clear that love for both God and neighbor "led Christ to undergo death."[117] As the Good Shepherd, Jesus loves his sheep and for this reason "gives his

114. Soskice, *Kindness of God*, 161.

115. In addition to the following examples from the *LSI*, Thomas claims from Dionysius that the ecstasy ingredient in divine love requires self-relinquishment for the perfection of *caritas* (Healy, "Christ's Eucharist," 7).

116. *LSI* 15.2009; see also 13.1738; Levering, "Does the Paschal Mystery Reveal the Trinity," 84.

117. *LSI* 14.1976.

life" for them.[118] In fact, it is in his death that "the love (*caritas*) of God for men appears most clearly."[119] By his use of 1 John 4:10 in the *LSI*, Thomas makes clear that the love of God is, in fact, expressed toward us as *amor amicitiae*: "Christ did not lay down his life for his enemies so that they would remain his enemies, but to make them his friends. Or, one could say, that he lays down his life for his friends, not in the sense that they were friends who loved him, but rather were those whom he loved."[120] The "execution" of God's love "*in finem*" is Christ's death, the greatest sign of his love.[121]

Amor amicitiae here moves intentionally beyond self-love in the revelation of God in Christ, as it is the self-denial manifest in Christ's act of dying for others that reveals divine *amor* most fully. *Amicitia* is the fulfillment of love in that *bonum* is not sought for oneself any longer but for the Other at one's own expense.[122] Love's truest nature is therefore revealed in the incarnation of the divine Word as necessarily relational in its self-giving nature, but to attribute this to the divine nature will require a reintroduction of the ecstatic elements of the operations and therefore a more material place given to the *unitas amoris*. These two adjustments call for two further and more fundamental revisions: the essential unity must include interpersonal diversity in its definition and the conceptual rendering of *esse* must admit of this definition of unity. What Thomas offers is the possibility of integrating the erotic desire for Good elicited in its self-diffusivity and the ecstatic yearning of love for the Other that reaches into the selfless love revealed in the Gospels within the trinitarian life itself. In short, the metaphysical framework of trinitarian theology must be recentered around *amor amicitiae*. While this concept goes further than sharing (already near or over the line for Thomas in *de Deo*) into a sacrificial idiom certainly at odds with Thomas's divine ontology, it is perfectly consonant with that of Hans Urs von Balthasar, to whom I turn in the next chapter.

118. *LSI* 10.1399, 1404–1405.

119. *LSI* 12.1673.

120. *LSI* 15.2009. For a sample of Thomas's use of 1 John 4:10 in the *LSI*, see 10.1422, 13.1735, 15.2020, 16.2159.

121. *LSI* 13.1738; see also *ST* III, q.46, a.3; Levering, "Does the Paschal Mystery Reveal the Trinity," 84.

122. See Healy, "Christ's Eucharist," 7.

3

Love, Kenosis, and Bonicity

The Possibility of Interpersonal Love in the Trinitarian Unity

Introduction

In his 1975 essay in honor of Hans Urs von Balthasar's seventieth birthday, Klaus Hemmerle provides a succinct evaluation of why Thomas's attempt to integrate the common and relative aspects of the divine life is insufficient: "Any understanding of Being in which the latter is taken for self-subsistence . . . is too thin to do proper justice to the Trinitarian idea of a Christian understanding of Being."[1] Specifically, the weakness is the focus on "self," and the correlated assumptions that tend to accompany it. This is demonstrated in a revealing way in Rowan William's essay "What Does Love Know?" While admitting that the language of self is "unhelpful," for Williams it seems unavoidable when "talking about life characterized by activity that is more like intelligent activity than any other, yet is neither the life of a single subject nor the history of several individual subjects."[2] Concealed within this last remark—that intellectual life is linked to a "single subject" while we must talk of something like "history" in regards to what goes on between several subjects—is the very metaphysical assumption Hemmerle is calling into question. Must the self be linked to the oneness of the divine *esse* in a manner that leads to tension with the threeness of the divine persons?

No, or so I have argued in the previous two chapters, as I sought to demonstrate from Thomas's own thought that there is more to be gained by

1. *Theses*, 33.

2. R. Williams, "What Does Love Know," 266.

conceiving of the divine *esse* as love before intellectual activity, and specifically love as a relational act, than there is to be lost. The concept of Being expressed in Thomas's *ipsum esse per se subsistens* assumes that true unity is self-subsistence, self-possession, and self-identity. In as much as this leads to hypostatizing the divine essence by the attribution of the rational operations, the danger arises of reducing the interrelationality of the divine Persons to the interior self-relating of a singular Person. From this, Hemmerle calls for more than a "mere *relecture* of the ontological pre-understandings which accompany faith" in favor of a "'new ontology,' . . . a 'Trinitarian ontology,' [as] a consequence of this faith itself."[3] In other words, we cannot simply reread the old categories of *esse*, *essentia*, *relatio*, and *persona* in light of the fact that in creation *esse* is always instantiated individually. Instead, a new understanding of *esse* must be established based upon the threeness of the one divine *esse*.

Hans Urs von Balthasar attempts this kind of revision by grounding the whole of his trinitarian speculation in the love between the Father and Son in the Spirit as it is spoken of in Holy Scripture.[4] While von Balthasar is committed to many of the same philosophical positions as Thomas, he applies them in fundamentally different ways throughout his corpus, considering Thomas's intellectualism a misguided importation of the created into the divine only maintained in order to provide some way to distinguish the divine processions.[5] Observing that it is "out of love" that "the Father hands over his Son to the World . . . (John 3:16)," he asks, "Does this not point, from the economy, to the theological fact of God's life, such that we can suppose that God also brought forth the 'Son of his love' out of love?"[6] Rather than love being "deferred until the procession of the Spirit,"[7] von Balthasar thinks that the scriptural language concerning the divine processions calls for a way to "differentiate God's all-embracing love . . . so as to

3. *Theses*, 33.

4. Von Balthasar carefully distinguished between natural love and what he called "absolute love," which is that of God who is "totally Other." While natural love for von Balthasar "never quite escapes its 'abysmal egoism,'" absolute love is understood "in terms of a radical opposition to egoism, self-love, self-interest, or the satisfaction of any need" (*Love Alone Is Credible*, 51–60); see also the discussion in Miner, "Thomas Aquinas and Hans Urs von Balthasar," 514–15. This marks a significant difference between von Balthasar and Thomas, as the latter identifies a proper place for *amor sui* while von Balthasar tends to identify this with a total lack of love.

5. See *TL*2, 162–63; see also Balthasar, *Razing the Bastions*, 29. For confirmation from a Thomist interpretation, see Malet, *Personne et Amour*, 112–13.

6. *TL*2, 162; see also *TL*3, 139.

7. See Nichols, *Balthasar for Thomists*, 54–58, 122–23, who notes throughout the Johannine cast of von Balthasar's theological method.

evidence, after all, something like a foundation for the distinction of the two processions within the one divine love."[8]

In this chapter, I will focus mainly on the trinitarian framework in the final two volumes of the *Theo-logic*, as these two are both the least studied and most mature trinitarian reflections from von Balthasar. First, I set the stage for von Balthasar's trinitarian reflection by demonstrating his commitment to locating the full extent of love's ecstatic action within the parameters of God's life *in se*, as well as the inability of both inter- and intra-personal trinitarian images to establish this love fully within a concretely unified divine life. After this, I overview von Balthasar's own trinitarian proposal through the lens of his consistent definition of "what is essentially divine: the giving over of self [*Selbstübergabe*],"[9] which is explained through his notion of the intra-trinitarian kenosis. For von Balthasar, the conception of love as giving is clearly prioritized over love as seeking, which he locates primarily within the relations between Father and Son. In the final section of the chapter, I present his mature pneumatology, interpreted through von Balthasar's reliance upon Ferdinand Ulrich to integrate the Thomistic concept of the Spirit as Bond with von Balthasar's preferred terms of Gift and Fruit. By prioritizing the finality of the Spirit, the trinitarian life of love can be understood as both seeking and giving, possessive and dispossessive, and the fulfillment of love is seen in the perfection of each divine person within the fecund context of *amicitia*, which is expressed and guaranteed in the Spirit.

God Is Love: Unity and Relationality

Just as von Balthasar viewed Thomas's real distinction between *esse* and *essentia* as fundamental to understanding the gift quality of created being, the lack of this distinction in God was equally important for von Balthasar's trinitarian theology.[10] Because the divine *esse* is the act of the divine processions ("*omnis processio sit secundum aliquam actionem*"), it must be

8. *TL*2, 163. Malet identifies the failure to do just this as the principal problem with Richard of St. Victor's attempt to describe the divine Trinity only through love, in which "*intelligence . . . est en quelque sorte noyée dans l'amour*" (*Personne et Amour*, 115). However, as I argued in the previous chapter, Thomas himself provides sufficient ground to see the movement of the intellect as itself a facet of love, but this can only work when love is not only understood as a function of the will but more fundamentally of existence itself.

9. *TL*2, 137.

10. Nicholas Healy makes this point extensively and draws out numerous implications related to this study in (*Eschatology of Hans Urs von Balthasar*, 19–89).

understood for von Balthasar as "coextensive with" and "as much 'in motion' as the event of the processions themselves."[11] Unlike Thomas, von Balthasar insists that any description of the divine *esse* must be "concomitantly determined by the unrepeatably unique participation of Father, Son, and Spirit in this event [that never exists] except as fatherly, sonly, or spirit-ually."[12] The common *esse* cannot be spoken of in a way that can be related to one divine person individually, but must consciously be described as an act that constitutes and includes the relations between all three divine persons.[13] In this, von Balthasar distances himself both from the material organization and conceptual separation found in the *Prima Pars*. Instead, the fact that the divine persons are identical with the divine *actus purus* means that just as God's *essentia* must be understood as an act, the unity of this act must be expressed in a simultaneous dialectic with the concrete life of the trinitarian persons.[14] Though von Balthasar leans heavily on Thomas's real distinction and the lack thereof in God, the way in which he works this concept out in his theology looks quite different. For von Balthasar "God's inmost being" must be further identified as love for the exact reason that it was not for Thomas, namely, that in its fullness it implies relations between persons by definition.[15]

11. *ST* Ia, q.27, a.1 *resp*; *TL*2, 136. In specific reference to his theological dramatics but with wider applicability, Nichols observes that von Balthasar's ontology is never divorced from a theory of act, whether in relation to man, Christ, or the Trinity (*No Bloodless Myth*, 63).

12. *TL*2, 136–37. Here and elsewhere, von Balthasar is quick to point out that the "last shadow of the lingering objection of a divine *quaternitas* finally vanish[es]"; see *TD*5, 191. See also Martin's helpful comments on how this identification between processions and essence "vivifies and makes dynamic a category—namely, essence—which has been rendered overly static and abstract" in "Consubstantial Otherness of God," 550–51.

13. Khaled Anatolios expresses this concept lucidly in reference to Rahner's concern over "centers of activity" in "Personhood, Communion, Trinity," 154–55.

14. See O'Regan's comments on the affinity between von Balthasar's trinitarianism and certain construals of Thomas's thought, particularly that of Gilles Emery, in *Balthasar and the Spectre of Hegel*, 224. However, this must also be balanced with von Balthasar's continuing desire to hold essential and existential language together, not allowing substance or essence to fade completely into the background in favor of language of action or relation. See his comments on Christian Personalists, especially Nédoncelle, in *TL*3, 148–51. See also Olsen, "*Exitus et Reditus*," 653.

15. *TL*2, 136. An extreme form of the consequences of radically prioritizing the divine unity and aseity found in Thomas can be seen in Sonderegger's opposition to logic like von Balthasar's: "[Divine] Love is free from the demand and need of an Object, divine or human. The Perfection of Love is not 'relation' or object centered in just this sense. . . . Love can exist without an object . . . [it] exists *A Se*, without object, relation, or act entailed. Almighty God is free over His objects, free over His relations. . . . Love

Simply adopting an alternative image for the Trinity alone does not satisfy this requirement. Von Balthasar illustrates this by juxtaposing the Augustinian-Thomist tradition with the interpersonal image preferred by Richard of St. Victor. Extending Gregory the Great's two-person requirement for love (*caritas*), Richard insisted that the love of the Trinity is not simply that of the Father and Son loving each other in "contrary directions," but is rather fulfilled in a *condilectio* of the Father and Son for the Spirit.[16] The joining together in loving a third that proceeds from them moves Richard's model from an I-Thou to an *imago trinitatis* able to counterbalance the emphasis on unity that locks the Augustinian model into single-subjectivity. However, while the psychological analogy struggles to provide language concrete enough to account for active relations of love between the persons, Richard's model leans too far in the opposite direction, "burst[ing] open the narrow confines of the self-enclosed subject, even as it fails to maintain the unity of the divine substance because of its emphasis on interpersonal love."[17] While the *unio substantialis* of the Augustinian-Thomist image is ultimately unable to "give an adequate picture of the real and abiding face-to-face encounter of the hypostases," von Balthasar believed that the Richardian *unio realis* of the persons is not finally able to "attain the substantial

is a Substance" (*Doctrine of God*, 481–82). For Sonderegger, if we do not confess that God is "Substance, whole and entire," that "God has and is a Nature," then "we fail in our question to begin with the One God" (*Doctrine of God*, 482, 483). Her argument continues in the same vein throughout her volume on the Trinity, for example: "We cannot satisfy the demand for a Supercelestial Unity, an Absolute and Transcendent Unicity, that Lateran IV codifies, by proposing as divine analogy the conversation among intimates, or the willing and eager obedience of the perfect servant" (*Doctrine of the Holy Trinity*, 455).

16. *TL*2, 40–41; quoting Richard of St. Victor, "*On the Trinity*," III.2.19.

17. *TL*2, 40. His discussion here addresses the common concern today that he is overly reliant upon the "I-Thou" model of his day (e.g., Kilby, *Balthasar*, 102–4). As McInerny notes, it is the reciprocity ingredient in von Balthasar's understanding of trinitarian love that makes the divine persons "appear as individual self-conscious subjects" (*Trinitarian Theology*, 24). Von Balthasar also includes lengthy discussions concerning various ways in which philosophers and theologians have discussed the relation between an I and a Thou and its application to an understanding of the divine relationality and its life of love. This includes Martin Buber, who talks about the space "between" or the "inter-" (*TL*2, 54–55), various German Idealists (Fichte, Hegel, Schelling) and Feuerbach (*TL*3, 149–50; Balthasar, *Love Alone Is Credible*, 43–44), and Christian personalists such as Maurice Nédoncelle and Gerhard Gloege (*TL*3, 150–51). Above all, however, McInerny is correct that Balthasar finds support for speaking of God in these terms primarily in Richard of St. Victor rather than the German tradition. Von Balthasar does not remain within this paradigm though, as becomes clear in his pneumatology, which I will discuss in the last half of this chapter.

unity of God."[18] The failure of each is rooted in the "naivety" of an analogical application of one human pattern or another to the "divine mystery," either that of human relationships or of the human self.[19] For von Balthasar this does not mean that these "complementary counterimage[s]"[20] must both be cast off, but rather that theology "must look upward to the incomprehensible archetype through the irreducible polarity of these two intraworldly images."[21]

Though the Victorine image supports von Balthasar's emphasis on the vis-à-vis relations within the trinitarian life, the divine essence is not sufficiently redefined to allow for these vis-à-vis relations to subsist in substantial unity. Specifically, what is needed is a more thoroughgoing relational ontology of love. Though Thomas's rational-self model for the essence is problematic, his theory of subsistent relations still provides von Balthasar with a mechanism for concretely defining the divine *esse* by the *rationes* of the divine persons. Rather than having to separate between the *esse* and *rationes* of the divine relations, the divine *esse* includes the *ratio* of each real relation.[22] As Hemmerle suggests, if *relatio* is freed by the emphasis on love to be no longer only a category or accident of being and elevated to the level

18. *TL2*, 38–42; see Nichols, *Balthasar for Thomists*, 123. Von Balthasar notes that Augustine himself identified a similar problem with his mature trinitarian analogy of *memoria*, *intellectus*, and *voluntas* (*TL2*, 40; quoting Augustine, "Sermon 52"). While McInerny correctly signals that von Balthasar does not think that Richard himself did not confess and teach the divine unity, it seems questionable to say that Balthasar contradicts himself here within two pages (*Trinitarian Theology*, 69–70). Rather than reading von Balthasar as conflicted, it would be more charitable to say that just as Augustine was not a modalist, though von Balthasar sees his model as unable to account for the fully personal nature of the divine persons, Richard is not a tritheist, though von Balthasar likewise sees his model as undermining the very divine unity that Richard sought to establish. This better explains why neither Augustine's and Richard's models can be taken as a final solution, though McInerny is right to note that Richard's model is given much more attention and development than is Augustine's in the following pages.

19. Balthasar, *Person in Christ*, 526–27. For a different expression of von Balthasar's thinking, see the introductory note to his essay "Spirit and Institution" (*Spirit and Institution*, 209).

20. *TL2*, 40.

21. *TL2*, 42. While von Balthasar does indicate that the "*communio* view of the Trinity represents the very best that the tradition has to offer" (O'Regan, *Balthasar and the Spectre of Hegel*, 209), this does not mean that the contributions of the Augustinian-Thomist tradition are left to the side, as McInerny suggests (*Trinitarian Theology*, 49).

22. While von Balthasar is dissatisfied with the way in which Thomas applies this theory to the Augustinian intramental conception of the trinitarian processions, he draws two general concepts from it: "the 'being' of the relations, which can only be identical with the being of the divine essence, and their 'sense' (*ratio*), their 'toward' . . . *both* concepts are necessary to grasp the divine mystery (to the extent that we are able)" (*TL2*, 133; see McInerny, *Trinitarian Theology*, 20–21).

of being itself, *esse* may take on a radically relational shape, removing the pressure that leads to the operations being restricted within a single subject conceived as a rational self without lapsing into tri-theism.

In effect, this would allow Thomas's *unio substantialis*, which normally only obtains in a singularly hypostatized rational nature, to exist as a true vis-à-vis *unio secundum affectum* in which, to adapt Thomas's phrase, the Lover relates to the Beloved as a true "other self."[23] As Hemmerle observes, to so strongly identify God's *essentia* and *actus essendi* with the *actio* of love leads to the "displacement of the center of gravity from the self to the other."[24] Said differently, in order for God to be considered as love, God must truly be able to relate to God as an Other, because love is fulfilled in *amor amicitiae* and not *amor sui*. If the divine *esse* is redefined as a singular act in which the divine persons truly relate to one another in Love, each sharing in the one divine act, *unio substantialis* need not be in competition with a kind of *unio realis* sought in *amicitia* within God. The essential unity of the divine *esse* might in this way be understood more directly as nothing but the personal unity through the mystery of divine love. A true vis-à-vis of generosity and receptivity may then no longer threaten to undermine unity but constitute it instead.[25] It is to the shape of the threefold personal participation in this singular act of love that I now turn.

Self-Giving: The Relation of the Father and Son

Von Balthasar's trinitarian account begins and continues as "elaboration of the claim that 'God is love' (1 John 4) and its surrounding context of the visible mission of the Son," which for von Balthasar includes the presence and activity of the Spirit.[26] Returning continually to the emphasis on giving in the Gospel of John, von Balthasar makes the notion of self-giving central to his understanding of the love that God "is" in the trinitarian relations.[27] Von Balthasar's basic understanding of love as an act of giving aligns with Thomas's understanding of *amor amicitiae*, which requires both *benevolentia* and *communicatio*. This communicative language of giving between the

23. *ST* I–II, q.28, a.1 *ad* 2.

24. *Theses*, 35.

25. Furthermore, from this, the nature of love as this common esse could not be determined in any other way than its self-disclosure in the activity of the divine persons themselves, as it is what it is only in its concrete enactment in their personal relations. Though I will not elaborate this epistemological claim, it is an important point to state against Thomas's preference for the least determined and most universal terms for God.

26. K. Oakes, "Gathering Many Likenesses," 887.

27. See *TL*2, 14–15, 136, 154, 299–301, 317; *TL*3, 162–63, 217–18.

Father and Son, used reticently by Thomas and (markedly less reticently) by Bonaventure, can be seen in von Balthasar's use of the second canon of Lateran IV.[28] The original canon reads:

> For the Father, in begetting the Son from eternity, gave [*dedit*] him his substance . . . . It cannot be said that the Father gave [*dederit*] him part of his substance and kept [*retinuerit*] part for himself since the Father's substance is indivisible, inasmuch as it is altogether simple. Nor can it be said that the Father transferred [*transtulerit*] his substance to the Son, in the act of begetting, as if he gave [*dederit*] it to the Son in such a way that he did not retain [*retinuerit*] it for himself; for otherwise he would have ceased to be substance.[29]

The three important aspects of this canon can be put positively as: (1) the Father gives the Son his substance; (2) the Father gave him his whole substance, not one part while retaining another part; (3) the Father gave his whole substance to the Son in such a way that the Father still retained it for himself. Von Balthasar paraphrases this:

> The eternal Father gives his entire Godhead, without holding anything back, to his Son (that is, the Father does not merely give the Son some divine essence distinct from, and excluding, the Father's Person), yet without losing his Godhead in this act of self-surrender.[30]

The initially paradoxical concept of the Father giving "entire Godhead . . . without losing his Godhead in this act" is explained through the language of the persons as relations subsisting in the divine *actus essendi*.[31] To be a

28. For example, see von Balthasar's comments in *TD*5, 64–65.

29. The English text of this canon can be found in Schroeder, *Disciplinary Decrees*, 207–9. Von Balthasar quotes this in full in *TL*3, 158.

30. *TL*3, 225; see also *TL*3, 158. Though there are only two explicit quotations from this council in *TL*3, the concepts derived from it are ubiquitous.

31. *TL*2, 133. Here, von Balthasar rehearses Thomas's conceptual distinction between the "being" and "'sense' (*ratio*)" of the *relationes subsistentes*. This allows Thomas to say elsewhere, in what may well be a gloss on Lateran IV, that "the Father . . . communicates His whole nature to Him [the Son], *the distinction only of origin remaining*" (*ST* Ia, q.41, a.3 *resp*, emphasis mine). See discussion concerning Aquinas's requirement to comment on this council's trinitarian decrees, ratified by papal decree in 1234, in Riedl, *Companion to Joachim*, 144, 149. However, as is evident in *ST* Ia, q.28, a.2 *resp* and *ad* 1, although the substantial and relative modes of predication, respectively related to the *esse* and *ratio* of each person, "do not differ from each other, but are one and the same," Thomas is forced to separate them because the substantial level (*esse*) has been defined in a way that excludes the *ratio*, rather than allowing the *ratio* (here, the Father's *paternitas*) to define the way in which each person subsists within the one act that is the divine *esse*.

divine person is not to subsist in the divine essence as "merely 'something'" but as the act of self-giving itself.[32] Thus, the Father's person is his act of giving the divine *esse* to the Son, in which he simultaneously gives his very "self" (as a relation subsistent in the very *esse* that is given) and enacts his personal relation of *paternitas* (in giving to the Son).[33] This self-donation is the act that von Balthasar identifies as "essentially divine," and the Father's subsistence is this act according to his paternal mode of "always already giving himself away."[34] The divine substance is "both given and not given"—given in the Father's enactment of the essential divine act of self-giving, not given in that the Father retains himself in his subsistence in that act as the relation of paternity established in its enactment.[35] As the "principle of 'giving all,'" the Father enacts the essential truth of the divine *esse*: "God, from his very origin in the Father, is the miracle of that love whereby he can *be* himself in *giving* himself."[36]

Bonaventure's influence is seen in von Balthasar's preference for describing the Son's procession as the *expressio per modum exemplaritatis* of the "entire trinitarian love."[37] As the divine nature is simply the trinitarian love, the Father giving it is nothing but an expression of that act which proceeds as exemplary of its origin. Once again, this provides a helpful way to distinguish von Balthasar from Thomas while drawing on important commonalities. Von Balthasar is uncomfortable with the image of the *verbum mentis* that Thomas adopts from Augustine largely due to the implication

32. *TL*3, 226.

33. Hence, von Balthasar insists that the gift given from Father to Son is not "merely 'something' (for example, the divine essence), but the self-giving Father himself" (*TL*3, 226).

34. *TL*2, 137; see also 136, 148; Moser, *Love Itself Is Understanding*, 152; Walker, "Love Alone," 534.

35. *TL*3, 158; see also McInerny, *Trinitarian Theology*, 22–23. The concept of a gift that contains the giver himself while still being truly given relies on Ulrich's distinction between the Giver and the Gift (see *TL*3, 225; Ulrich, *Leben in Der Einheit*, 79–81). It is only when the gift is actually relinquished and given *away* that what is given in the Gift is no longer considered the Giver's and can be received by the Beloved as Gift. But if, as in the case of the Father, the only thing that he has to give away is his very nature, then the distinction between the Gift and Giver becomes necessary for the divine nature to be truly *given* to the Son in a way that includes the Giver in the primal unity of the Giver and Gift while establishing the Father's own identity as Giver as distinct from the Gift. See Tourpe, "Positivité," 93.

36. *TL*3, 158–59.

37. *TL*2, 154. See also Hayes, "Introduction," 3; McInerny, *Trinitarian Theology*, 25. For detailed discussions regarding Bonaventure's influence on von Balthasar, see Johnson, *Christ and Analogy*; McInerny, *Trinitarian Theology*.

of hypostatic interiority to the divine essence.[38] Referring specifically to Augustine, von Balthasar is "careful not to connect this total self-surrender (in the Augustinian manner) with God's 'self-knowledge.'"[39] While truth does belong primarily to the Son, this "rests upon the wonder of the Father's generative act, which, considered from the standpoint of the hypostasis of the Logos, is groundless love."[40] Bonaventure himself, von Balthasar's preferred counterpart to the Thomistic tradition, cites Augustine to link intellect and love: "'the Word is the understanding of the Father insofar as it is bound with love and omnipotence.'"[41] However, the way in which von Balthasar relates the divine intellect, the generation of the Son, and the divine *esse* as love is carefully balanced in the midst of three theological antitheses.

The first, which von Balthasar situates between Anselm and Thomas, concerns the location and role of generative fecundity in God. Specifically, the question posed is "whether God the Father knows himself by virtue of eternally possessing the divine essence or whether he knows himself (as Father) by placing his meaning-word, the Son, vis-à-vis himself." Representing the first option, Anselm held that the Son proceeds as the self-knowledge of the Father, coming close to amalgamating the paternal origin and the common divine essence. Von Balthasar thought that this radical "primacy of the one essence over the plurality of the hypostases" would lead to Arianism if taken to its logical conclusion.[42] Further, and more central to von Balthasar's own concern, Anselm's position ultimately "fails to explain why the Father

38. Von Balthasar is not careful enough in his claims that Thomas views the divine knowing as the Father's "the Father knowing himself" (*TL*2, 165), or as the processions taking place "within the one divine mind" (*TL*2, 132). This characterization of Thomas is precisely what R. Williams, "What Does Love Know," and Emery, "Essentialism or Personalism," take issue with. Yet, given what I have argued previously about the effects of Thomas's attribution of intellect and will to the *esse* along the lines of a rational substance, it seems to me that—uncareful language aside—von Balthasar is signaling the same issues I identified.

39. *TL*3, 158.

40. *TL*2, 155. See also *TL*2, 177; *TL*3, 442. For an account of the perichoresis of the transcendentals, the convertibility of being and love, and love as the "inner depth or intrinsic ground of the ratio entis," see Walker, "Love Alone," 530–35; Nichols, *Balthasar for Thomists*, 206. Walker also observes that Balthasar does acknowledge the "undeniable truth contained in the Augustinian-Thomistic appropriations of the truth to the Son and the good to the Spirit—while simultaneously allowing us to take better account of the way in which the circumincession of the persons is required to unfold the ratio of the divine being in its fullness as love" through both his adoption of Bonaventure's schema and his account of the transcendentals. This qualifies McInerny's claim in *Trinitarian Theology*, 69–70, that the Augustinian model plays no significant role in Balthasar's immanent trinitarian theology.

41. *TL*2, 164; quoting Bonaventure, *Sententiarum* I, d.10, a.1, q.2.

42. *TL*2, 129; see also *TL*2 117.

generates the Son and breathes the Spirit."[43] On the other hand, for Thomas the divine persons are subsistent relations that are the resulting terms of the processions, which allows von Balthasar to speak of the persons both in their relation to one another and in their identification with the processions. On the basis of Thomas's position, von Balthasar denies any fecundity to the divine essence itself, saying, "There is nothing fruitful in God other than the Father."[44] However, while Thomas allows von Balthasar to avoid the threatened conflation of the Father and the divine essence he finds in Anselm's position, Thomas's argument tends toward the opposite danger, that the Son's generation is necessary for the Father to know himself as God, which would ultimately be Hegelianism.[45] Von Balthasar feels constrained to disagree with both, taking them as one more set of countervailing propositions from which to progress. McInerny expresses this well:

> If Anselm seemed to err by providing no logic as to why the Father generates the Son (and together with him breaths [*sic*] the Spirit), Thomas errs by locking the Trinity into the supposedly necessary logic of the intramental analogy . . . . Contra Anselm, Balthasar believes like Thomas that there is a logic to the generation of the Son and the breathing of the Spirit. However, contra Thomas, Balthasar does not think this logic is that of necessary intramental activity.[46]

Instead, von Balthasar thinks that the logic of God's life is only that of "groundless love," itself the only possible ground of "the self-surrender or self-expropriation thanks to which the Father *is* Father."[47]

Yet von Balthasar is committed to honoring the link between the Son and truth. This leads to the second antitheses, which continues his move away from a purely intellectual understanding of the procession of the Word. While von Balthasar observes that Thomas's catalogue of the various names of the Son "culminates" in the concept of *verbum mentis* because the Son is "generated in a purely intellectual manner," Bonaventure explains

43. McInerny, *Trinitarian Theology*, 20.

44. *TL*2, 131; see *TL*3, 56, quoting Durrwell, *Esprit Saint de Dieu*, 162: "In God there is no nature to develop and show itself fruitful in Persons: it is God's nature to be Trinity."

45. See *TL*2, 177; see also *TL*3, 139, 158.

46. McInerny, *Trinitarian Theology*, 21.

47. *TL*2, 177. Earlier in the same volume, von Balthasar says that making love the "primal mystery" of the divine life "communicates [this] groundlessness to everything that, qualifying its plenitude closely, can be called a 'property' of God. Everything inside and outside God proceeds '*a secreto Patris arcanoque*' [from the secret and mystery of the Father]," which is simply the Father's self-giving in love; see *TL*2, 137.

that *logos* is most fundamentally an *expressio*, the "integrative attribute . . . which recapitulates the sense of all the other names."[48] Though Thomas includes the possibility of created imitation in the divine ideas, Von Balthasar values the bridge that *expressio* provides between the Son's procession *per modum exemplaritatis* from the Father as the divine love expressed and his "disponibility for every creative resolution of God" by which God's nature is communicated to the world in creation and, ultimately, in the "cosmification of the Logos" in his incarnation.[49] This dual sense of *expressio* is the most "suitable medium" for the Father's expression of the divine love in all senses that relate to the Son, a *similitudo* both "expressive" and "expressed."[50]

The third antithesis, once again between Thomas and Bonaventure, completes von Balthasar's attempt to express the connection of the Son's generation to truth. Here, the question concerns whether the concept of generation is most properly understood in God based on an analogy from procreative generation (thus relying on paternity and filiation) or from the expression of words (thus relying on an act of the intellect). While Bonaventure realizes that expression happens in both ways, he prefers the analogy from paternity and filiation for the simple reason that in creation "the bringing forth of a person takes place naturally, and not by means of a mental act."[51] Thus, he makes "the Father's 'nature' responsible for the generation of the Son in God."[52] This is a problem for Thomas because natural generation only communicates a part of the nature in question, whereas the nature of God is both "indivisible" and "entirely intellectual," which leads to his specification of the *verbum mentis*, which von Balthasar has already rejected.[53] The only reason that the link between generation and nature in Bonaventure is not problematic for von Balthasar is that it remains understood as an act of love expressing itself, that is, enacting itself as self-giving love. The Father does not know himself in the generation of the Son except as the expression of the love that the Father is in that very act. The connection between the generation of the Son and truth is retained in the identification of the Father with his own subsistent act in the divine *esse* of love, which is his expression of the truth of the divine *esse* both in his act of generative self-giving and in the *expressio* of the Word proceeding from him *per modum exemplaritatis*.

48. *ST* Ia, q.34, a.2 *ad* 3; *TL*2, 165.

49. *TL*2, 167–69.

50. *TL*2, 166–67.

51. *TL*2, 167.

52. *TL*2, 167.

53. *ST* Ia, q.41, a.3.

As the recipient of the Father's self-expropriation, the Son is not a static expression of the Father as an externally spoken word (*vox*). Instead, in receiving the Father's "primal act of love," he receives both the self-giving Father and "the 'giving' in the 'gift,'" the very same act of self-giving love.[54] Because the gift received is an act, he "receives it . . . not 'passively' as the Beloved, but (since he receives the Father's substance, his Father's love) actively as a Lover, returning love, as one who responds to the totality of the Father's love and is ready to do everything in love."[55] His unique relation of filiation is an active reception that returns itself back to the "'Person' who '*principaliter*' . . . gives himself over, the Father."[56] However, it cannot be said that the Son's responsive self-giving is a reciprocal generation of the Father, giving him back the *esse* that he gave to the Son. The Father retains his Godhead in his own act of self-giving precisely in the mode of the self-renunciatory positing of the Son. The Son's return to the Father springs from this "initial act of begetting," but its mode, that of disposing himself totally to the Father's will, is unique to the Son's own subsistence, which is determined by his subsistence in the divine act of love as the relation of filiation.[57] The Father and Son "interpenetrate in their reciprocal loving-surrender," both "renounc[ing] being a mere 'I' without a 'thou.'"[58] Here, the reciprocal self-giving reveals the "identity of poverty and wealth in the divine love; for wealth and fullness are found in the self-surrendering Other."[59]

54. *TL3*, 226; here, von Balthasar is alluding to Adrienne von Speyr's insights surrounding the economic offering of the Son to the Father, but it is clear from other methodological statements that von Balthasar makes that all that we see relationally in the economy also teaches us to know the mystery of the immanent Trinity. For example: "No one doubts that, as the New Testament tells us, the Father's act of giving up the Son and the Spirit in the economy is pure love, as is the Son's and the Spirit's act of freely letting themselves be given up. But how could this fundamental claim about the economy of salvation have no foundation in any property of the essence of the triune God" (*TL2*, 136). See the discussion of von Balthasar's doctrine of antecedence in McInerny, *Trinitarian Theology*, 74–82.

55. *TL3*, 158.

56. *TL2*, 137; see also McInerny, *Trinitarian Theology*, 34, 62. On passivity and activity in the divine life, see E. Oakes, *Pattern of Redemption*, 286–87.

57. See McInerny, *Trinitarian Theology*, 62.

58. *TL3*, 226.

59. *TL3*, 226. The language of the identity of wealth and poverty is taken from Ulrich, *Mensch Als Anfang*, which is quoted in *TL2*, 178, as a complementary image for Bulgakov's intra-trinitarian kenosis.

The Kenosis of the Father and Son

Controversially, von Balthasar refers to the act of self-giving that characterizes the subsistence of the Father and Son as the "first, intratrinitarian *kenosis*."[60] Though this particularly fraught term is relatively rare in von Balthasar's treatment of the trinitarian life, it is identical to the "positive 'self-expropriation' in the act of handing over the entire divine being in the processions," and the "selflessness" of the self-giving love of Father and Son. Ultimately, all these expressions define von Balthasar's mature understanding of divine love as the Trinity's organizing concept.[61] The love that the Father "is" is "nothing other than the pure surrender of himself," and the Son, who is "the same God (the Father's self-utterance, his 'Word')," likewise renounces "being a mere 'I' without a 'thou,' giving his 'self' back to the Father as 'gift in return.'"[62] Thus, love is only expressed absolutely "where there is this surrender of what is one's own," and only where this surrender is undertaken fully for the sake of the Other can "absolute love . . . guarantee the unity of essence."[63]

As the topic of kenosis often elicits discomfort, it is fitting at this point to mention a handful of observations from a recent volume specifically on

60. *TL*2, 177; see also *TD*5, 84–85. This concept of kenosis is introduced in *TL*2 in conjunction with the sole mention of Bulgakov in the whole of the volume, but there is no citation in either *TL*2 or *TL*3 related to Bulgakov's own understanding of kenosis, though Bulgakov features even more prominently in the third and concluding volume. For a superb overview of von Balthasar's use of Bulgakov, especially of the connection between his influence and that of Thomas, see Leamy, *Holy Trinity*.

Though the doctrine of intra-trinitarian kenosis is arrived at through the rule of antecedence (see *TL*3, 241, 300), it belongs materially before the explorations of creative and Christological kenosis within the next chapter; see K. Oakes, "Gathering Many Likenesses," 877–78.

For two succinct histories of the concept of kenosis within the doctrine of God, see K. Oakes, "Gathering Many Likenesses," 871–73; Schwöbel, "Taking the Form." See also von Balthasar's own summary of this in Balthasar, *Mysterium Paschale*, 29–36. Not surprisingly, von Balthasar does not use the term "kenosis" to refer only to the "handing over of the entire divine being in the processions" (*TL*2, 178), but also to the act of creation and to the mission of the Son, especially his death. In this he follows Bulgakov, who specifies in addition that the incarnation of the Son and outpouring of the Spirit constitute an additional kenotic element in distinction from the Paschal mystery. It is important to note here that the kenosis of creation and that of the Paschal mystery are "new expressions of this triune way of being"; see Nichols, *Balthasar for Thomists*, 125. This is to say that any kenotic element of God's action toward creation is derivative of, not constitutive of, his triune life of kenotic love.

61. *TL*2, 178, 284, 300; Nichols, *Balthasar for Thomists*, 73; McInerny, *Trinitarian Theology*, 43; K. Oakes, "Gathering Many Likenesses," 880–81.

62. *TL*3, 441, 226.

63. *TD*5, 85.

the topic of kenosis with the particular aim of unpacking its relation to the primary scriptural text, Phil 2:7.[64] Von Balthasar mentions this passage only infrequently compared to the ubiquity of the concept of kenosis, but a handful of passages make the connection explicit, warranting further examination. To include one example in full:

> The Son "lays up" his "form of God" with the Father, "emptying himself and taking on the form of a slave," demonstrating that readiness to perform the Father's will which is eternally present in his loving response to him. This attitude of readiness is fitting for the pure creature, but its prototype is and was always found in the eternal Son, so that, without alteration to his Godhead, he could be "born in the likeness of [or equality with] men. And being found in human form he humbled himself and became obedient unto death, even death on a cross" (Phil 2:7–8).[65]

In his essay within the recent volume, John Barclay offers two observations that reorient the concept of kenosis in the text of Philippians in a way that illuminates von Balthasar's usage of the concept. First, the entirety of the hymn must be understood not simply as an ethical drama, "exemplifying the heroic self-humiliation that the Philippians are to imitate," but rather—and more importantly—as a soteriological drama, "a depiction of how 'God was in Christ reconciling the world to himself' (2 Cor 5:19)."[66] This means that the telos of kenosis in the Christ-hymn is not being ultimately self-less, as in lacking a self because it has been emptied, but instead being the "'self-for' that is also the 'self-with,' the self whose commitment to the other is not ultimately at the expense of the self (properly configured) but aims at shared benefit and conjoint flourishing."[67] While the "acme of [Christ's] kenotic path is death . . . the acme is not the *telos*," but only the highest moment of dramatic commitment.[68] This complements von Balthasar's expression of kenosis as the intra-trinitarian refusal to be an I-without-a-Thou, which viewed positively is a commitment to relate as a "self-for" and "self-with."

Secondly, Barclay offers a powerful rereading of the relatively strange Greek contained in this hymn, including the "rare noun *harpagmos* and the odd expression *to einai isa theō*."[69] Addressing the latter, Barclay suggests that the substantive phrase ought not to be taken as indicating status, as it

64. Nimmo and Johnson, *Kenosis*.

65. *TL*3, 204; see also *TL*3 48–49, 229–31; *TL*2, 141.

66. Barclay, "Kenosis," 9.

67. Sherrard, "Review," 336–38.

68. Barclay, "Kenosis," 22.

69. Barclay, "Kenosis," 15.

normally is, but rather "mode or quality of being."[70] Pointing out that *isa* is an adverb not an adjective, he translates the broader phrase as "he did not consider *harpagmos* to be a manner of existence equal/equivalent to God."[71] This then sets up *harpagmos* to be read as an act rather an object, which he points out is its "most common" meaning.[72] Rather than "something to use for his own advantage," which is seen in modern translations such as the Christian Standard Version even though it is, as Barclay puts it, "an almost unparalleled meaning for the term," Barclay renders *harpagmos* as "seizing."[73] Thus, Phil 2:7 reads, "being in the form of God, Christ did not consider seizing to be a manner of existence equivalent/equal to God."[74] For Christ to empty himself and take on the form of a servant was not to give up "an equality he securely possessed."[75] On the contrary, and in support of von Balthasar's own reading and understanding of the divine life, for "Christ to 'empty' himself as a human being would mean that he renounced the capacity to exercise power as humanly understood, humbling himself to the epitome of powerlessness."[76] The result of this is that the "powerlessness" of Christ's incarnation and submission to death is the divine power "operating on a different plane" than the one on which humanity typically defines power. Divine power and human power are incommensurable, and thus Christ's incarnate kenosis is a revelation of the truth of God's power, and indeed, of God's perfection.[77]

Lastly, in harmony with Barclay's argument for the transcendent quality of divine power over our conception of the same, Hanna Reichel argues that the kenosis of the first part of the hymn is not reversed in the glorification of the second part. For the Father to elevate Jesus and bestow on him the name above all names (Phil 2:9) is an "extension of the same movement"

70. Barclay, "Kenosis," 15.

71. Barclay, "Kenosis," 15.

72. As Barclay points out, the scholarship surrounding this word has taken its cues for a half-century from one article (Hoover, "*Harpagmos* Enigma"), which his interpretation challenges.

73. Barclay, "Kenosis," 16.

74. Barclay also notes that Moule, "Further Reflections on Philippians 2:5–11," and Vollenweider, *Horizonte Neutestamentliche Christologie*, support his view.

75. Barclay, "Kenosis," 15.

76. Barclay, "Kenosis," 17.

77. As Graham Ward says, "Kenosis is a doctrine of divine representation . . . Christ's kenosis is not concerned with the abandonment of divine properties. It actually reveals something about God that would otherwise be concealed—his powerlessness in his giving of himself as servant" ("Kenosis," 20–21).

as the Son's kenosis.[78] The movement of the Son's incarnate life is "the display of the true divinity that he already had." In this sense, she agrees with Bruce McCormack that, as the Father gives God's own name to the Son in his vindication, kenosis is attributed to the Father, such that "God . . . is essentially kenotic."[79]

These three observations help clarify von Balthasar's intent in attributing kenosis to the relationship between the Father and Son *ad intra*. Kenosis is not a diminution of any divine quality, but is the manifestation of the divine nature itself, of the Father as well as the Son. At bottom, *Ur*-kenosis is self-emptying in the sense of surrendering one's supposed right to live for, and therefore alone with, oneself. Both Father and Son renounce being an I-without-a-Thou, emptying their self-for-itself. This kenotic act is attributed to both Father and Son as the basic orientation of unselfishness, or lack of selfish self-preservation, that is expressed in God's humble participation in the lot of sinful humanity in the incarnation and Passion. Though von Balthasar's language surrounding kenosis is often striking in the intensity and directness of the concepts such as emptiness, suffering, self-expropriation, self-surrender, and self-denial attributed to the Father and Son, even going so far as "super-death" and "sacrifice," these dramatic concepts identify in the kenotic relation of the Father and Son the ground for the possibility of God to enter into those realities that exist in creation under sin.[80] Said in the opposite way, "There is only one way to approach the trinitarian life in God: on the basis of what is manifest in God's kenosis in the theology of the covenant—and thence in the theology of the Cross."[81]

Within the divine life, the concept of kenosis identifies the ingredient of unselfish regard for the Other necessary for truly self-giving love to take place. Though kenosis invokes a concept of distinction, or separation,

78. Reichel, "End of Humanity," 306.

79. Reichel, "End of Humanity," 306; see McCormack, *Humility of the Eternal Son*, 207.

80. See especially Balthasar, *Action*, 324, 327; *TD*5, 84, 245, 251; see also McInerny, *Trinitarian Theology*, 32, 82.

81. Balthasar, *Action*, 324. See Ward, "Kenosis," 40–49, for a fuller explication of how kenosis is the "condition for the possibility of theo-logic itself and its very form." Von Balthasar also identifies kenosis in the act of creation and in the Son's mission, most especially in the Paschal mystery itself. As Nichols points out, rather than these created realities being determinative for the divine being, they are "new expressions of this triune way of being" (*Balthasar for Thomists*, 125). In this way, Balthasar differs from Jürgen Moltmann and approaches Aquinas's position on God's perfection; see K. Oakes, "Gathering Many Likenesses," 874–78; Nichols, *Balthasar for Thomists*, 124–25; R. Williams, "Balthasar and the Trinity," 38. For an approach to this issue that employs Thomas and is critical of von Balthasar, see Schwöbel, "Taking the Form."

between persons, Martin Bieler rightly suggests that "we should not think first of all of a separation from the other, but of a separation toward the other . . . understood not as an estrangement but as a positive letting be of the other, which connects with the other."[82] This act of love, though, has too often been spoken of in the metaphysically questionable terms of separate acts of kenosis attributed to each of the divine persons, leading to further fears of tritheism.[83] McInerny rightly corrects this tendency in recent interpretation, guiding the conversation back in a direction more faithful to von Balthasar himself and more likely to accomplish the goal of maintaining the unity of the divine *esse* through, not in spite of, the mutuality of the kenotic act:

> The *first* kenosis [of the Father] expands to a kenosis involving the whole Trinity. Because the Son *is* and *gives thanks* in his being begotten, and he is begotten in the kenosis of the Father, the Son *is* and *gives thanks* in the kenosis of the Father. There is thus only "the kenosis (or selflessness) of the love of Father and Son," not two distinct kenoses of the Father and the Son. The Son's self-surrender in thanksgiving and obedience is "kenotic," but never is *another* kenosis symmetrical, as it were, to the Father's.[84]

The Father and Son are both identical to the divine substance, which is the movement of loving self-emptying in favor of another, here "enacted" by the persons of the Father and Son as they relate to one another in a mutual self-expropriation grounded in the Father's kenotic fecundity.[85] Further, the Father and Son enact the divine self-expropriation according to their uniquely relational modes of subsistence, the Father as the "principle of 'giving all'" and the Son as the "one who responds to the totality of the Father's love and is ready to do everything in love."[86] In each mode, both persons enact the essential self-giving of divine love in a way that constitutes the reciprocity that is necessary for a true vis-à-vis relationality in the divine life, the possibility of which von Balthasar identified as lacking in the Augustinian-Thomist tradition. Each person has their being in their respective mode of divine action, each of which is necessarily in reference to the Other.

The concept of the Son's reciprocal self-giving, while always retaining an asymmetry appropriate to the trinitarian taxis, allows the trinitarian

82. Bieler, "*Analogia Entis*," 332n11.

83. For a summary of interpretations, see McInerny, *Trinitarian Theology*, 33–34.

84. McInerny, *Trinitarian Theology*, 33–34, 62; citing *TL*3, 300, and Balthasar, *Epilogue*, 90.

85. See *TL*2, 137.

86. *TL*3, 158.

persons to be described not only as relations of origin—their "whence"—but also according to their "whither," "deduced implicitly at most" in the medieval models.[87] Christoph Schwöbel also saw this as a requirement, suggesting that we cannot leave the trinitarian relations simply as "originating relations," but instead must construe them as "mutual and reciprocal relations *so that the relationship of the Father to the Son is acknowledged and endorsed in the relationship of the Son to the Father*."[88] For Schwöbel, this is a "crucial requirement of construing the trinitarian relationship as a relationship of love."[89] Thomas also claims that the ability to return love is an essential element in the definition of friendship, which I have argued is the fulfillment of love.[90] The taxis of origin is not left behind in this reciprocation but complemented by the mutual return of the Son to the Father, which itself is not equiprimordial as a relation (as the Father is his self-giving *principaliter*) but is an "acknowledgement" and "endorsement" of the paternal relation that is the Son's relational origin. The mutuality of the relations does not erase the relations of origin, for the Father remains the fecund principle of the Godhead, but rather demonstrates precisely what the divine *esse* is.[91] Neither does this render the Son's subsistent love as only receiving and returning the Father's love as *amor debitus*, as Richard holds, a love that simply owes itself to the Father and therefore gives itself back to its origin.[92] Instead, the Son's "returning love," understood in terms consistent

87. *TL*3, 149.

88. Schwöbel, "God Is Love," 323.

89. Schwöbel, "God Is Love," 323.

90. *ST* Ia, q.20, a.2 *ad* 3, though in relation to rational creatures rather than the distinct persons of the Godhead.

91. See *TL*2, 131; see also *ST* Ia, q.39, a.5, which von Balthasar quotes as evidence against the fecundity of the divine essence itself.

92. See *TL*3, 441; Richard of St. Victor, "*On the Trinity*," V.16, 18. McInerny identifies a shift between von Balthasar's early essay "Summa Summarum" in Balthasar, *Creator Spirit*, especially p. 372, and *TL*3, claiming that von Balthasar wants to "retain the language of gratuity but discard the reduction of the persons to a schematic combination giving/receiving love" found in Richard (*Trinitarian Theology*, 54). This is true insofar as von Balthasar presses further into the identity of the act of love common to the Father and Son, but the groundlessness of this love that he identifies in both the Father and Son at the end of *TL*3 does not do away with the taxis of the trinitarian processions to which giving and receiving point. The Father remains, in the final pages, the "groundless abyss of love" that we may only glimpse through the Son and Spirit (*TL*3, 447). The way that von Balthasar emphasizes the consubstantiality of the Father and Son in the act of divine love is through the Thomistic idea of subsistent relations, either explicitly or by adopting the same conceptual structure, which gives the lie to McInerny's earlier claim that "[von] Balthasar nowhere adopts characteristically Thomist trinitarian concepts" (*Trinitarian Theology*, 49). This tendency to portray von Balthasar as Franciscan over against Thomas and Augustine, while popular, has already

with the doctrine of subsistent relations, identifies the Son as the same act of love that is the divine *esse* and has been given and received fully by him, but identifies this love as "returning" insofar as this is the Son's own unique mode of subsistence within the divine *esse*. The Son's act of giving is the same identical act of love as the Father's but differentiated according to the relations of giving, receiving, and returning.

The Spirit

The importance of the person of the Spirit for von Balthasar, as yet largely unmentioned, can hardly be understated. This is especially true of the developments seen in *TL*3, though these have not garnered the attention they deserve.[93] His pneumatology can be summarily organized by a sequence of four terms: Bond, Gift, Fruit, and Bonicity (*bonitas*, or goodness). The first three are integrated within the Spirit's Bonicity, but the role of this final term has not been given sufficient attention in scholarship on von Balthasar. For this reason, I will provide an overview of Bond, Gift, and Fruit as a prelude to a longer treatment of Bonicity.

Spirit as Bond, Gift, and Fruit

The first term, Bond, refers to what von Balthasar terms the "subjective" role of the Spirit, in which the Spirit is the *relatio* established by the mutual self-giving of the Father and Son, inhabiting the "space" or "distance" (*Abstand*) between them.[94] The Spirit does not only "bind" the Father and Son

been identified as unbalanced in O'Regan, *Balthasar and the Spectre of Hegel*, 209–10, and directly contradicts von Balthasar's own statement of purpose in *TL*2, 40.

93. While this is especially true in English literature on von Balthasar, there are currents in French scholarship that are pressing toward more robust interpretations of von Balthasar's thought as well as his use of certain sources, such as Thomas Aquinas, that will be cited and relied upon in the section that follows, for example, the work of Emmanuel Tourpe and Jean-Noël Dol.

94. *TL*3, 17–18; see Wigley, *Balthasar's Trilogy*, 133–34. See also McInerny, *Trinitarian Theology*, 36–40, for his helpful discussion concerning the most helpful interpretation of *Abstand*, correcting a previous suggestion by Rowan Williams. Karen Kilby offers repeated critique of von Balthasar's use of the image of distance in the Trinity, which she fears is both overly speculative and unhelpfully vague in light of consubstantiality; e.g., *Balthasar*, 109–22, esp. pp. 107–8, 110–11. E. Oakes is correct to point out, however, that "in the Trinity distance and separation are always positive realities; in the Trinity, and there alone, distance comes to be because of love: God the Father's love is so total that there is 'nothing left,' so to speak, when he generates his Son in love; and the Son returns that love so totally, also holding nothing back, that he too is

together in love as in the standard Augustinian-Thomist construal, but is the *relationis oppositio* that also serves to distinguish them from one another in their mutual act of love. Going ever further, von Balthasar identifies the Spirit himself as the very "act of reciprocal love between Father and Son" by which they are united and distinguished.[95] Von Balthasar considers the relation between the Spirit and the divine act at the beginning of *TL*3 by surveying two accounts from contemporaneous theologians. First, von Balthasar mentions Louis Bouyer's suggestion that to understand the Spirit as the bond of love implies that we might better understand the Spirit as the love of the divine life itself. Building off Marius Victorinus's description of God as motion ("*esse est moveri*"), Bouyer describes a threefold movement wherein the Holy Spirit is not only the "copula" between Father and Son but is the return ("*regressio*") of God back to himself between them.[96] In this sense, the Spirit expresses "what is deepest in God" as the "'motion' (Victorinus) that drives the Father to go out from himself and generate the Son (and so become the Father)" and "moves the Son to gratitude to the Father for everything and drives him to give it all back to the Father (thereby becoming Son)."[97] Because the love of the Father and Son is perfected in the Spirit in this way, von Balthasar takes Bouyer's suspicion of the "inherited distinction between love as essence and love as personal" seriously.[98] The suggestion is then taken another step forward by F. X. Durrwell's claim: "God is love, and the Spirit is love. All God's attributes are hypostasized in the Spirit; he is God himself in his innermost depths."[99] The Father and Son relate to one another in the Spirit as their "bond of unity," so the Spirit can

---

totally 'emptied' . . . . And that same Spirit [that is spirated from this 'eternal exchange'] is so much and so totally the Spirit of the Father and Son that he is able to bind them in loving union even when their loving self-bestowal is so total that they have 'lost' themselves" (*Pattern of Redemption*, 188–89). On the "primordial positivity" of this space, see Martin, "Consubstantial Otherness of God," 556–57. Tourpe helpfully identifies Siewerth's influence on this point in "Thomisme Ontologique," 473.

95. *TL*3, 242.

96. See *TL*3, 54–55, relying on Bouyer, *Consolateur*, 425, 439; see also von Balthasar's later comments to the same effect in relation to Thomas in *TL*3, 142. Though there are intertwined aspects of *theologia* and *oikonomia* within Victorinus's understanding of the *regressio*, it is clear that von Balthasar reads any economic return through the Spirit as love as implying a return, or at least a motion, within God's life itself, that can be correlated to the Spirit as the love between the Father and Son.

97. *TL*3, 55.

98. *TL*3, 55.

99. See *TL*3, 55–56, where von Balthasar quotes from Durrwell, *Esprit Saint de Dieu*.

be described as the "personalizing Person in the Trinity-in-Unity."[100] For von Balthasar, both thinkers rooted the "mysterious affinity of divine nature and Holy Spirit" in the fact that the Spirit functions as the medium of the Father and Son's relation: the Spirit is the "relatedness of the Father and Son . . . in terms of essence."[101]

If the Spirit remained only the *relatio* established by the mutual self-giving of the Father and Son, the Spirit would be equivalent to Hegel's "Unity of Both," in which the Spirit fails to attain to true divine personhood. The Trinity could thereby be reduced to either a binity established in reciprocal love or the single subject of an Absolute Spirit.[102] It is through sustained attention to the concept of Gift, aided by Ferdinand Ulrich, that von Balthasar avoids these dangers, specifically by turning not to the act of giving but rather to the reception of that Gift. Since the act of divine self-giving is selfless, the Gift given *gratis*, any expectation of reciprocation cannot be a required condition for their self-giving. Thus, the true Gift that is received in the unexpected mutuality of their love is not the Other but the event of the mutuality itself. Von Balthasar expresses it in this way:

> Both [Father and Son] renounce being a mere "I" without a "Thou": this allows us to glimpse the identity of poverty and wealth in the divine love; for wealth and fullness are found in

100. This does not mean that Durrwell ignores the traditional trinitarian taxis: "The Spirit is *at* the origin, in the generating Father, and he is *at* the end, in the generated Son. *Although he proceeds from both*, he comes neither after the Father nor after the Son, for it is in him that they are Father and Son" (Durrwell, *Esprit Saint de Dieu*, 160). Adrienne von Speyr helps von Balthasar to navigate this tension, reminding his reader from her works that the taxis is eternal and that the processions are therefore just as eternal as the existence of the three persons. Thus, von Balthasar says, "The *taxis* must not be understood in any temporal sense whatsoever, because the processions of the Son and Spirit are just as eternal as their existence: 'The Son even cooperates in his begetting by *letting* himself be begotten, by holding himself in readiness to be begotten'" (*TL*3, 58; quoting Speyr, *World of Prayer*, 65). This is only possible in an atemporal understanding of the processions that allows for the person to be eternally constituted even in the act of his constitution.

101. *TL*3, 141, 157.

102. *TL*3, 46–47. This calls Levering's comments into question concerning the equation of the Spirit with the "'We' arising from the 'I-Thou' of the Father and Son" ("Holy Spirit," 127–28n6). Von Balthasar rejects this construction from Mühlen as insufficient in *TL*3, 174 (see also 56n84, 140–41, 155), although he seems to have considered it earlier in his career (see *Creator Spirit*, 127). The incommunicability of the personhood of Father, Son, and Spirit resists their *communio* being construed as an identical vis-à-vis among all three persons, but his emphasis on the Spirit as Fruit decisively shows that the Spirit is not simply a collective consciousness. The emergence of a third is the "superabundant perfection" that prevents the "'dialogical' relationship of Father and Son within the Godhead" from collapsing into a "We" (*TL*3, 232).

> the self-surrendering Other (this also applies to the Father, since without the Son he could not be Father). Since this wealth—with its implicit renunciation—is experienced by both as a single gift, and neither keeps account of the renunciation it demanded, the wealth of both (which in each case is a *received* wealth) coincides in a oneness. For both, the event of this oneness is a gift: the *bonum* of a mutual love is a *donum* for the lovers. Thus both, the loving Father and the loving Son, receive this mutuality as a gift.[103]

Because the Gift of mutuality is received by them as a single Gift that exceeds what either demanded, the received Gift cannot express either the "calculable total" or "resultant identity" of their love.[104] Instead, the Gift that is given ("*donum doni*") and received is "an unfathomable *more*, a fruit . . . an 'overflowing.'"[105] The Third emerges from the mutuality of the Father and Son as the "objectivized subjectivity" of their mutual giving, a *donum* that is not only within but also "beyond the reciprocal giving" of Father and Son as the Fruit of their love.[106] In the "miracle of fruitfulness, of 'gift' above and beyond," what von Balthasar calls the "objective" aspect of the Spirit comes into focus, the distinct terminus of the *relatio* of the Father and Son's love.[107]

Von Balthasar's preferred image for the Spirit's emergence as a miracle of fruitfulness is the miraculous appearance of the child as "the fruit of the 'one-flesh' relationship of man and wife."[108] Though he is aware that this image has been almost universally avoided by theologians, even being expressly rejected by Augustine, Von Balthasar argues that this image in one stroke "transcends Augustine's self-contained I" and allows Richard's *condilectus* to "spring from the intimacy of love itself" rather than being "posited as some third entity outside the reciprocal love of the two lovers."[109] Though the analogy of the child initially seems like a poor fit for the Spirit, as it is the Son's generation that is normally portrayed analogically in this way, his

103. *TL*3, 226.

104. *TL*3, 226.

105. *TL*3, 162, 227, 230.

106. Balthasar, *Spirit and Institution*, 237; *TL*3, 161. This is the basis for von Balthasar's extension of this identity of Gift into the intra-trinitarian relations, wherein the economic gift of the divine through the Spirit is based not only on a tendency to be given in creation, as in Thomas (*ST* Ia, q.38, a.1), but upon a true giving within the trinitarian relations as the *donum doni* (*TL*3, 161–64, 226–27).

107. *TL*3, 46; see also pp. 160–61.

108. *TL*3, 227; see also *TL*2, 59–62, 163, 177–78; *TL*3, 46, 141, 155, 159, 160, 241–43; Balthasar, *Creator Spirit*, 15–55; Balthasar, *Unless You Become like This Child.*

109. *TL*2, 62.

point is simply that the procession of the Spirit from the Father and Son is the "proof that this loving indwelling has succeeded, just as the human child is both the proof and the fruit of the reciprocal love of the parents."[110] The principle presented by this *imago Trinitatis* is that "fecundity is the law, not only of organisms, but . . . also of the life of the spirit," which provides the "inner 'logic'" lacking in Richard's original image.[111] For von Balthasar, the fecundity of divine love must exceed the expected fecundity of self-giving. While the Son's procession from the Father is the "expected" outcome of the Father's self-gift, the Spirit's "unexpected" emergence reveals that divine love is not exhausted in the mutual kenosis of Father and Son but is "more, and more fruitful, than had been envisaged."[112]

An Unfinished Pneumatology

By way of summarizing von Balthasar's pneumatology thus far, the subjective aspect of Bond is bridged to the objective aspect of Fruit by the concept of Gift: the Gift that is given by Father and Son in divine love is received by them as the Fruit of their mutual Bond. Though this Fruit is the Third, it has been described primarily as a result, however unexpected, of the I-Thou relation of the Father and Son.[113] In the final volume of the *Theo-logic*,

110. *TL*3, 159; von Balthasar quotes Tertullian to show that the image of fruit is not without precedent, though in Tertullian it is "fruit of the tree is third from the root" (von Balthasar's translation of *Against Praxeus*, §8).

111. *TL*2, 62; *TL*3, 237. Because love for the Other carries no expectation of return, the "logic" of love must not be one that can be traced from the beginning (prospective) but rather one that must be understood only in its fullness (retrospective). It is for this reason that von Balthasar refuses to accept a Neoplatonist "law of Being" that explains in advance the return of the Spirit, such as Dionysius's diffusivity of the Good understood *per modum naturae* apart from the freedom of love ("*nihilominus ut dilectus*"); see Balthasar, *Studies in Theological Style*, 285–88; Balthasar, *Man in God*, 126; Nichols, *Word Has Been Abroad*, 87–88; McInerny, *Trinitarian Theology*, 58–59. Instead, the Third must proceed from the mutual selflessness of the Father and Son in a way that is "unexpected" from their point of view; it must be a triadic logic constructed in light of the fruit itself. On this, see Tourpe, "Dialectic and Dialogic," 320.

112. O'Regan, *Balthasar and the Spectre of Hegel*, 209; see also Nichols, *Balthasar for Thomists*, 125.

113. See Buckley's comments on von Balthasar's balanced critique of Thomas and the tradition of the Filioque debate in reference to Spirit's own personhood in Buckley, "Balthasar's Use of the Theology of Aquinas," 536; see *TL*3, 441. The enduring strength of the tendency for the Spirit's personhood to be confined to the I-Thou relation of the Father and Son is underscored in that Clarke, a main proponent of the personalist turn in modern Thomism, even while quoting von Balthasar allows the Spirit's personhood to be fully defined within the parameters of the giving-receiving relation of the Father and Son's I-Thou (Clarke, *Creative Retrieval*, 229–31).

however, von Balthasar introduces a dense section applying Ferdinand Ulrich's concept of Bonicity to the Spirit by insisting that "there is still more to be said" about the nature of the Spirit.[114] The importance of this section is underscored by Tourpe, who calls it "a central and decisive moment for von Balthasar's entire pneumatology."[115] However, commentators have consistently failed to attend to the way Ulrich allows von Balthasar to integrate the Spirit more fully into his trinitarian thought, leading to an incomplete presentation of his pneumatology that has opened his thought up to various critiques.[116] Thus, it is not surprising that Karen Kilby has asserted that he "shares in the weakness of much modern western theology when it comes to the role of the Spirit," who shows up "as a kind of afterthought, an addendum; the Spirit rarely seems as central and necessary to the account as are Father and Son."[117]

114. See especially *TL*3, 225–29. This section, entitled "Gift," is a terse paraphrase and adaptation of large swaths of Ulrich's expansive treatise, itself on St. Thomas, which in turn functions as a metaphysical framework for Speyr's mystical prose. Both authors function as the "hyper-text" behind von Balthasar's theological argument here, making clear that this is not simply a "principled solution" but rather a "careful argument"; Tourpe, "Positivité," 93, 95, my translation; see also pp. 88–89, 98; Tourpe, "Thomisme Ontologique," 469, 485.

115. Tourpe, "Positivité," 96, my translation. He begins this essay by suggesting, "Bien des critiques urgées de Hans Urs von Balthasar devraient méditer cette proposition centrale, qui éclaire l'ensemble de son œvre: 'Le pur fruit [de] l'amour (renonçant à son être propre) ne repose pas comme tel sur une exinantition, mais il est las pur positivé du bien'" (86).

116. One of the only English exceptions is a recent essay that mentions von Balthasar's use of Ulrich in this section but still does not observe the explicit and important link to the Spirit in his immanent aspect (Servais, "Balthasar," 213–14). Otherwise, it is ignored in English literature. For instance, while Ulrich is mentioned a handful of times in O'Regan, *Balthasar and the Spectre of Hegel*, it is never in relation to this final concept from Ulrich employed by von Balthasar. Though Moser intends his book *Love Itself Is Understanding* to fill the "noticeable lacuna" of "English-language scholarship on . . . the three volume *Theo-logic*," there is no mention of Ulrich at all in connection with the Spirit. The same can be said for Aidan Nichols's summary volume on the *Theo-logic* (*Say It Is Pentecost*), which skips directly over the most conceptually pertinent (and perplexing) part of the section, as well as López, "Eternal Happening," and Wigley, *Balthasar's Trilogy*, 133–42. Rowan Williams goes so far as to assert that in *TL*3, "there is nothing here that the attentive reader of any of the earlier works will find surprising" ("Balthasar and the Trinity," 47).

117. Kilby, *Balthasar*, 104n30. It is noteworthy that Kilby rarely cites the *Theo-logic* in her book, and not at all in the chapter addressing the Trinity, in which she accuses him of an underdeveloped pneumatology. This is a serious oversight, especially if E. Oakes is correct that "issues of the Trinity . . . receive their most natural treatment, in the *Theologik*" (*Pattern of Redemption*, 277n1), though he himself goes on to hardly quote it at all in the chapter dedicated to it. Vogel, who notes that *TL*3 is entirely devoted to the Spirit, is surely correct that the "charge often leveled against Karl Barth . . .

It must be admitted that von Balthasar himself did not unpack how this final aspect of his pneumatology integrates all that has gone before, not least because it only comes to the surface of his thinking at the very end of his trilogy, and indeed close to the end of his life. Nonetheless, there are two ways that the relative inattention to the role of *bonitas* in his pneumatology threatens to undermine the constructive potential of the rest of his trinitarian thought, which are worth identifying before I expand upon Ulrich's system and its impact in more detail. The first lies in the failure to integrate the Bonicity of the Spirit into the identity of poverty and wealth, a concept also derived from Ferdinand Ulrich. For instance, although O'Regan does identify the fact that the Spirit as Fruit reveals that fruitfulness is not limited to the mutual kenosis of Father and Son, he still maintains that the identity of poverty and wealth seen in the Father and Son's I-Thou cannot be "further unpacked."[118] This renders the *coincidentia oppositorum* of poverty and wealth as a simple equation, which threatens to evacuate concepts like perfection or *actus purus* of any meaningful content. In Schwöbel's terms, von Balthasar's *Ur-kenosis* initially seems to threaten to destroy the divine *plerosis.*[119] Because poverty has been effectively equated with wealth within a closed dyad, it is difficult to see how the Spirit's emergence truly exceeds kenosis, which is necessary for the life of the Trinity *in se* finally to be seen as "full rather than empty," as O'Regan puts it. This increases the temptation to identify the created economy as the return of God to God, making the divine life dependent upon creation in a Hegelian sense.[120] Thus, the alternative option of leaving behind the language of poverty when speaking of the trinitarian relations is taken.[121]

However, even if the development of the Spirit's Fruit-aspect is considered by observing that the *coincidentia* is not simply the reciprocal self-satisfaction of Father and Son because it is exceeded in the Spirit, the nature of this Fruit must be considered to avoid the second set of issues that arise, specifically in relation to the concept of Gift. As Tourpe points out, even if

that his theology is effectively 'binitarian,' does not apply in the case of von Balthasar" ("Unselfing Activity," 117).

118. O'Regan, *Balthasar and the Spectre of Hegel*, 209.

119. Schwöbel, "Taking the Form"; see also Schwöbel, "Generosity," 285.

120. O'Regan, *Balthasar and the Spectre of Hegel*, 207.

121. For instance, see Schwöbel, "Taking the Form," 64; this position is more nuanced in his later essay, "Generosity," 285–87. Schwöbel's critique of von Balthasar is related to what has become the standard Thomist critique, the most extreme example being Mansini's evaluation: "The Trinitarian kenosis of Balthasar destroys the Trinitarian theology of the Church" ("Hegel and Christian Theology," 999). For a catalogue of these critiques, see Betz, "Humility of God"; White, *Incarnate Lord*, 432–34; Marshall, "Personal Distinction."

the Spirit is understood as "excess" in relation to the Father and Son, if the Spirit is similarly kenotic, there is a risk of the "abyssilization of the gift."[122] The Gift continues to be given but never truly received, and love therefore remains solely ecstatic. Wealth continues to be something always possible but never present, being reduced all the same to poverty in the experience of the divine persons. If the Gift never arrives, it is not truly given but creates an abyss of giving that leads to poverty that is euphemistically referred to as wealth. This danger evokes the Derridean concern that a true gift—defined in terms with significant resonance to von Balthasar's own insistence that the kenotic gift is given with no demand for return—cannot be given or received at all except in the case of death.[123] While one could respond to this concern by appealing to von Balthasar's language of the *Ur*-death involved in kenosis, the concept of *bonitas* offers a better solution.

Bonicity: The Pure Positivity of Fruit

This brings us to the core of von Balthasar's Ulrichian insight: while the Spirit is the Bond and Fruit of the self-giving of the Father and Son, the Spirit himself "does not, as such, rest on a self-emptying but is the pure positivity of the Good."[124] Quoting Ulrich's *Homo Abyssus*, von Balthasar claims: "There is no self-emptying (*exinanitio*) in the case of the Holy Spirit," for Good must be "prior" and "superior" to "all self-emptying."[125] To this end, Ulrich suggests three "ontological moments": Reality (*Realität*), Ideality (*Idealität*), and Bonicity (*Bonität*), understood not as "discrete 'phases' in time, each extrinsic to each other," but "co-constitutive parts of a whole, and indeed of each other."[126]

Reality refers to the finite substance, already existing as a unity of essence and *esse*. As Schindler points out, insofar as Reality signals the "already subsisting *unity*" of the concrete *res*, Thomas's real distinction "falls away" in a certain sense, emphasizing that a *res* is not "*composite* in the

122. See Tourpe, "Positivité," 92, my translation. Coakley's comments on the dangers of referring to the Spirit as an "excess" approximate a similar concern (*God, Sexuality, Self*, 24, 56).

123. See Coakley, "Why Gift," 226; Leung, "Transcendentality and the Gift," 89n48.

124. *TL*3, 227.

125. *TL*3, 227–28; *HA*, 464. For discussions concerning von Balthasar's reading of *HA* in this section, see Tourpe, "Positivité"; Schindler, *Companion*, 21–48.

126. Schindler, *Companion*, 28. Much of this section is reliant on Schindler's excellent analysis of *HA* in this volume. On the three ontological moments, see especially pp. 29–48; see also Bieler, "Introduction," xx–xxi; Tourpe, "Thomisme Ontologique," 487–88.

sense of a conglomeration of two discrete realities" but a "(nonreductive) unity" in which *esse* and essence are joined together in a mutually kenotic movement.[127] *Esse*, infinite but non-subsistent in itself, gives itself over to essence, allowing itself to be limited by its reception in finite essence as *actus essendi*. In turn, as a "kind of obedient space that esse releases from itself" in its self-gift, essence provides the condition of the subsistence of *esse*.[128]

Ideality intimates the *a priori* character of *esse* as such as the "actuality of all acts" and "formality of all form," not an act or form in itself but that which "'precontain[s]' all possible things and so all possible concepts."[129] In relation to Ideality, Ulrich speaks of both the "vacillation" and "crisis" of being. While "vacillation" (*Seinsschwebe*) suggests the temptation to think of "a sort of hesitation or indecisiveness, a reluctance to give oneself away" on the part of infinite *esse commune*, "crisis" does not signal a cataclysm or critical situation but a positive and decisive judgment (in the sense of κρινειν). To hold Ideality and Reality together is to "recognize being [*esse*] as having always already given itself away" and "beings" as essence that has received it.[130] Ulrich develops Thomas's understanding of *esse* as "*completum et simplex sed non subsistens*" into a concept of being (*esse*) as "pure mediation" in the sense that "being is fullness *given away*."[131] Infinite being's movement of finitization is the transnihilation of *esse*, a "decision" to give itself away to finite essences that does not annihilate it but allows it to become truly "manifest in actualization."[132] This reveals the "perfect 'given-away-ness'" of being that flows from "the total, unhesitating generosity of God," which constitutes the *proportionalitas* between Ulrich's three ontological moments and the trinitarian life, which is based in Thomas's real distinction.[133]

If Reality is thought of in isolation from Ideality, then being is reduced to essence and the radical givenness of the whole *ens*, signaled in Ideality, is lost. Dynamism becomes static, life becomes death, infinitude is reduced to nothingness. On the other hand, if Ideality is thought of alone, effectively giving over to selfish vacillation, *esse* is hypostatized as a "thing" over

127. Schindler, *Companion*, 29.

128. Schindler, *Companion*, 31, 32.

129. Schindler, *Companion*, 36; citing *ST* I–II, q.2, a.5 *ad* 2. The relation of Ideality to ideas follows a similar pattern, such that Ideality signals the "absolute simplicity of esse and, beyond this, the simplicity of God himself," the simplicity that is presupposed in the radical generosity of the designation of ideas themselves; see Schindler, *Companion*, 35.

130. Schindler, *Companion*, 39.

131. *DP* q.1, a.1; *HA*, 28, 30.

132. *HA*, 70; see Coleman, "Thinking the 'Nothing' of Being," 11.

133. Schindler, *Companion*, 39–40.

against both *essentia* (as created) and God (as infinite). From this, *essentia* are reduced to "so many discrete ideas, co-eternal with God," and *esse* must become the "mere facticity" of a thing existing.[134] These two "moments" must be kept together, a task only possible by the mediation of a third. Thus, it is here, finally, that the third moment of Bonicity appears in its full importance. The starting point of both thought and being cannot be either being's vacillation or the brute essence but rather "the paradox of love, which celebrates the tension and the resolution at the same time."[135] Bonicity preserves and presents this paradox, indicating not only "the concrete thing" (*res*) but the creature (*ens*) "in the doing of its being."[136] While Bonicity marks a return to Reality in that it denotes the actual creature, the *res* of Reality is present here now as *ens*, the enactment of the essence through the *actus essendi* given over in the finitization of being (Ideality), such that the *ens* "makes manifest the mystery of being that *exceeds* the creature" in that it exists as itself "only in its giving to and receiving from other things."[137] *Esse* communicates its self-giving nature to essence such that the *ens* enacts this same form in its interaction with the other *entia* that with it comprise the communion of beings in Being.

Lying in the background to this conception of Bonicity is Thomas's link between goodness, perfection, actuality, and being in *ST* Ia, q.5. Whereas being is prior to goodness in thought, goodness lies at the end of the chain, signaling the ultimate perfection accomplished by attaining to the full actuality of their being. This means that a thing is most properly good when it enacts its being, that is, the *actus essendi* of self-gift revealed in the real distinction. A thing is most properly itself—truly good—when it offers itself to others in the enactment of its finite essence.[138] The Good (Bonicity) is not the self-gift of being in its crisis (Ideality) nor the reception of that Gift (Reality) but the "pure positivity" of the subsisting *actus essendi* of an *ens* giving and receiving itself. It is not "juxtaposed" to self-emptying but is the actuality of that very act, an actuality that does not empty itself but is the fullness of the ongoing act of relational giving.[139]

As Ulrich approaches the end of his task, the identification of the Good with the concrete and actual *ens* gives way to a final observation,

134. Schindler, *Companion*, 38. By this, Ulrich shows how the same concept lies at the root of rationalistic essentialism and empirical nominalism.

135. Schindler, *Companion*, 41.

136. Schindler, *Companion*, 41.

137. Schindler *Companion*, 41–42. See *HA*, 381–91.

138. See Schindler, *Companion*, 46–47.

139. *TL*3, 228; see *HA*, 465–80.

again drawn from *ST* Ia, q.5. While the "necessary sense of being comes to a head in the moment of the good" as the fecund Fruit of the real distinction, the Good is likewise "prior to being's kenosis and its transnihilation in the crisis."[140] Thus, Good structures Being as its *ratio finis*: "although the end is first in intention, it is last in execution."[141] Thus, the Good is "prior" to the self-emptying of which it is ultimately the Fruit, and it is "superior" to it as its "ether," "vital element," and the "power that inspires" it.[142] The Good as concrete act of love "accompanies [the crisis of being] without being identified with it."[143] Instead, the Good is the dimension that envelops the relations of self-giving and fecundity within itself, not as a whole made of individual parts (such as *esse* and *essentia*) but as the unity of diverse ontological realities that only exist in dependence upon the other. The Good is at the same time a Third that proceeds as the Fruit of the two and their inner unity, being both "end and beginning" of being as love.[144] As such, the Good reveals that love does not mean either unity or fecundity but both at the same time in the mutually fulfilled act of self-giving love. As the *causa finalis*, the Good is present as an intention even within the gratuity of being's kenosis: the self-disappropriation identified by Ulrich in both Reality and Ideality is aimed at and contained in the actuality of Bonicity, which is in the power of neither alone except through the other. Thus, the pure positivity of love's act in the fecund Third "is what 'guides' the movement of finitization to its end," the "abiding 'unoriginateness'" of the Good that animates the mutual kenosis of Ideality and Reality in which it is revealed and enacted.[145]

Love: From Ulrich's Bonicity to von Balthasar's Spirit

While it is tempting to appropriate these three ontological moments to the three trinitarian persons, Ulrich cautions against doing so "immediately," lest all difference in God and in creation collapses into the "absolute subjectivity" of the Spirit, as in Hegel.[146] Instead, the crisis of infinite being's

140. *HA*, 463.

141. *DP* q.7, a.2 *ad* 10; see *HA*, 464–65; *ST* Ia, q.5, a.2 *ad* 2. Von Balthasar first raises the question this concept poses in his third prelude, "Can There Be a Spirit-Christology?" (*TL*3, 33).

142. *TL*3, 228; see *HA*, 436, 465.

143. *TL*3, 228. See Tourpe, "Positivité," 87; Ide, "Être comme Amour."

144. Tourpe, "Positivité," 107; the second quotation is taken from *HA*, 151.

145. *HA*, 464–65.

146. *HA*, 158. Tourpe misses this caution and claims that Ulrich proposes a direct attribution in "Positivité," 108.

finitization, in which the "difference" of the real distinction is unified in the concrete act that perfects the creature through its relational act of self-giving, finds its "ultimate condition of possibility" in the "unfathomable unity and differentiation of Person and Nature in God."[147] Creaturely difference, both the real distinction and the distinctions between *entia*, is grounded in the unity-in-distinction of the trinitarian persons who together as one are the trinitarian life. However, Ulrich does draw a direct (if only parenthetical) line from the non-kenotic nature of Bonicity to the nature of the Spirit, which von Balthasar then cites at a crucial moment of clarification in his pneumatology: "There is no self-emptying [*exinanitio*] in the case of the Holy Spirit."[148] As the "pure fruit" of mutually selfless love, the Spirit is the "pure positivity of the Good."[149] As the final end of all things, the Good is the fulfillment of being, actuality, and perfection. The Spirit, occupying a role within the act of trinitarian love similar to Bonicity's final causality within created being, is "prior" to the divine kenosis as its fulfillment and "superior" to it as that which both contains and exceeds it.[150] It is not that the Spirit "presupposes" the act of mutual kenosis of Father and Son as its extrinsic fruit; rather, the Spirit "contains" their mutual kenosis, accompanying it intrinsically as the Good accompanies the "crisis of being" with which it is "indistinguishable" yet not "identified."[151]

In this way, Ulrich's concept of Bonicity allows von Balthasar's twofold schema for the Spirit—his subjective role as the "innermost fire of love of Father and Son" and objective role as the fruit of this very love—to be integrated under one concept.[152] Subjectively, as a final cause "accompanies" the entirety of the act by which it is attained by nature of its self-diffusivity, the Spirit is indistinguishable from the personal act of the Father and Son that is the ground of the Spirit's procession as Fruit, while not being identical with it for the very same reason, that is, by its procession as its Fruit. The Spirit is the very *donum doni* who in himself communicates the self-gift of Father and Son, each to the Other, and as such the Spirit personalizes and maintains both Father and Son as the space in which they enact their mutual love. Just as Bonicity "saves the entire span of the movement of finitization" because neither *esse* nor *essentia* come into being apart from the

147. *HA*, 161.

148. *TL*3, 227; see *HA*, 465. Tourpe has provided an impressive analysis of the importance of this concept to von Balthasar's broader metaphysical project in Tourpe, "Positivité."

149. *TL*3, 227.

150. *TL*3, 228.

151. *TL*3, 228, 235; see *HA*, 436.

152. *TL*3, 243–44.

mediating moment of Bonicity, the Spirit guarantees the mutual kenosis of Father and Son by carrying each to the Other in the form of divine Love as the mediating reality of perfect goodness, which can only be attained by this perfect union.[153] Objectively, this perfect goodness is not the calculable total of their mutual exchange, "containing" it in mathematically demonstrable manner (Father + Son = Spirit), as this would only reveal mutual love to be the calculated selfishness of a pair who, so to speak, meet each other's needs perfectly. Instead, the Spirit's emergence as Fruit signals the success of their love in the excess that miraculously springs from the "interplay of absolute love that would seem to be eternally self-sufficient" (and possibly self-enclosed by its equilibrium) if not for the Third that springs from it and surpasses it.[154] In the attainment of the final cause in the Spirit, divine love is revealed as truly selfless, in which each gives themselves to the Other *gratis*, and from this mutual selflessness, divine love is revealed as fecund. Therefore, as both Father and Son unexpectedly receive from the Other, the Gift that they receive is not only themselves as a return but a Fruit in excess of their mutual love. The Spirit's presence as Fruit validates that the love of each was not calculated for their own gain but truly carried out for the sake of the Other, and that this love was truly mutual, because when truly selfless love is reciprocated it finds its fulfillment in the miraculous and ecstatic movement of new life.

Since the Spirit is divine love "lived out in personal terms," both in the "innermost center" and "highest point" as the divine person who "concludes and rounds out God's entire being as love," neither divine personhood nor divine love itself, contrary to many of von Balthasar's commentators, can be reduced to or sufficiently defined by kenosis.[155] Papanikolaou's claim that "the divine persons are constituted in and through movements of kenotic self-giving and receiving" can only apply to the Spirit in a limited manner, as his person is explicitly said not to be constituted in self-giving like Father and Son, instead resting on the mutual kenosis of Father and Son as the pure

153. *HA*, 465.

154. *TL*3, 159.

155. *TL*3, 228; 161–62. See McInerny, *Trinitarian Theology*, 34, though he does not note that von Balthasar is reliant upon Ulrich here, hence the absence of any consideration of *bonitas* in his work; contra Nichols, *No Bloodless Myth*, 167; E. Oakes, *Pattern of Redemption*, 290; Levering, *Scripture and Metaphysics*, 123; Lefsrud, *Kenosis in Theology*, 154–56; to a certain extent, Papanikolaou, "Person, Kenosis, Abuse," 47.

positivity of being, constituted by pure reception, that is itself the Gift of love between Father and Son.[156] Thus, the Spirit gives, but not kenotically.[157]

156. Papanikolaou, "Person, Kenosis, Abuse," 47. This is only possible, however, if receptivity is attributed to the divine love as a perfection equal to that of gratuitous giving, such that we do not "ascribe more perfection to human love than to God's love" (Healy, *Eschatology of Hans Urs von Balthasar*, 81). This relates to the Father and Son in their mutual kenosis, but even more absolutely to the Spirit who receives from both and is the medium of their reception.

The discussion of receptivity as a perfection in God received significant attention among those engaged in both Thomist-Balthasarian conversations in the early 1990s, beginning with W. Norris Clarke's Aquinas Lectures, published as *Person and Being* in 1993. Healy summarizes and continues the discussion, which included thinkers such as David L. Schindler, Stephen A. Long, and George A. Blair, concluding that there is good reason to see "receptivity as a metaphysical perfection" that obtains in the divine *actus essendi* itself (*Eschatology of Hans Urs von Balthasar*, 72–83). Paul O'Callaghan objects on the grounds that because receptivity is a "consequence of the 'real distinction' between being and essence" that signals creatures' dependence on God, it "could hardly be a perfection in a God who is self-sufficient" ("Can God Be Enriched," 192). As Schindler notes, von Balthasar seeks to emphasize both sides of the identification between *esse* and *essentia* in God in a way that does not only remove limitation and render a concept of undifferentiated plenitude but also signals the particular manner of the subsistence of that infinite *esse*, which is in three related *personae* ("What's the Difference," 25). In this sense, though there is no distinction in God between *esse* and *essentia*, this does not mean that reception has no place in God, but that it only obtains in the perfect mutuality of giving and receiving of the *modus essendi* of the divine Trinity, or, as Milbank puts it, in the "infinite *plenitude* of essential determination" in which "God's *essential* Being . . . is conceived as the full giving of Being as an infinitely determined essence in God" ("Can a Gift Be Given," 153–54).

157. Describing the Spirit by an inversion of kenotic giving, which von Balthasar identifies as what is essentially divine, draws attention to the significance of his willingness to adopt Ulrich's denial of kenotic giving to the Spirit. While there are sparing references to a kenotic aspect of the Spirit in von Balthasar's work, they are restricted to the economy, and specifically to von Balthasar's concept of the trinitarian inversion. In *TL*3, 147, von Balthasar expresses Theo Preiß's idea that the Spirit "gives place to the Father and Son in a kind of kenosis." Similarly, the Spirit is said to renounce "an aspect of his divine form: of being the overwhelming product of the love between Father and Son" (Balthasar, *Spirit and Institution*, 232). But von Balthasar clarifies that just as the incarnation is "not an alienation of [the Son's] loving readiness but only its metamorphosis in a soteriological form," just so is the subjective aspect of the Spirit as bond transposed into the encounter between Father and in the Son's mission, in which the Spirit's identity as the "overwhelming product" of that encounter comes under a "corresponding hiddenness" during the time of the Son's *descensus*, until the "Trinity's personified love becomes visible as fruit and gift in the Holy Spirit" opening up that encounter "beyond itself" in the Son's outpouring of the Eucharist of the world (*Spirit and Institution*, 232–34). The Spirit's proclivity to "give place" to the Father and Son is a function of the fact that their I-Thou relation—which only comes about in the bonicity of the Spirit—is an expression of the fact that the eternal reality of the divine life is being presented in the divine missions to bring the world into the eternal fullness of the fecund life of God. In other words, the trinitarian inversion is not a permanent feature

This means that kenosis is not a univocal concept under which the divine persons are subsumed.[158] Neither can kenosis be equated *simpliciter* with the divine *esse*, as the non-kenotic Spirit is equiprimordially subsistent in the divine love along with the Father and Son. Rather, kenosis is contextualized within absolute love as a necessary aspect, even representing the acme of absolute love in its poverty while remaining oriented toward the *telos* of fecund communion. The divine persons all subsist in the totality of divine love, but they do so incommunicably according to their respective modes of relation, which must be held together when considering any at all.[159]

---

of the economy but is an expression of the Spirit as bond that will ultimately be (and always already is in God) fulfilled in the fruitfulness of the Spirit's "liquefaction" of the Father's love and the Son's Eucharist for the whole world (*TL*3, 229; see also Balthasar, *Spirit and Institution*, 237). In this sense, the Spirit's economic expression of some "kind of kenosis" is itself safeguarded by his immanent and eternal lack of kenosis as the abiding origin-less-ness of divine love as *bonitas*, because his economic expressions are expressive of his role as *relatio* rather than *relata*.

158. See Balthasar, *Mysterium Paschale*, 28–29.

159. As the divine *esse* is determined by the concrete unity found through each divine person's reciprocal enactment of divine love, each person subsists in this concrete unity according to their own incommunicable *modus existendi*, "only definable in terms of relation, each vis-à-vis the other" (*TL*3, 136–37, 148; see *ST* Ia, q.30, a.4 *ad* 1–3; *DP* q.9, a.2 *ad* 2. See McInerny, *Trinitarian Theology*, 26–27, 33–34).

Gilles Emery argues that while Thomas did not reject Richard's emphasis on incommunicability between the divine persons, Thomas believed that this was included in the correct reading of "individual" in Boethius's definition of a person. According to Emery, Thomas did not pursue Richard's modification any further because he saw, as did Bonaventure, that Richard's definition ("an incommunicable existence [*ex-sistere*] of divine nature") failed, unlike that of Boethius, to provide the analogical connection between divine and created persons (*Trinitarian Theology of Aquinas*, 111; see also Solignac, "Personnes Selon Saint Bonaventure," 453–54). While Boethius's definition does provide the analogical concept that functions as the basis for reflection, it is Richard's definition that specifies the way in which the divine persons can be said to subsist individually apart from matter: "God cannot be called an *individual* in the sense that His individuality comes from matter; but only in the sense which implies incommunicability" (*ST* Ia, q.29, a.3 *ad* 4). To call a distinct subsistent reality a person "signifies that which distinguishes the determinate thing," which in humanity is matter and in the Godhead is only relation (*ST* Ia, q.29, a.3 ad 4; a.4 *resp* and *ad* 3). As the divine persons can only be distinguished through mutually constituted relation, Richard's modal incommunicability points out precisely the same clarification that Thomas must add to Boethius's definition to consider the divine persons, namely, the incommunicability of the divine relations. It is not that Thomas is unimpressed by Richard's definition but, on the contrary, that he has already taken this exact step himself in his consideration of God by clarifying a distinction necessary to applying Boethius's definition to God at all. Compare the argument for the similarity between Richard and Thomas on this issue in Malet, *Personne et Amour*, 38, 91.

For von Balthasar's part, this unique concept of each divine person existing in an

The interrelation of these modes helps to illustrate the reciprocal determination of *esse* and person at play in von Balthasar's thought. For the Spirit to be constituted by something other than the giving of his own self to another signals the fact that his possession of his own person is already established in relation to the Father and Son. The Spirit's person is constituted in absolute reception rather than a mutual giving and receiving, but this absolute reception issues in an absolute freedom that bends back to its origins in a dramatic transformation of the Father and Son's relation, imbuing the concept of kenosis from the beginning with the promise of absolute freedom only realized in the whole trinitarian life as its end. Von Balthasar expresses this by speaking of the "necessity" of the Father's willing self-gift to the Son and the Son's simultaneous necessity and freedom in consenting to "being begotten" and self-disposing for sake of the "Father's purposes."[160] The Father's "necessity" is his enactment of his "spiritual nature" as love, while the Son's free response "already has the contours of obedience" to the "Father's wishes, which count on his collaboration."[161] Both forms of "necessity" are transcended, however, in the surprise of the Fruit that emerges from the "encounter" of the Father and Son. As von Balthasar argues, "the concept of 'necessity' cannot be applied in the case of this 'third,'" which is the Spirit that enacts the absolute freedom of love: "The wind [πνευμα] blows where it wishes" (John 3:8). In this absolute freedom of the Spirit, the necessity in the first moment is revealed "as lying beyond all creaturely freedom and necessity," a phrase which von Balthasar quotes from von Speyr.[162]

incommunicable manner is a powerful rejoinder to the prevalent concern that trinitarian grammars derived from examples of interpersonal love tend toward social trinitarianism (which, the implication normally is, tends itself toward tritheism). One example of this is Karen Kilby, who suggests that von Balthasar is here "at one with . . . social theorists. He too envisages the 'persons' of the Trinity functioning as something not too far from 'persons' in our ordinary sense of the term, and so imagines the Trinity as closer to a small family than to differing aspects of a single psyche"; see "Hans Urs von Balthasar and the Trinity," 213; see also Kilby, *Balthasar*, 102–4; McInerny, *Trinitarian Theology*, 24. While it is true that von Balthasar rejects the absolute monarchy of the *intra*-personal model found in Augustine and Aquinas and prefers to speak (also) in *inter*-personal terms, it is difficult to see how each divine person existing in an incommunicable *modus existendi* as a relationally conditioned yet identical act of self-giving and receiving could be said to mirror our "ordinary" sense of the term "person." Von Balthasar does not understand "persons" as a univocal concept between creatures and God, or even between the three persons of the Godhead; see *TL*3, 134–37. Also helpful to resist the temptation of too quickly categorizing von Balthasar's thought in this way is Jennifer Newsome Martin's work on von Balthasar's commitment to a quite strong doctrine of divine simplicity in her essay "Consubstantial Otherness of God."

160. See *TL*3, 236–37.

161. See *TL*3, 236.

162. See *TL*3, 236.

The self-giving of both Father and Son are both enacted in the Spirit who is the *donum doni*, retrospectively revealing that the "necessity" of the spiritual enactment of divine self-giving is carried out in the freedom of the Spirit as *bonitas*.[163] The Father's self-gift cannot be thought of even *principaliter* without also implying the eternal return of the Son to the Father in the Spirit as Gift. Further, the Gift that is given by the Father and Son is both their very selves and the Spirit of divine love, who proceeds in absolute freedom from their selfless mutuality and as the totally free Beloved bestows the excess of divine love upon Father and Son. Though the Father and Son subsist in the divine nature as their relative acts of self-donation, the fact that the very subsistence of the Father and Son is constituted in this act of self-giving means that the divine love of the Trinity is fundamentally relational and reciprocal in nature, closer to Milbank's "purified gift-exchange" than Derrida's "pure gift." Not only can the divine Gift not be thought of apart from the relationality within which it is given—as in Milbank, they are coincident—the Gift that is given exceeds the self-giving of Father and Son as the Spirit who eternally guarantees the free reciprocity of this gift-exchange as the bonitic *donum doni*.[164] It is in total freedom, then, that the Spirit turns back to both Father and Son and bears witness to their love, testifying that the depth from which he emerges is precisely the free and absolute commitment to the Other of divine love.

As *bonitas*, then, the Spirit is clearly not "tacked on" as a "different kind of love" than the self-giving love of Father and Son because the "loving acts of self-gift by the Father and by the Son are apparently insufficient to 'bond' or unite them," as Pitstick surmises.[165] While von Balthasar does say that "the giving over of self" is "what is essentially divine," the assumptions behind Pitstick's analysis mark a subtle shift toward a univocally kenotic divine love ("If the divine essence is self-gift . . .") in which the Spirit gives himself in the same kind of kenosis as the Father and Son. Bonicity clears this confusion up. Far from being an add on to the love of the Father and Son, the Spirit's roles as Bond, Fruit, and Gift are intrinsic to the mutual love of the Father and Son. He is not a different kind of love but the fulfillment of the very same act of love between Father and Son, but this can only be seen if divine love is not reduced to the generic concept of self-giving. Instead, divine love is always selfless love that gives freely and receives the Other

163. It is only at this point in his pneumatology that von Balthasar would be able to respond sufficiently to Milbank's concern that the persons are subjected to "an impersonal negative logic of the essence emptied of all personality" in order to be free in their personal subsistences; see Milbank, *Suspended Middle*, 81.

164. Milbank, "Can a Gift Be Given," 137.

165. See Pitstick, *Light in Darkness*, 287–88.

as an unexpected gift of unity that exceeds what was given. Divine kenosis issues in an "always more" that reveals the bounty of divine wealth in the absolute self-giving of Father and Son. The reciprocation of the Father and Son is contextualized with the Spirit as both *donum doni* and *causa finalis*, which gives kenotic love a new horizon where the self is not lost in the vacillation of a zero-sum exchange but is received in the Spirit as Gift through the gratuitous love of the Other that exceeds what was initially given away with no demand for return.

This also allows the coincidence of poverty and wealth to be grasped more fully. Without the Spirit, the Father and Son would be trapped in the past and present of mutual kenosis and uncertain of the future of its success; the identity of wealth and poverty would therefore be reduced to the calculable total of co-dependence. The only wealth that could be found "in the moment" would be in the return of their own selves, such that both could never fully exist. In a sense, unless kenotic love blossoms in mutuality into a truly free Fruit, there would be only one divine self that is shared and passed back and forth in a mutuality that would ultimately lead to the dissolution of one or the other, or both. In the emergence of the Spirit, then, selfless, absolute, and mutual love is revealed to be miraculously fruitful. What is received is more than was given—each gives himself as his enactment of the divine *esse* and accepts, in dramatic terms, that the wealth of this act of selfless love is a sufficient enactment of their subsistence, but what each receives is the Other's gift in the Spirit as something more than was expected.

Furthermore, because this wealth is the reception of self within the entire event of being as Love, the Spirit does not trail off into an abyss of self-giving but marks the reciprocal sublation of the mutual self-giving of Father and Son by exceeding their own "acts" of love in the return of their selves. The Father and Son are not thereby lost, negated, or subsumed by the Spirit's emergence but are constituted in the Spirit's Bonicity, the ever-present excess within God's absolute love that carries the love of God for the Other (the Father and the Son) to its completion in the divine unity.[166] Thus, the identity of poverty and wealth is revealed only in the Spirit who breaks free of the reciprocal emptying as the fullness that each receives. Poverty is not wealth simply because it is the enactment of the divine nature as self-giving,

166. This invokes a concern similar to von Balthasar's own concern that divine love must be an immanent surpassing rather than (contra Marion) constituting some external "beyond"; see *TL2*, 134n10; see Tourpe, "Positivité," 90. It seems from this, too, that Milbank's assessment that von Balthasar "forgets" the simplicity of God and contradicts Lateran IV by speaking "of the Father as handing over 'the entire substance' of the Godhead to the Son, such that the divine essence remains in a kind of suspense," does not attend closely enough to the fulfilling role of von Balthasar's pneumatology (Milbank, *Suspended Middle*, 81).

paradoxically equating the fullness of actuality with the emptiness of the specific act that is actualized. This would mean that wealth was reducible to the actuality of *ipsum esse per se subsistens*, the *primus actus* considered apart from the *ultimus actus*.[167] To leave the coincidence of poverty and wealth underdetermined in this way allows the possibility that the Trinity becomes enclosed, and for all intents and purposes, static. It is only when the divine love is seen as not only self-giving but miraculously overflowing with life that God's wealth can be understood as a true and beneficent plenitude and not simply divine self-satisfaction.

Nevertheless, the aspect of kenosis remains at the heart of this act of absolute wealth because the selflessness of true poverty is nothing but an acknowledgment of the fact that true wealth is only that received in love from the Other. To not embrace poverty would be to vacillate and fail to come to subsistence, so to speak, and in embracing the kenotic poverty of self-giving, the divine persons possess the wealth of relational reception. Whereas Derrida sees gift-giving as totally one sided and disinterested and Milbank argues that it must establish reciprocity, von Balthasar provides a way to see it as absolute self-giving so that reciprocity cannot be constitutive of kenosis yet truly obtains in the Trinity. Even for the Father, poverty is the only possibility of his wealth, for the enactment of his being as self-giving love cannot exist in isolation. The "risk" of the "sacrifice" of both Father and Son that von Balthasar speaks of indicates the reception necessary for them to truly be, which is fulfilled in the Fruit who fills each up as their mutual excess. But the wealth that is identified with poverty is not simply possessive return but the excess of love that overflows from mutual selflessness. In the return to each Giver, this excess is not kenotic but plerotic, the revelation of kenotic, or selfless, love's ultimate fecundity that freely gives "objective testimony to the effect that this love takes place eternally."[168] To return to von Balthasar's favored image, just as a child "demonstrates that its father and mother were united in love," the Spirit's testimony to the love of the Father and Son is grounded in the fact that he proceeds as (objective) Fruit from their love of which he is the (subjective) "innermost fire of love."[169] The Spirit

167. This concern lies behind Hemmerle's claim that any ontology that stops at self-subsistence is insufficient for the trinitarian revelation of God's identity (*Theses*, 33); Olsen, "*Exitus et Reditus*," 849.

168. *TL*3, 243.

169. *TL*3, 141; see also *TL*3, 55–56. Von Balthasar's polemic against Hegel, which runs throughout the *Theo-logic*, helps to clarify the difference between their uses of very similar categories; see Moser, *Love Itself Is Understanding*, 194–95, 201–4. Unlike Hegel, von Balthasar insists that these categories cannot be ordered in a sequence such as "*subjective-objective-absolute Spirit*" which is "read off from a theory of 'becoming' that does correspond to the trinitarian *taxis*" (*TL*3, 243). Instead of "moments in the

is not kenotic in that he does not renounce "being for himself alone"; rather, the Spirit is the revelation of the free, divine act of being for the Other. This retrospectively situates the kenosis of both Father and Son as a similarly free act that is "contained" and "secured," and indeed represented to us as a self-emptying that is eternally full in the mutuality signified and enacted in the bonitic Spirit, the "nutritive and life-bringing milieu" which expresses the true sense of Being which it envelopes and accompanies throughout.[170] The kenosis of Father and Son is not *nihil* but *actus purus* when seen in the light of the continual mediating presence of the pure positivity of the Spirit as the *causa finalis* of their mutual love. This rescues divine kenosis from the danger of making love into an abyss of self-giving, revealing it as an eternally replete act of self-giving love by which the gratuity of the self-gift miraculously issues not in a loss of self but an overflowing of self to and from the Other. In God, kenosis is not loss, but the condition of the gain found in mutually selfless love.

Conclusion

I have taken three significant steps toward describing God's life as relational love in this chapter. First, I adopted von Balthasar's description of love as kenotic self-giving as an appropriate expression of the sacrificial *amicitia* identified by Thomas as the fulfillment of *caritas*. This intra-trinitarian kenosis is not destructive but wholly dispositional, such that it is the rejection of self-sufficiency in favor of giving to the Other. Secondly, the coincidence of poverty and wealth was identified as necessary for God's life to remain plerotic, but wealth may not be understood simply as the enactment of self-impoverishment, which is self-contradictory, or as that which is received in the impoverishment of the other, as this is ultimately destructive and reducible to *amor sui*. Instead, the identity of wealth and poverty in God is found in the miraculous emergence and reception of wealth that exceeds their mutual love through the surprising fruitfulness of kenotic poverty. The emergence of the Spirit as Fruit is what rescues kenosis from being ultimately dispossessive. The third and final step was establishing the importance of

self-realization of absolute Spirit" considered as a monad, the Spirit's subjectivity and objectivity are simultaneous aspects of the "eternally realized being" of the Spirit, ultimately indistinguishable but able to be distinguished only through a "logic of love" that expresses both the self-giving and fecund aspects of love (*TL*3, 243).

170. Ide, "Être comme Amour," 284, my translation. Ide identifies the concept of *enveloppement* as fundamental to rightly denying being's *extranéation* to the Good (with Ulrich) without making the Good completely external to Being. See also Dol, *Esprit de Vérité et d'amour*.

Ulrich's three ontological moments for interpreting von Balthasar's mature pneumatology. The emergence of the Spirit as Fruit is not a "surprise" in the sense that it is ontologically disconnected from the kenosis of Father and Son. On the contrary, the bonitic emergence of the Spirit revealed the secret of kenotic love that accompanies it in all its ways. Divine love is not only kenotic, but plerotic. Kenosis is a first and necessary aspect of true love for the Other, but in perfect mutuality kenosis reveals itself to be the ground for the possibility of the infinite expansion of life, being, and love.

This leads to final point: von Balthasar's stated concept of divine love must be expanded. Love is not simply *Selbstübergabe*, as he sometimes claims, though that is a necessary aspect. Absolute Love remains one act while involving a multitude that exceeds the Lover and Beloved. In the next chapter, the insights garnered from Thomas, von Balthasar, and Ulrich will be gathered together with Klaus Hemmerle's trinitarian ontology to suggest a way in which unity and plurality can be expressed in a single divine ontology of love that avoids denigrating any of the divine persons while maintaining their true essential unity.

4

Plerosis in Kenosis

The Fecundity of Divine Love as the Union of Unity and Plurality

Introduction

THOUGH FERDINAND ULRICH'S INFLUENCE can be seen in von Balthasar's work throughout the triptych, it is not until *TL*3 that he explores the pneumatological implications of Ulrich's three moments within the trinitarian life, which then play a consistent if covert role in his short *Epilogue*.[1] Identifying the Spirit with *bonitas* gestures toward the Spirit's accompanying presence of the Father and Son's mutual kenosis and the consequent transcendence of the polarity between poverty and wealth. But it is not yet clear how the Spirit's "mysterious affinity" to the divine nature should be configured in the metaphysical terms of the common and distinct, that is, the divine *esse* of love and the divine person of the Spirit. Questions concerning the nature of divine personhood depend on clarifying the metaphysical form of divine love suggested in von Balthasar and Ulrich, as the Spirit is associated with the *esse* in ways that the Father and Son seemingly are not.

In this chapter, I will take up Hemmerle's ontology to explore three ways that these metaphysical questions might be answered.[2] First, it provides

1. For instance, see Balthasar, *Epilogue*, 55–57, 76, 82–86. For previous appearances of Ulrich's influence, see Balthasar, *Realm of Metaphysics in Antiquity*, 38; Balthasar, *Realm of Metaphysics in the Modern Age*, 625–27; Balthasar *Man in God*, 256–57; implicitly in *TD*5, 72.

2. Balthasar summarizes Hemmerle's *Theses* in *TD*5, 73–75, but they do not enter materially into the fuller discussion of the Spirit in *TL*3. See Eduard Fiedler's excellent essay situating Hemmerle in his philosophical and historical context, "Klaus Hemmerle on the Trinitarian Ontology."

a structure and vocabulary to express an ontology of love that includes both common and distinct, act and identity, *esse* and person. Importantly, Hemmerle's work is not simply a speculative ontology. According to Hemmerle, it is exactly the opposite; what is new about his proposed ontology is that it approaches the depth of being in a way that follows the divine revelation of the "threefold mystery of God" in faith.[3] The "mystery of this mystery is love, is self-giving," but it is fundamentally the gift of God himself in the self-giving of Jesus Christ for us in which it is revealed.[4] In this gift, "everything is transformed—life and the world, the meaning of Being, everything whatever—because the gift is given from His origin, from the rhythm of His self-giving."[5] Many have attempted to construct analogies from below that shine some light on the divine nature and have sought like Thomas to demonstrate how these analogies are shaped by Scripture. In distinction from this, Hemmerle attempted to frame the entire analogy of self-giving love by the divine self-gift of God in Jesus Christ, reading the immanent "rhythm of *His* self-giving" from his relations to the Father and Spirit, which are the "inner justification, and, indeed, the necessity, of a Trinitarian ontology."[6] The economic acts of the Trinity are established as the revelatory "unfolding" of the immanent life of God, from which creation flows, to which its *oikonomia* is ordered and in which it finds its "fulfillment and completion."[7] This divine disclosure forces a relecture of all other analogies, in which theological thought "learns how to think anew in this 'phenomenology'; it is transformed by becoming a going-along with the way of self-giving, the way of love."[8] Theological thought is thus moved from simply containing the trinitarian ontology to carrying it out; to think along with trinitarian ontology is to "enter into its rhythm oneself."[9] Since for Hemmerle knowing something only happens in the simultaneous permission of receiving that thing ("receptive understanding") and the giving of one's self over to it ("giving projection"), to know this trinitarian ontology is to enact it in the very movement of thought.[10] It is a "spiritual performance" of the very thing that one is performing, and so we can only conceive of this divine love as a

3. *Theses*, 50.
4. *Theses*, 50.
5. *Theses*, 51.
6. *Theses*, 51.
7. *Theses*, 55.
8. *Theses*, 50.
9. *Theses*, 61; see also p. 52.
10. *Theses*, 62.

performance that only exists as it is enacted or "performed" in the Trinity.[11] In this way, Hemmerle's trinitarian ontology is simultaneously practical and philosophical, scriptural and natural, a human representation of the divine life.

Second, Hemmerle's ontology also offers an alternative way of construing personhood that is built on the identity between being and act. His theory of identity through intensification explains how the enstatic and ecstatic fulfillments of each person are a part of the same process. Not only does intensification provide a philosophical structure for many of von Balthasar's trinitarian statements, it also suggests a way in which the rational operations found in Thomas's theological anthropology might rightly be understood as an analogy of the distinction in unity between the divine persons without leading to three distinct "centers of consciousness" that divide the divine unity.

Finally, and most importantly, Hemmerle provides a way in which to understand the Spirit's personhood as both particular and, in some sense, representative of the whole. In his concept of the "performance of the We,"[12] Hemmerle provides a personal model of a unity of the one and many that does not reduce either one to the other, allowing the individual fulfillment identified as beatitude to truly obtain in and through the context of the unity of the whole. In this, he pushes past von Balthasar to supply more robust analogies for how the Spirit exemplifies the whole of the divine life other than through the metaphor of a child.

By incorporating and building upon Hemmerle's trinitarian ontology in this chapter, I will offer the reconfiguration of the notion of the divine *esse* according to the concept of *amor* called for in the previous chapters, so that what is common to and identical with the three divine persons is the eternally plerotic movement of mutually kenotic love. If, as Zizioulas claimed, Love is the "supreme ontological predicate," it calls us to abandon the fundamentally nonrelational concept of essence that, in the end, is "a metaphysical symbol for the misguided worship of independence . . . [and] self-sufficiency" inherited largely from Aristotle and the Neoplatonic idolization of Oneness. Instead, we end with an understanding of the divine in which the Trinity "defines the Christian's social existence through its own consummate sociality even as it fundamentally reveals the character of God."[13]

11. See *Theses*, 61–62.

12. *Theses*, 62.

13. Zizioulas, *Being as Communion*, 46; Mirus, "Relation Is Not a Category," 194, 198; Marsh, "In Defense of a Self," 278.

Unity in Plurality

As soon as the concept of three consubstantial and equal divine persons began to enjoy a relatively stable dogmatic acceptance around the time of the first Council of Constantinople in 381, the concept of transcendental number was applied to the issue of trinitarian unity and plurality. For instance, St. Basil argued that the divine persons are innumerable in the sense that they cannot be counted in the same way that composite, circumscribed beings can.[14] Instead, the hypostases are only identified and distinguished according to the relational terms "fatherhood, sonship, and sanctification."[15] Thomas continues in this vein by removing measure from how the divine persons are numbered. While the concept of transcendental multitude provides Thomas an avenue to posit a kind of plurality in the divine unity, he only takes this to signify that each divine person identified is "undivided in itself."[16] In other words, the relations which constitute the respective persons do not inform the kind of unity in which they exist.[17] Von Balthasar, though following the general trend of denying numerical measure from the divine persons, insists that this innumerability means that their relational plurality must be materially included within the concept of their unity rather than simply allowed.[18] This requires that an "absolute positivity of difference," a concept taken from Gustav Siewerth's reading of Thomas, be attributed

14. See Basil's "Letter 13" in *Letters and Select Works*, 116; Lingua, "Trinity, Number, Image," 1309–10. See also Gregory Nazianzen's "Oration 28" in *Gregory Nazianzen*, 290. Quantity is one of Aristotle's ten categories of how matter, or being, can be known; simple substances cannot be counted in the same way. Basil is arguing that innumerability does not preclude, but in fact allows for, triune simple being. Non-simple substances could never be triune in this way.

15. Basil, *Letters and Select Works*, 278; Gregory Nazianzen, *Gregory Nazianzen*, 307. Basil does use the terminology of relations intermittently, such as in Basil, *Against Eunomius*, 94, 164, but he uses the terminology of cause and effect more frequently, which Gregory also picks up.

16. *ST* I, q.30, a.3 *resp*. See *ST* I, q.30, a.2 *ad* 5; *TL*3, 439.

17. See *ST* I, q.28, a.3 *resp*: "Hence, there must be real distinction in God, not, indeed, according to that which is absolute—namely, essence, wherein there is supreme unity and simplicity—but according to that which is relative."

18. See *TL*3, 217: "the name of 'Love,' given to God by John (1 Jn 4:8, 16), . . . must presuppose, not numerical, but transcendental plurality, if it is to go beyond mere self-love (*dilectio*) and become *caritas*—the highest of the perfections created by God and which is found supereminently in him"; see also *TL*3, 121–23, 439. This contrasts with the distinction Thomas must maintain, as seen in *ST* I, q.39, a.1 *ad* 1: "But in God relations are subsistent, and so by reason of the opposition between them they distinguish the *supposita*; and yet the essence is not distinguished, because the relations themselves are not distinguished from each other so far as they are identified with the essence."

to the relations of the divine persons in God.[19] This "greatest of differences does not violate the unity or simplicity of being," but reveals that the divine "act of being is accordingly 'equi-primordially unity and nonunity,'" where the unity is "the unifying ground of the equally original nonunity."[20] That is, the divine act of being must be understood as the relational unity in which the nonunity of the distinct persons is grounded in the common act of love by which they are all both constituted and distinguished.[21]

The common act of love which is envisaged here can be conveyed in Ulrich's terminology as "God's absolute actuality in the actuality of a difference," which expresses the Father's ability "to hand over the entire fullness of the Godhead to the Son so perfectly that he may breathe forth the Spirit together with the Son."[22] Though McInerny is right that the *relatio* subsisting as a divine person does not signify an act ("to relate") but a "state of being" for Thomas, Katy Leamy is also correct that von Balthasar nonetheless intends to bring these together "to mean that relation *is* the divine essence, which determines the divine persons and divine activity."[23] All four concepts involved in Thomas's account—the divine *esse* as *actus essendi*, the *actio* of the processions, the relations that are constituted in these processions, and the persons that are designated by and subsist as these relations—are thereby integrated within a new image.

However, von Balthasar refrains from sketching a truly new framework that can "get beyond" the countervailing propositions of the inter- and intra-personal images.[24] A promising attempt at this kind integration is found in Klaus Hemmerle's essay written in honor of von Balthasar's seventieth birthday, *Theses Towards a Trinitarian Ontology*, not published in English until 2020.[25] Hemmerle's fundamental goal is to develop an ontology that is

19. *TL2*, 185, quoting Siewerth, *Thomismus Als Identitätssystem*, 104.

20. *TL2*, 185, quoting Siewerth, *Abstraktion Und Das Sein*, 60, and Siewerth, *Thomismus Als Identitätssystem*, 91.

21. See *TL3*, 136–37, for Balthasar's comments (following Mühlen) on the relationship between proximity and "distance" between the divine persons.

22. Bieler, "Introduction," xxxiv; see *HA*, 104–7.

23. McInerny, *Trinitarian Theology*, 52; Leamy, *Holy Trinity*, 51.

24. See *TL3*, 157: "Any approach to the mystery must proceed by statements running in opposite directions. (Nor must it be thought that we can 'get beyond' this insight.)"

25. For the rest of this paragraph, see *Theses*, 35–37. See also Balthasar's positive summary and appropriation of Hemmerle's work as early as *TD5*, 73–75, 84. My interpretation of Hemmerle follows the general shape of what Fiedler calls a "hermeneutics of continuity" ("Klaus Hemmerle on the Trinitarian Ontology," 69). This is exemplified in Coda's attempt to expand Thomas's *relatio subsistens* through the "intersubjective dynamic . . . of *agápe* as reciprocal self-gift, as intuited by Augustine and recovered by Richard of St. Victor" (*From the Trinity*, 491).

"distinctively Christian" and therefore necessarily trinitarian, which cannot be limited either to the concept of self-subsistence or self-consciousness.[26] Because love as an act provides the conceptual density required for a trinitarian ontology, the "substantive term in such a thinking is no longer the noun, but the verb."[27] The starting point of thought is the "event" (*Geschehen*) of love itself, the "process" (*Vorgang*) that the verb represents. Thinking along with the process or event of love reveals "what is going on, who is going on, and whence and whither the process is going." The process of love reveals that "all 'things' . . . can only be understood, and can only be fulfilled, in [their] action [*Akt*]." Because all things are constituted and exist only in the "relationships" (*Beziehungen*) established in this process, it follows that "nothing 'is' outside of its action." Therefore, a "process" (*Vorgang*) is not an "undivided flow" but a "relationship which happens" (*geschehende Beziehung*) through "the mutual movement towards each other, in each other, and out of each other of the poles [*Pole*] between which this relationship is in play." These "poles," or "points of connection," are "bound up" in the process, in "what takes place" (*Geschehens*), in such a way that "they are *in* what takes place. More than this, they *are* what takes place." And what takes place is that these poles communicate themselves, relate (*bezeihen*) themselves, give (*hineingeben*) themselves to and receive themselves from the process (*Vorgang*). The result is that the "whole process (*Vorgang*) is in each pole; the whole process (*Vorgang*) is the Being (*Sein*) of each of the poles." The poles are only distinguished by the way in which the process (*Vorgang*) "proceeds" (*hervorgeht*) from them and the way in which they proceed (*hervorgehen*) from the process (*Vorgang*), but the distinction between the poles is only "the distinction of the process itself; this means its articulation, from which the process acquires its unity and its divisibility, its structure." From this, finally, it follows that the replacement of an ontology's "substantive term" with the verb, Love, rather than a noun, "then the single subject [*einen Subjekts*] is displaced by a plural origin [*Mehrursprünglichkeit*]." The process or event is the mutual movement "in which the poles of the one process are related to each other." Unity is found in "the many poles, which, simultaneously, each from a different direction, allow each other, one upon another, to proceed [*hervorgehen*] to the whole process [*Vorgang*]."

26. Interestingly, as Betz also observes, Hemmerle's mention of self-consciousness (*das Selbstbewußtsein*) is omitted from the English translation with no explanation ("What's New," 141); see Hemmerle, *Thesen Zu Einer Trinitarischen Ontologie*, 37; *Theses*, 33. Nonetheless, as Betz notes, "[Hemmerle's] approach is more Thomistic," which offers further legitimacy to situating his proposal as a development upon both Thomas and Balthasar ("What's New," 142).

27. Note the similarities to Kerr, *After Aquinas*, 190, 200–201.

Just as Ulrich's ontological moments explicate the *similitudo divinae bonitatis* of created Being and therefore suggest new images through which to express the life of the Trinity, the relational framework of Hemmerle's trinitarian ontology allows the one and the multitude to be integrated together within the concept of love without losing either. In the language of the trinitarian life, the common divine *esse* is the relationship that happens (*geschehende Beziehung*) in the processions (*hervorgehen*) of self-giving (*sich hineingeben*) between the particular persons (*Pole*). This relationship is an event (*Geschehen*), or process (*Vorgang*), which simultaneously proceeds from the persons and from which the persons proceed, as the *esse* is simultaneously the act (*Akt*) of each person in which and as which they exist, and the process (*Vorgang*) in which and through which they find themselves united and distinguished in relation. Relation is what happens in the act of processing, which is a personal act of self-giving, which is a particular subsistence in the common event of "that movement which *agape* itself is."[28] Thus, if God is love, and if love is the "rhythm of giving that gives itself," then God's *esse* is likewise understood as a "relationship which happens" in the "mutual movement towards each other, in each other, and out of each other of the [persons] between which this relationship is in play."[29] In its concrete enactment between the persons who subsist in that very act, this divine Love is "the source of both unity and difference between the persons."[30]

Thus, the unity of the divine *esse* is not something that happens "underneath" the *relata* or on some other essential register but is precisely and only the interrelationality of the subsistent divine persons.[31] The perichoretic unity that Moltmann recommended does not need to be, as von Balthasar seems to have feared, a unity that only emerges ("at best, if at all") as a result of the *circumincessio* of the divine persons, reliant upon the logical antecedence of an act. Rather, it is the unity of the one act in which Father, Son, and Spirit are themselves constituted in their interrelationality.[32] Or, to adapt the words of philosopher Christopher Mirus, the actuality of the divine *esse*

28. *Theses*, 35.

29. *Theses*, 35, 38. It is precisely Pitstick's misunderstanding of this point—of the identity and distinction of the persons only through and within the one divine act of love—that ironically leads her to accuse von Balthasar of re-establishing the divine essence as a fourth thing (*Light in Darkness*, 281–83).

30. Leamy sees this point as the point of coalescence for Thomas, Bulgakov, and Balthasar (*Holy Trinity*, 72). See also Betz, "What's New," 146.

31. Surprisingly, it seems to me that this still satisfies Thomas's requirement that the plurality of the divine persons be derived from relational distinction rather than "difference" or "diversity," both of which imply difference of essential form (*ST* Ia, q.31, a.2).

32. *TL*3, 157.

is truly the "interactuality" of the divine persons, who are only "posited as relata" insofar as they "find their fulfillment in one another."[33] *Esse* is Love, the one fundamental reality that is itself the three divine persons in their self-giving and receiving. Thus, the unity does not emerge "from" perichoresis but is the absolute perichoretic state of the persons ecstatically giving and enstatically receiving.[34] The identity upon which von Balthasar insisted between the processions and essence in the end leads back to the possibility that the *unio realis* between the persons is precisely the *unio substantialis* of the common act of love of the divine *esse*.

Of course, there remains the important task of identifying the *maior dissimilitudo* within which these *similitudines* might properly sit. Both von Balthasar and Thomas identify the real distinction between *esse* and *essentia*—and the lack of this distinction in God—as the primary way to ground this ever-greater difference.[35] For Thomas, this allows him to consistently maintain the distinction between God and creation by emphasizing the transcendence of God's *modus existendi* over that of creatures, who exist within an ineradicable relation of receiving from God who gives existence to creation from the infinite plerosis of the divine *esse*.[36] Within creation, this manifests itself in the process of what Ulrich called the transnihilation of being, in which infinite *esse commune* only comes to subsistence in finite *essentiae*, and vice versa. Thus, the finitude of created essences expresses their dependency on the finitization of *esse commune*, and this whole process in turn depends upon the gratuity of divine creativity *ad extra*. This

33. Mirus, "Relation Is Not a Category," 194. Though what he says must be put through a careful trinitarian *analogia proportionalitatis*, his insights developed from Aristotle provide intriguing images for my own suggestions: "Such interactivity, in which both substances become fully what they are, and apart from which they cannot be what they are—this interactualization, we might say—is the fundamental type of relation. Substances—or perhaps better, *hypostases*, so as not to confuse our theology—are the beings defined by such relations." Could we illustrate the *similitudo divinae* by saying that the interactuality of the divine persons is absolute in a manner that coincides in a single, perfect "substance" rather than three finite interactualized substances? This kind of account helps avoid what Marsh critiques some accounts of personhood that shy away from personal interiority of any kind of falling into, namely, the destruction of the "I" ("In Defense of a Self," 281). See R. Williams, "Interiority and Epiphany," for an example of the kind of accounts Marsh has set in his sights.

34. What Marsh says of Jüngel's rather different account of trinitarian personhood is an apt description of what I am proposing here: "Inasmuch as each person becomes what it is only in its togetherness with the other two persons, God in his triune mystery is Godself by *coming* to his other" ("In Defense of a Self," 278).

35. See E. Oakes, *Pattern of Redemption*, 31; Nichols, *Word Has Been Abroad*, 142, 144.

36. See *ST* Ia, q.13, a.7; q.44; *LSI* 1.133; Emery, "*Theologia* and *Dispensatio*," 525–26; Oliver, *Creation*, 48.

produces three sets of relations involving creation: (1) the relation between Creator and creature; (2) the relation between *esse* and *essentia*; and (3) the relations between individuated creatures.

In Thomas, all three relations take on negative functions within the *analogia entis*, primarily identifying what from created reality is denied of God.[37] From the same distinction of *esse* and *essentia* in creation, von Balthasar offers positive readings by replacing the divine *essentia* identified by Thomas with the trinitarian life of the persons as the divine analog.[38] For example, the first relation above, the difference between God and creatures, is also understood in positive terms as it is taken up into the difference between Father and Son through the Word's cosmification in creation and the incarnation. The abyss between divine and created being is not thereby obviated but is made more deeply understandable as an immanent intimacy in light of its inclusion in the trinitarian difference between Father and Son, one relation being set in relation to another relation by the Word's union with creation as source and telos.[39] Ulrich's philosophical expansion of Thomas identified how the second relation, the transnihilation of being in *esse* and *essentia*, participated in the kenotic movement of the Father and Son in the *bonitas* of the Spirit through similar avenues. Further and in a similar fashion to Hemmerle, Ulrich identified how the individually subsistent *ens* enacted the kenosis of *esse* by existing in giving and receiving relations to one another, the third relation established by Thomas's real distinction.[40]

37. See Tabaczek, "Trace of Similarity," 107–9; Knasas, *Being and Some Twentieth-Century Thomists*, 7.

38. Even though these trinitarian readings expand the *similitudo* between God and creatures, instead of ultimately bridging the abiding *maior dissimilitudo*, they emphasize it by identifying the "ultra-positive prototypical distance between God and God in the fruitful generation of the Word" that in its infinity is always wider than the longest bridge built by any *similitudines*. See especially *TL2*, 180–81.

39. See *TL2*, 180–82, for von Balthasar's discussion of *Abstand* in the divine life and its relation to the abyss between divine and created being; see also Nichols, *No Bloodless Myth*, 73; E. Oakes, *Pattern of Redemption*, 22–23.

40. Nichols's summary of this *similitudo* is worth quoting at length: "And so a chain of self-giving, of outpouring, runs from God to existents—God in his fulness rendering himself 'poor' by communicating being; being delivering itself to existents, and existents themselves experiencing both the power to shelter being and yet also their own limitedness—from which they should learn the lesson that they must let being be further handed on through them, in which alone will they find fulfillment. The analogy of being proves itself to be in the last analysis an analogy of giving, an analogy of love" (*Word Has Been Abroad*, 182). See also Tourpe, "Thomisme Ontologique," 467–91, for a discussion of Ulrich and Siewerth's influence on von Balthasar's understanding of the role of transnihilation in being as love; *TL2*, 183.

This third relation identifies the question of *unio substantialis* and *unio realis* I have been exploring. In this case, the first proportion of the *analogia proportionalitatis* is the relation between essential *unio substantialis* and relational *unio realis*. The other side of the analogy is the relation between the unity of the divine *esse* and the unity of the divine persons, which I have argued are identical as a substantial unity of absolute interpersonal unity actualized in love. The two sides of this *proportionalitas* may once again be bridged by the relation between *esse* and *essentia*, which in creatures means that the *unio realis* never fully attains to a *unio substantialis* between creatures, while in the Trinity they are identical. Nevertheless, the distinctions that remain between creatures should not "be thought of merely as 'sheer *dissimilitudines* opposed to the divine actuality' but rather as grounded ultimately in the life of God."[41]

This is justified by the identification of *esse* as *amor*, understood as *caritas* mutually fulfilled in *amicitia*. Both require interpersonality; the love by which *esse* is understood cannot be *amor sui*, for God or for creatures. Charity is that love by which a good is both wished and communicated to the Beloved, and when this is mutual, friendship is established.[42] Thomas sought to position *amor sui* in the primary place as the metaphysical love of the Good and the ground of *amicitia* that finds its fulfillment in the love of God, but all that he sought to secure by this is found in the Spirit who enables and secures the true and selfless transfer of self to the Other and the kenotic expression of agapeic love by the Father and Son. Eros is fulfilled relationally rather than individually. To be is not simply to have oneself but to be fundamentally in relations of receiving and giving with others.

The *maior dissimilitudo* between God and creatures is that God is—absolutely, freely, and without derivation or antecedent reference—this loving movement of giving and receiving in the bountiful Spirit, while creatures participate in this movement fundamentally and irrevocably by receiving it—their existence in the relational event of love that is being—from God.[43] Piero Coda expresses this beautifully, saying:

> Of themselves, created persons are not able to live fully the nonbeing of love [transnihilation] precisely because they are created: and that is that they receive being from God and do not have the possibility to deprive themselves of it ontologically. At most it is possible for them to give themselves intentionally (at the level, that is, of the act of knowledge and of love), but not

41. Martin, "Consubstantial Otherness of God," 556; quoting *TL2*, 83.

42. See *ST* II–II, q.23, a.1.

43. See Betz, "What's New," 153–58.

> as far as giving up their own being as being. This means that in the creature, being and *agápe* do not coincide: only God in fact "is" *agápe*.[44]

The trinitarian love *in se* flows kenotically outward in creation, revelation, and redemption, and in all things is ordered toward bringing creation into mutual plerosis with the Godhead. Divine relationality is freely bountiful *in se*, while creation finds its source and fullness in its relation to God. It is by the vertical relation that creation receives its first act of existence, the form of its movement in appetite, and the movement itself in *amor*, and from this creation moves in relationality horizontally within itself and vertically back toward God. The finitization of *esse commune* into the particularity of a creature's *actus essendi* does not lead to the dissolution of being's commonality but rather to its further expression in the self-giving love that obtains between each particular and its friends, revealing the ground of their common existence to which they are destined to return.

Trinitarian Person as Actor

Elevating *relatio* to the level of essential act in the divine life in the way suggested by Hemmerle's ontology clearly requires a different description of trinitarian personhood than that typically offered in either the intra-personal or interpersonal models.[45] Hemmerle posits that the "self-contained I" of the intra-personal model "is displaced by a plural origin," which does not equate to the plurality of subjects of the interpersonal model.[46] The difference is that a Subject, whether conceptualized in reference to the divine essence or the divine persons, cannot be established upon a self-containing, self-possessing, or self-referencing.[47] Rather, the divine existence ought to be understood as a relational life involving a plurality of relatively identified loci of relational action. Each divine person is identified by and as its participation in the relationality of the divine act. Divine persons are "actors" because they are their enactment of the divine life. No longer can the divine person (or the created person, for that matter) be a Subject that is definable

44. Coda, *From the Trinity*, 496.

45. See Van Nieuwenhove, "Trinitarian Indwelling," 388–403, for an example of this language.

46. *Theses*, 39.

47. See the way in which Fiedler situates Hemmerle within the various trinitarian ontologies of the twentieth century that attempted to integrate some form of personalism within an *analogia trinitatis* in "Klaus Hemmerle on the Trinitarian Ontology," 60–65.

in itself and thus identifiable apart from its act of relating to an Other, as this makes the person's act something that mediates between other persons rather than something included in the constitution of the Subject itself. Relations remain extrinsic to the person *per se* as a relatively weak category of being. To the extent that this remains in force, the violence done to the primordial coinherence of divine unity and multiplicity is inescapable.

The way von Balthasar navigates between Bonaventure's "processional" account and Thomas's "relational" account of the proper way to relate the Father and the act of generation is an instructive example. In Thomas's relational account the Father generates the Son because he is Father, while in Bonaventure's processional account the Father is Father because he generates the Son. The issue von Balthasar takes with both is that they try to identify the Father in a way prior to his primordial act of self-giving. Bonaventure does this through imbuing innascibility with a positivity that enables him to identify the Father logically prior to the act of generation.[48] Thomas relies on his theory of subsistent relations to claim that the divine paternity (which is the Father) can be understood both as a relation dependent upon the act of generation (similarly to Bonaventure) and as it signifies the person of the Father as subsisting in the divine *esse*, where it identifies the person who acts in generation.[49] Through this second perspective, Thomas identifies the Father before his notional act of generation. Though von Balthasar shares inclinations with both medieval thinkers, he takes Thomas's concept of subsistent relations and radicalizes the statement of identity such that the Father becomes identical with his act of generating love.[50] For von Balthasar, the Father "'is' Father by eternally giving his all," for "as Father, he is nothing other than the pure surrender of himself."[51]

48. Contra McInerny, *Trinitarian Theology*, 52–54, the fact that von Balthasar sometimes uses conventions associated with Bonaventure's processional account, such as referring to the Father as the "origin" and "principle" of the divine love, should not be understood as evidence that von Balthasar adopted this view rather than the relational account of Thomas. It is true that von Balthasar does adopt language consistent with the processional account: the Father is the "very origin" in God (*TL*3, 159); the "principle of 'giving all'" (*TL*3, 158); the "'Person' who '*principaliter*' . . . gives himself over, the Father" (*TL*2, 137). However, see, for example, *TL*2, 136, where Balthasar cites Lateran IV ("what the Father is, he is, not in relation to himself, but to the Son") to tie the Father's identity solely to his act of "eternally [giving] over to the Son all that is his." This contradicts McInerny's claim that von Balthasar saw Bonaventure's innascibility as sufficient to identify the Father.

49. See *ST* Ia, q.40, a.4 *resp* and *ad* 1; *TL*3, 161.

50. See *TL*2, 129–33, 153.

51. *TL*3, 158, 441; see also the essay "The 'Beatitudes' and Human Rights" in Balthasar, *Man Is Created*, especially p. 448; *TL*2, 136, 141; McInerny, *Trinitarian Theology*, 22–23.

Said differently, the Father is the Father only in and as his act of self-giving. The relation of *paternitas* and the Father's identity as such can neither be thought of as consequent upon or the ground of generation but rather, as subsistent in and identical with the divine *esse* that is that very act of generation, it must be considered only as the Father's personal mode of subsistence in the act of divine love.[52]

Thus, von Balthasar avoids the horns of the dilemma by refusing to distinguish between the Father's person, his act of self-giving, his relation of paternity, and the divine *esse* in a way consonant with Hemmerle's trinitarian ontology.[53] As in von Balthasar's interpretation of Lateran IV, the Father does not lose himself in giving himself because, as von Balthasar summarizes Hemmerle, self-giving is instead "the essential realization of oneself," in which "*ekstastis* and *enstasis* are one, simply the two sides of the same thing."[54] The Subject-Object dichotomy is thus resituated as two articulable moments within the act of loving self-gift that identifies the two poles. The Father has himself (*enstasis*, or subsistence) in giving himself (*ekstasis*), because the Father "is" Father in going out of himself to the Son. Likewise, the Son has himself in receiving the Father and surrendering himself to the Father; the Son is Son is his act of self-transparency to the Father. Their "subjectivity" is located in the action beyond themselves, and so the Subject-Object dichotomy that is expressed is incompatible with the modernist Cartesian subject insofar as it is dependent upon its ecstatic mediation to and with the Other.

Trinitarian identification through the enactment of self-giving, such as I have described here in Hemmerle and von Balthasar, precludes the description of only one trinitarian person at a time, as the divine persons as *Pole* do not possess "any isolated position outside what takes place."[55] In this way, the problem of how the "subject"—at risk of remaining self-enclosed in self-referentiality—"manages to go beyond itself" is avoided by finding the subject's identity only in its act by which it goes beyond itself as a pole established in and thereby establishing the process of self-giving love.[56] The trinitarian persons are ontologically inseparable and epistemologically indescribable apart from the inherently relational event of divine love. Rather

52. Incidentally, my claim comes close to Jordan Wood's reading of Bonaventure, where he claims that "paternity and innascibility resolve into the Father's fecundity," which ought in von Balthasar's terminology to be thought of as the Father's primal self-giving ("Father's Kenosis," 27).

53. See Betz, "What's New," 142–43.

54. *TD*5, 74; see O'Donnell, *Hans Urs von Balthasar*, 70.

55. *Theses*, 38, 41–44; see also Betz, "What's New," 148.

56. *Theses*, 36.

than contravening doctrines such as divine simplicity or unity, however, this assertion expands them by making them, as Jennifer Newsome Martin has shown, compatible with the "dynamic eventfulness of inner-trinitarian life."[57] As Love, the divine life requires the distinctions among the persons to be fundamentally positive in nature for the gift of each person to "comprise" rather than "compromise" the divine unity and simplicity. No longer must the "simple unity of the infinite divine Being" be juxtaposed to the language of ecstatic personhood.[58] When the divine *esse* is conceptualized in this manner, the simplicity of the divine nature becomes a simplicity of love, the absolute perfection of an act requiring relation and true distinction, rather than of *esse* understood as naked *actus* that cannot be spoken of in terms of relation.

The concept of trinitarian personhood as actor renders some of von Balthasar's most enigmatic statements more understandable, such as: "The divine essence is not a blank, homogenous block of identity but a giving (in the Father), a receiving (in the Son), a gift given to the Spirit by Father and Son together, and a cause of thanksgiving by Son and Spirit . . . the Divine Persons are *themselves* only insofar as they go out to the Others (who are always Other)."[59] Because the "self" in self-giving is found in the very act of giving oneself, the position, or self, of each divine person is found only within the process that is the divine "relationship that happens." The identity of each divine hypostasis is its particular enactment of relating within the divine event of love, and this identity is more truly defined by its "plural origins" because it is identified in the relational acts by which the other persons are also identified, rather than as Subjects that have their "selves" first before relating through going out of their "selves." The "whole" is not something from which a Subject can be abstracted, nor something that can swallow up the individuals constituted by the relations within that whole.[60] In this way, the conceptual distinctions utilized by Thomas to distinguish between essential and personal description of God, such as *processio*/*relatio* and *esse*/*ratio*, are integrated within the single horizon of the event of love concretely determined by the essentially perichoretic unity of the divine persons.[61]

57. See Martin, "Consubstantial Otherness of God," 555–56; see also Leamy, *Holy Trinity*, 73; *TL*3, 136–37, 158; *TL*2, 82.

58. Kwasniewski, *Ecstasy of Love*, 283n271.

59. *TD*5, 76.

60. See *Theses*, 42; see Healy's comments on the relation between person and being in Balthasar's meta-anthropology in "Christ's Eucharist," 5.

61. Leamy argues for a similar claim, specifically in relation to Balthasar's own reading of Thomas's *relatio* and Bulgakov's kenosis, in *Holy Trinity*, 51–68, 72–73.

Hemmerle's perichoretic concept of the *Vorgang* and *Pole* also provides a divine image of the differentiation and unification that Thomas's rational operations map between created finite persons. While Thomas emphasized the possessive aspect of understanding in the divine life *in se*, attending to the final element of *iudicatio* suggests that understanding is simultaneously enstatic and ecstatic, especially when occurring between two distinct persons. Though the Other that is known is present within the Knower intellectually, the Knower is nevertheless beholden to the Other's willingness to be known, and that which is known remains hypostatically ecstatic to the Knower.[62] "Only by remaining who he is and by not becoming who I am," von Balthasar says, can the Other be known, and as the "appearance" of the Other is manifested within the Knower, it is the Knower who is more properly "claimed" by the Known than the other way around.[63] The concept of self-donation is operative on both sides of the intelligible act in what von Balthasar describes as "the will to self-revelation from the side of the object and the will to self-opening for the understanding of the object from the side of the subject," both sides of which are particularly necessary for an understanding of beatitude that only obtains within friendship.[64] If viewed in this way, Williams's aim for the Father to "know himself in generative relation to another" can be realized. When the Father knows the truth of his subsistence in the divine *esse* as *amor*, what he knows is nothing but his act of giving himself—his own good—away to the Son in true *amor amicitiae*, the love in which the Lover considers his own good to be only the act of giving his good to his Beloved. What is known is the truth of love in the ecstatic relation to the Other, a relation that is one of kenotic self-giving rather than the self-seeking of *amor concupiscentiae*. Hence, the Son's procession may still helpfully be understood as *per modum intellectus* within a trinitarian ontology of love as "a procession of love" that proceeds "*by* intelligence," if this intellective mode of procession is understood as the ecstatic self-differentiation involved in apprehending the Other in the kenotic self-gift of

62. Kwasniewski raises this question at the very end of his book on *extasis* in Thomas, asking, "The difference between knowing and loving has been strongly emphasized, but what of the other side—the loved *in* the lover, and knowledge is always knowledge *of* something" (*Ecstasy of Love*, 316).

63. Balthasar, *Epilogue*, 52.

64. *TL2*, 225; see Nichols, *Say It Is Pentecost*, 29; *TL1*, 118. This is not far from the non-possessive theory of knowledge Schindler develops from von Balthasar in response to Thomas, in which truth is not located in either the knower or the object, but rather in the *Gestalt*, a concrete "third" that mediates between the knower and object as the appearance of the object to the intellect that emerges in the mutuality of "knowing" and "being known" ("Towards a Non-Possessive Concept of Knowledge," 589–98).

divine love.[65] And though the mutual self-gift is absolute between the Father and Son, the nature of knowledge is not solely the presence of the known in the knower but also the ecstatic extension of the knower toward the known. Thus, to speak of the divine persons knowing is to identify them in their own act of identifying and relating to the other divine persons, whom they know each in their respective subsistence in the divine act of love.

If the perfection of the intellect in knowing truth is not restricted to the inward possession of that truth, then it becomes easier to see how the act of knowing is fully and perfectly enacted between the Father and Son within the love of the divine life. The love of absolute self-giving is dependent on the notion that intellectual possession does not exhaust the act of knowing the Other, but rather that it forms the basis for the absolute desire for the Good of the Other that is known. This mutual desire, which in this way truly follows knowledge, traces the procession of the Holy Spirit from the Father and the Son in his reciprocal movement as the Gift in which the immolation of kenosis and the generativity of mutual reception coincide in the bonitic Fruit of their union. Here, *eros* and *agape* coincide in total self-giving born out of true personal fulfillment in the Good of the Other, the freedom and fullness of which miraculously gives rise to the Spirit. It is the abiding weakness of Thomas's account of divine love and the Holy Spirit that desire is opposed to giving *in se*, such that the divine persons cannot truly love one another with the fullness of love that God expresses toward creation and that creatures are called to return to God. As Schwöbel once observed, relational love of this kind cannot be a "simple alternative" to other accounts of love such as erotic desire or agapeic gift-giving, but rather it must be their fulfillment.[66] Love for the Other gives desire its true shape, and thus for the divine persons to possess themselves, they cannot do so apart from the enactment of the divine *esse* in kenotic self-giving and plerotic fecundity.

Hemmerle's trinitarian ontology provides a helpful expansion to von Balthasar's image of the divine life: as love, *esse* is intrinsically relational and secures the place of each person not only within the whole but as the whole, that is, an enactment of divine love. Each is mutually dependent upon the self-giving of the other poles, which seen together are the plural origins of the self-giving act of each pole. The self-giving constitutive of each pole is grounded in the self-receiving of each pole. By consequence, the unity of the divine life of Love admits of the "transcendental plurality" necessary, in von Balthasar's words, to go beyond "self-love (*dilectio*) and become *caritas*—the highest of the perfections created by God and which

65. Malet, *Personne et Amour*, 121, my translation.

66. Schwöbel, "God Is Love," 313.

is found supereminently in him."[67] But in Hemmerle's framework the vis-à-vis required between each of the divine persons initially presents once again the problem of the Spirit's unique personhood. If, as characterized by Ulrich and von Balthasar, the Spirit is bonitic and therefore does not enact the divine love kenotically but only receives the self-giving of the Father and Son, how can the Spirit be identified as a true Third in Hemmerle's sense of a *Pol*, a truly distinct third divine person identified by its act of self-receiving and self-giving? Is the Spirit once more flattened into the copula between Father and Son?

Trinitarian Personhood: Particular, Whole, and Spirit

When approaching the moment of describing the Spirit's unique *modus existendi*, von Balthasar tended to retreat by appealing to the concept of incommunicability. For instance, at one such point he says, "The way in which the Spirit is Person is beyond our grasp."[68] In support, he cites the Dominican theologian B.-D. Depuy: "There are no words that would enable us fully to express the Spirit's Personhood and role."[69] For von Balthasar, this means that the Spirit can be "understood in his operations, but only 'apophatically' in his essence."[70] Citing Depuy again, he affirms that the Spirit's "Person transcends all that is personal."[71] Similarly, von Balthasar quotes Mühlen's assertion of the "absolute impenetrability of the Holy Spirit's personal distinctiveness."[72] However, one of Ulrich's central contributions to von Balthasar's later pneumatology was that the Spirit contains and expresses the self-giving of the Father and Son as the bonitic Fruit of their unity, which is neither kenotic nor juxtaposed to *kenosis* as its negation. As the Third who simultaneously recapitulates the Whole, the Spirit's *modus existendi* as Bond, Gift, and bonitic Fruit promises to enlarge the concept of "all that is personal" rather than transcending it in total impenetrability. That is, what is personal comes to be most truly understood within a relational and trinitarian metaphysic that integrates the one—the divine *esse* as the *Geschehen* of love—and the many—the divine persons identified in and as their relational acts of love—through the Spirit that mediates and recapitulates the Whole as Third.

67. *TL*3, 217–18.
68. *TL*3, 144.
69. *TL*3, 144.
70. *TL*3, 144.
71. *TL*3, 144.
72. *TL*3, 111.

Within his ontological framework, Hemmerle attempts to concretely illustrate the trinitarian nature of created reality by providing multiple examples of triadic structures that cohere into a unity in which "the many poles . . . simultaneously, each from different direction, allow each other, one upon another, to proceed to the whole process."[73] A word, for instance, "has, at least, the three origins 'I,' 'language,' 'you.'"[74] These three origins "spring up *mutually*, each in a distinct manner."[75] They are distinct yet inseparable without losing the whole from which they arise. Similarly, time can be understood as the interplay between past, present, and future.[76] These concrete examples deepen the concept of the trinitarian persons as (en)actors of the divine love, as the identity of any one pole is "experienced as an intensification, as a dramatic transformation" in the interplay between the action carried out among the poles.[77] Life, language, time; each is identical with itself and its constituents "in so far as it goes on, in so far as it grows"—life into more life, language into conversation, time into the future.[78] In each, the continuation of the whole is dependent upon each pole and is experienced as an excess, as a surprise. The continuation of the process is not about any one pole alone but about the whole that is the interplay, or "inter-action," of all the poles together. In this way, the subsistence of each pole is not an "endpoint" of the process but a "limit," a point at which "what happens flows back into itself" and coalesces as a discernible point of relational action within the process.[79] Each pole is permanent only as a "givenness from which the origin . . . can be found . . . in such a way that it goes beyond itself in relation."[80] In this way, each pole exists in the others, just as Thomas's divine persons must in some way be understood to exist outside of themselves in the others as subsistences of *esse ad*.[81]

73. *Theses*, 39.

74. *Theses*, 40.

75. *Theses*, 40.

76. See *Theses*, 41. This image has interesting resonances with Robert Jenson's expression of the temporality of the trinitarian life. Though Hemmerle, like Jenson, is epistemologically focused on God's revelatory action within the created order, it is his additional willingness to speak of the happening of the Trinity in relation to itself that I am capitalizing on here.

77. *Theses*, 41.

78. *Theses*, 41. Ulrich expresses a similar concept linked to kenosis as the "super-death" of love in the Triune "prototype" (*Leben Und Tod*, 29–30, 132); see also *TD*5, 84–85.

79. *Theses*, 44.

80. *Theses*, 44.

81. In this way, Kwasniewski's intimation at the end of his study of *exstasis* in Thomas is confirmed: "Might the Persons be defined as 'subsistent *extases*' for the same

Hemmerle's concept of dramatic intensification appears again later in his *Theses* as the "spiritual performance" that moves along "the three lines of the away-from-me, the towards-me, and the including and distinguishing mutual relation of these two."[82] These three "positions" are "disclosed in the way the Trinity happens," in which the I of the away-from-me and towards-me is exceeded in "the performance of the in between."[83] By this the Father and Son are identified by their self-enactment in the augmenting process of divine love as the "away-from-me" of self-giving and the "towards-me" of self-reception. The third relation—"the including and distinguishing mutual relation of these two"—is the Spirit, who most truly represents the nature of the whole process as the medium of all relation by which Father and Son continually receive themselves anew and give themselves away. As such, the Spirit is the *Pol* in whom the process of identification by intensification is exemplified and by whom it takes place.

When placed into conversation with the various aspects of von Balthasar's pneumatology, the resonance between the positions is clear. Especially apparent is the similarity to Durrwell's description, mentioned by von Balthasar, of the Spirit as the "personalizing person,"[84] the Third who continually presents a new "self" to each of them from the Other by newly "reveal[ing] the affiliation of each to the other."[85] Or in terms more accordant with Ulrich, the Spirit's divine personhood is not defined and constituted by his own self-giving, in which his own person is given, but in the fact that he gives to the others their own selves in excess and newness. The image of time as Hemmerle uses it plays similar notes: the Spirit is the constant and eternal "future" of the Trinitarian performance to which the Father and Son are eschatologically open for the reception of their own persons. The similarities here to Jenson's later descriptions of the Spirit as both the future of the Father and Son and, as such, the one "as whom God is future to himself" are striking, especially in light of the fact that Jenson also describes the trinitarian persons as "*dramatis dei personae*."[86] It is important to note with

---

reason that they are 'subsistent relations,' the being of which is a being toward, *esse ad*? What implication might this have for an understanding of person or personhood? Is the category of relation somehow the category of ecstasy? . . . Can *being* itself—the act of being, *esse*—be defined as ecstatic?" (*Ecstasy of Love*, 316).

82. *Theses*, 62.

83. *Theses*, 62.

84. *TL3*, 55; see Durrwell, *Esprit Saint de Dieu*, 54.

85. *Theses*, 54.

86. Jenson, *Triune God*, 89, 158, 171. Though in many ways different from (and more radical than) von Balthasar and Hemmerle, Jenson shares their commitment to developing his trinitarian framework from God's action in creation, an important

Schwöbel, however, that these kinds of temporal indicators do not imply "temporal succession but simply the taxis of the relational unity of the three Trinitarian persons."[87] Taken in this sense, it is even more intriguing that the Spirit can be seen as the "future" in three ways that align with the pneumatology I have been developing here: the "in between" of the Father and Son as the future of the past that gives way to the present; that which proceeds from both as Third as the future of both past and present; and the future of both in which the past and present are included and fulfilled, which invites comparison with Ulrich's concept of Bonicity.

These three ways in which the Spirit can be seen as the trinitarian "future" ground the potential for a more robust description of the Spirit's unique personhood, which is perhaps most helpfully framed as the way in which the Spirit can be conceived of as the trinitarian We. First, from the Spirit's position "in between" the Father and Son, the Spirit presents the We of the Father and Son as their *nexus amoris*. But to leave the Spirit as a "mere 'we'" in this way, as Hegel did, is not sufficient to recognize the Holy Spirit as a divine person, as von Balthasar observed.[88] Here, the Spirit is only We.

Second, from the position of the future as the third moment in succession, the Spirit relates to the We of the Father and Son as the Thou who proceeds from their common act of spiration.[89] Von Balthasar rejects this possibility because he does not recognize any economic relation between the Father or Son and the Spirit. This is only partially true, though, as the counterexamples in John 14 and 16 show. There the Son refers to the Spirit as "another" (ἄλλον), one who is distinct from the Father and Son and is sent by either one or both.[90] This establishes the vis-à-vis relation of the Spirit to both the Father and the Son, together and individually, as the Thou-of-the-We. As this clearly expresses the classic trinitarian *taxis*, as well as the filioque, there seems to be sufficient warrant for retaining this mode of speaking.

However, a core element of the mission of the Spirit is to continue revealing the divine unity of the Father and the Son by bringing about a

---

epistemological discussion I have left largely to the side here.

87. Schwöbel, "Eternity of the Triune God," 350.

88. See *TL*3, 155n40.

89. This is similar to Heribert Mühlen's suggestion, which von Balthasar identifies various times; see *TL*3, 137, 155. Mühlen himself gestures beyond this toward the way in which it is in the Spirit, as the "We in Person, that the Actus Purus attains its *plenitudo* . . . its ultimate fulness" (*Heilige Geist Als Person*, 162; translation from *TL*3, 56n84). The link to the divine *actus purus* reinforces that the bond of personal unity established in the Spirit cannot be separated from the way in which the divine *esse* is expressed.

90. See John 14:16, 26; 15:26; 16:7.

derivative unity between the Son and the disciples.[91] This brings us to the third aspect of the Spirit's identity as We, which integrates the previous two: the We-as-Thou in which the unity of the Whole is contained and expressed in the Spirit's bonicity as a true Third. Hemmerle expresses this in his concept of spiritual performance, naming the in-between relation the "performance of the We."[92] This requires a distinct conception of the We, a "new society" that is neither a totalitarian "collective subject" in which the "mutual relations of all individuals are alienated," nor a "product of a merely functional series of bonds" that "does not lead beyond the synchronization of egoisms and solitudes."[93] These would lead to a Hegelian modalism or a social tri-theism, respectively. Rather, the Spirit expresses the trinitarian We in the form of a society that "has a single, common life" that "is nevertheless the life of each individual."[94] This We has its origin in the other poles, the Spirit proceeding from Father and Son, while also enacting its own life that is "more than the sum of individuals" and as such stands vis-à-vis to each of them. As the "enveloping" *Pol* of the trinitarian performance, the Spirit expresses his own identity, the distinct identities of the Father and Son, and the identity of the whole movement of divine love. Since the Spirit contains the whole, the Gift given through his mediation outstrips what is given in the enactment of either Father or Son, such that what they receive is more than they are in their self-giving. Only as We and Thou—a We-as-Thou in which both terms reference the Spirit—can the Spirit become the Giver of Self for the Father and Son in a way that allows the Trinitarian life to be expressed in a way that includes both the unity of the whole and the distinctiveness of each person, a "unity of fruitfulness transcending the differences" in his identification as the fecund superabundance of the Gift given through his mediation.[95]

91. See John 14:10, 23; 17:20–21.

92. *Theses*, 62.

93. *Theses*, 62–63.

94. *Theses*, 63. Hemmerle's concept of this "new society" was certainly influenced by the "charism of unity" central to the Focolare Movement, which Hemmerle embraced in 1958; see Coda, "Unity of Reciprocal Love."

95. Balthasar, *Epilogue*, 86. This serves as an answer to Sonderegger's question to what she calls "event metaphysics": "Just where is the 'natural' implicature between Father and Spirit, or more pressingly, between Father, Son, and Spirit? We do not seem to discover a Relatio that entails the Two (or Three), and we do not seem invited to meditate deeply on an Act, even Procession, that leads us to distinguish and relate the Spirit to the Father or Son" (*Doctrine of the Holy Trinity*, 525–26).

Conclusion

In the perfect reciprocation of kenotic love mediated, expressed, and enacted in the emergence of the Spirit as bonitic Fruit, ecstatically oriented *caritas* becomes *amicitia*. In the perfectly and eternally fulfilled *amicitia* of the divine life, the beatitude of each person is accomplished through the bond of the surpassingly full mutual gift given and received by all. The Whole exists in a perfect *unio substantialis* by the perfect unity of the single event of relational love, in which each pole exists within and continually seeks the *unio realis* established in their mutually ecstatic self-giving. This unity is as singular as Thomas's *unio substantialis* while admitting the constitutive character of the trinitarian multiplicity that he denies.

To be sure, Thomas would not follow much of anything that I have said in this chapter, but it is the job of students to identify the tensions and ambiguities in their master's thought and to try to provide a solution that is faithful to Scripture and reason. The challenge—other than the sheer immensity of Thomas's intellect—is that the way that we regularly conceive of being is so far from how we regularly conceive of love. If, though, we start with Scripture, reading Thomas's anthropological and metaphysical insights, von Balthasar's trinitarian focus on love, and Ulrich's expansion of the finality of the Spirit through Hemmerle's ontological categories offers a promising framework with which to understand the trinitarian relations revealed in the Gospels.

Conclusion

Summary: A Paradigm of Trinitarian Love

SPEAKING OF THE LOVE that God "is," according to St. John, requires one to negotiate each of the five aspects of the paradigm presented in the introductory chapter. Each layer presents a Scylla and Charybdis who threaten to derail the delicate process of constructing a properly trinitarian metaphysic, namely, one that maintains that the unicity of the divine essence is not a unity arrived at solely through the negation of division but a triunity constituted by the interrelations of the three distinct but perichoretically existing divine persons. The problem of integrating the one and the many has always been the foundational metaphysical problem for the Christian confession of the Trinity, but this problem has been exacerbated by the relatively unrevised hegemony of the Aristotelian and Platonic metaphysical systems used to express the church's theological confession.

In this present book, I have argued for a concept of trinitarian love that integrates both sides of the fivefold architectonic developed in the introduction. Though Thomas and von Balthasar often lean toward opposite sides of the paradigm's dichotomies, Ulrich's Thomasian philosophy of being and Hemmerle's constructive trinitarian ontology allowed Thomas and von Balthasar's contributions to be integrated into a coherent trinitarian metaphysic of love. First and most importantly, I have argued that bringing together the essential and personal aspects of love requires revising the categories of substance metaphysics adopted without significant change by Thomas, especially when used within theological speech about the divine life. Though Thomas's strategy of *redoublement* allowed him to offer a coherent picture of three hypostases in one divine essence, the control exerted by his concept of *unio substantialis* had the unfortunate effect of restricting the relationality that could be spoken of between the divine persons, especially within the context of love. While *amicitia* with God is the end of created persons in which they most fully possess their final good in beatitude, Thomas cannot speak of the trinitarian persons in this way. Von Balthasar refused to follow Thomas in this direction, instead strongly identifying the divine *actus essendi* itself with the act of love lived as Father, Son, and Spirit. Thus, the essential and personal aspects were brought together under the relational aspect of love, which is the prerequisite for the rest of the dichotomies to then be resolved.

The move from Thomas to von Balthasar required both metaphysical and methodological adjustments. Though philosophical categories are necessary to express the meaning of our theological vocabulary and grammar, the role of concepts such as *essentia* and *substantia* must be open to revision by the language and events of divine self-revelation. Thus, though the concept of *essentia* identifies something that is describable precisely in its individuation, the corollary concepts of unity, goodness, perfection, and so on, cannot be attributed theologically to a tri-hypostatic God without being significantly revised. When this is allowed, however, theological language is given further clarity along with greater adherence to the revelation of God's life.

When the relational act of self-giving love is identified as the very *esse* of the divine life, the ecstatic movement inherent in love no longer contradicts the enstatic emphasis found in Thomas's defense of divine aseity. Love is not an act that can be fulfilled internally for one person, as the fulfillment of love's act cannot be described apart from the Good being given by the Lover to an Other. While the metaphysical basis of love can be identified in a tendency toward the good absolutely considered, love finds its true expression between persons, specifically in the regard for the Beloved over the Lover. In God's triune life, essential love is nothing but its mutual enactment between the persons, and so their ecstatic movement toward the other in an erotic desire for the good of the Other never transgresses the boundaries of their essential love.

The seeking of Eros and the giving of Agape are brought together in the kenotic relinquishment of self-subsistence when the Good is erotically sought not for oneself but for the sake of the divine Beloved, apart from whom the divine Lover has no self. It is not the self-possession of substance that characterizes the goal of Love, but the union with the Beloved obtained in the Lover's relinquishment of self-sufficiency. Thus far, however, I have only paraphrased the common reception of von Balthasar. As I have argued, by deepening our understanding of the finality of the Good—identified by Ulrich as the *bonitas* of the Spirit—the kenotic relinquishment of self-sufficiency attributed to both Father and Son can be seen in its eternal fullness as both a true letting-be of the Other and a true receiving of self. The mutuality of love is included and transcended in the miraculous fecundity of that love in the emergence of the Spirit as the perfectly expressive Fruit that bestows upon both Father and Son an identity that exceeds their person taken in isolation.

Integrating Ulrich's pneumatological insight into the categories of Hemmerle's trinitarian ontology finally opens the door to a unique and robust expression of the trinitarian life. To be understood in its final form, the act of love must be expanded into the event of *amicitia*, the process of self-giving, self-receiving, and self-finding between the divine persons, in which the unity of the divine *esse* is found not in an underlying substance but in the interactuality of the divine persons in this absolute act. Unity neither precedes nor emerges from this act, but is the perfection of this act itself, remaining within itself in its very ecstasy. The divine persons each remain fully identical with this act, the whole being in each, while each remains distinct from the others by virtue of the same act. The creaturely acts of knowing and willing are the finite manifestations of this act of love, which in God is absolute, disclosing the divine ground for the distinctions between the dividing and uniting movements of the rational operations. The Spirit's finality is revealed as the ultimate unity of the divine life, in which neither person nor essence is obscured in the relational performance of the trinitarian We.

Though I have covered extensive terrain, I have focused almost completely on the divine side of the *analogia proportionalitatis trinitatis* of love that I have developed. The purpose of an analogy of this kind, however, is not only to illuminate the life of God but also to come back down cataphatically to illuminate the life of creation as it relates to the divine in its own movement. In fact, *TL2* is structured in precisely this way, beginning *ana*-logically by "looking up" to the divine life from the revelation of God in Jesus Christ and then shifting decisively in the middle of the volume to a *kata*-logical approach that looks down from the divine to re-make sense of the divine revelation of God in Jesus Christ.[1] Further, as that divine revelation takes place in the God-man who unites God and creation in one person, this *kata*-logical perspective must also include the nature of created being itself, encompassing the entirety of creation in its union of *esse* and *essentia* and incorporating it into the movement of the trinitarian life. Ultimately, *theologia* and *oikonomia* are put into what McInerny calls a "hermeneutical relationship," so that "neither can be interpreted without the light of the other."[2]

1. See the sections entitled "Ana-logical Logic in the Worldly Realm" and "Kata-logical Aspects" in *TL2*, 35–62, 171–218.

2. McInerny, *Trinitarian Theology*, 17.

In fact, sketching the *oikonomia* in this way is the true focus of the works of both Ferdinand Ulrich and Klaus Hemmerle that I have turned around as *ana*-logical lenses to develop a further description of the divine life. In what remains, I briefly sketch the *kata*-logical implications of my account of divine love for the nature of created being, both in its relation to the divine and its internal relations. This will allow for a short consideration of a concrete example of these relations coming together in the sacramental act of baptism, which I argue ought to be understood as a divine act of love in creation oriented toward unity between God and creation derived from the unity exemplified in the divine life.

Theologia and *Oikonomia*

Turning to the world, Ferdinand Ulrich's description of the created realities of *esse*, *essentia*, and *bonum* are clearly present in my sketch of the trinitarian relations. Apart from its subsistence in finite *essentiae*, *esse* is thought of as *esse commune*, the infinite and uncircumscribed plenitude of existence that is simultaneously *actus purus* and total potentiality. Because *esse commune* cannot subsist apart from its transnihilation, however, it must empty itself of its infinitude and give itself over to the finitization of *essentia*, mirroring the kenotic generosity of the Father in giving himself completely to the Son. *Essentia* receives the gift of the infinite in its finitude, bringing it along with itself into subsistence, thus mirroring the kenotic reception of the Son who gives himself simultaneously to the Father. Though Ulrich resists these parallels, it is difficult not to see how the moment of Ideality expresses the generative self-dispossession of the Father and the moment of Reality the reciprocating reception of the Son. While it is true that these moments in creation identify the temptations of *esse commune* and *essentia* to refuse their kenotic movement toward the other, either remaining in infinite non-subsistence or finite stasis, respectively, for the Father and Son these temptations are eternally and decisively rejected by the absolute nature of the Love that is the divine life. It is in the third moment of Bonicity that created reality truly exists as the expressive fruit of the kenotic giving of the other two moments, miraculously maintaining both *esse* and *essentia* within itself and reflecting the Spirit's identity as both Third and Whole in which Father and Son give and therefore are.

The *analogia* goes further than only offering a construal of created being; it describes—without determining—the *proportionalitatis* itself, the third relation which tethers the divine and creation together through God's economic act. Though the chasm between the divine and creation is unsurpassable, this chasm only exists because God has already crossed it in the act of creation, meaning that while the chasm is unsurpassable for creatures, for God there is no chasm, only divine action. This action must be understood only as the action of the Trinity, and one way to do this is to extend the alignment between Aristotle's four modes of causation and the relations of the trinitarian life.[3]

This is likely to raise concerns over the doctrine of inseparable operations, which resists any neat attribution of distinct actions to the divine persons. There is only one creative act, as it is nothing other than the divine act turned toward a way of being that is not the divine life *simpliciter*.[4] These modes of causality, therefore, cannot identify distinct divine actions, but rather interdependent aspects of the one divine act, in which the divine persons participate according to their mode of relation.[5]

Thus, in the Genesis account of creation and its theological expansion in St. John's Prologue (John 1:1–18), each of the persons of the Godhead is textually identified, the Father speaking the world into existence through the Son as the Word, and the Spirit hovering over the face of the deep as his divine power. It is from the Father's primordial rejection of being alone in giving himself to his Son that the possibility of the effective act of creation arises, which is then seen in the Father's speaking of his Son as *verbum* and his desire to spread his Son's beauty throughout a created realm by the effusive power of the Spirit. It is fitting that the Father is often identified as Creator by the Scriptures and the creeds, but the Father does not act alone, instead creating through the Son as Word and the Spirit as Love. In the Son's reception from the Father as his perfect *verbum*, all the forms of creation are found in him by virtue of his expressive procession from the Father, but only in the Father's efficient bestowal of *esse* to the *essentiae* expressed in the Son does creation arise in the likeness of the Son. And it is the Spirit, enabling the self-giving of Father and Son by the guarantee of his emergence as the fruit of their love, who provides the full and final illustration of all that might be created by them. Thus, the Spirit is the motive power of love in which the Father moves to efficiently grant *esse* to the *essentiae* known formally in the Son, as it is the truly concrete *bonum* of the Son's perfections

3. As noted in ch. 1, Thomas structures the relation between God and creation in exactly this way in *ST* Ia, q.2, a.3, though this lacks the "express indication" of "Christian content" that so troubled Barth (*Church Dogmatics: Creation*, 101).

4. For a helpful essay on the relation between the two, see Webster, "*Non Ex Aequo*."

5. For an expanded discussion on the connection between these four types of causality, see Dewan, "St Thomas and the Principle of Causality"; Falcon, "Aristotle on Causality," §2.

displayed that is the final cause of creation, toward which the Spirit moves both Father and Son in the act of creation.[6]

The only remaining mode of causality, the material cause, identifies the *maior dissimilitudo* within which the three causal modes mentioned above identify the *similitudines* between the trinitarian life *in se* and divine creative action. For good reason, Thomas reduced the material cause to God in the third of his *Quinque Viae*, as the matter which is joined to form to constitute created beings does not possess its own necessity.[7] This means that all matter which is acted upon efficiently, formally, and finally by God is given as a gift by the divinity who has "of itself its own necessity, and not receiving it from another, but rather causing in others their necessity."[8] In this way, the material cause differentiates between the infinite, groundless love of the trinitarian life and the finite movement of created being in which the Trinity is revealed. Because the movement of love in created being is grounded in the trinitarian life as its externalization, created being repeats the pattern of the triune life in its asymmetric relation of dependence upon God.[9] While the divine being exists "*ex se et secundum se et propter se*," creation exists "*ex alio et secundum aliud et propter aliud* . . . and thus owes itself to a first origin (the Father), to an archetypal image (the Son), and to a perfective end (the Holy Spirit)."[10]

The love of the Trinity is therefore simultaneously revealed in creation and hidden in its groundlessness, never being reducible to the causality of divine action in creation yet never being separable from it. Identifying the divine pattern which creation follows reveals both God's inseity and promeity because that pattern is a pattern of self-giving love. The perfect love of God's life (inseity) renders the divine persons absolutely free in their eternally fulfilled desire for the Other (aseity), but this freedom pours itself out into creation (promeity) because the act of love fulfilled in the Trinity extends itself outward in the Spirit, needing nothing but being free to give from its depths the movement of a completely dependent world. As divine transcendence over creation is rooted in aseity, divine immanence in creation is rooted in the character of God's perfect life *in se*. The interdependent aspects of creation identified in *esse*, *essentia*, and *bonum* are the

6. For a similar suggestion that relies upon Thomas's categories entirely, see Emery, "Personal Mode." For more recent discussion, see also Spencer, "Causality and *Analogia Entis*"; and White, "How Barth Got Aquinas Wrong."

7. See *ST* Ia, q.2, a.3; Hankey, *God in Himself*, 55.

8. *ST* Ia, q.2, a.3.

9. This mirrors Thomas's doctrine of a mixed relation between God and creation without reducing it to a mental relation in God.

10. *TL2*, 175.

creaturely effects of the gratuitous self-giving of the trinitarian persons to creation, received by creation in the medium of material subsistence that depends upon the bonitic fecundity of the Spirit. In the Spirit's absolute goodness, the divine act of creation is an act not of love's necessity but of its freedom to freely posit and love the Other. This mirrors Thomas's doctrine of a mixed relation between God and creation, but also opens the possibility that creation's dependence upon God may not need to be reduced to a mental relation in the divine life, as creation is an Other both as included in the Son's exemplarity and truly distinct in the Spirit's freely fecund power to mediate true vis-à-vis relations between the two.[11] The two sides of the relation are two sides of the divine act, where "in theological logic what is from the creature's side participation is from the Creator's side revelation."[12]

Going one step further, the basis for a truly relational ontology can be established through the trinitarian causality just sketched. The ontological categories of *actus essendi*, *essentia*, and *bonum* do not exist abstractly but concretely in the distinct subsistences of all created *entia*, which do not primarily express this *imago trinitatis* in their individuality but in their existence as individuals within the whole. They are bound together through their universal reception from the fatherly *esse commune*, in which reception their *essentiae* subsist interdependently in their relations of giving and receiving from one another. To receive the gift of *esse* is, after the likeness of the Son, to receive the giving in the gift, such that for a creature to subsist is simultaneously for it to be enstatically grounded in reception and to proceed ecstatically toward others "by virtue of a dynamic given to it in order to realize itself (its innerness) in the very act of expressing."[13] Being mutually defined in these relations, all creatures are bound together in the movement of the Spirit toward the telos given in the divine act of creation, that of *unio realis* among themselves and with God in *amor amicitiae*. Thus, all created being is love, as Ferdinand Ulrich has argued, as it is received from God as a *similitude divinae bonitatis* in which *esse* and *essentia* only cross the abyss of nothingness in their mutual return to one another in the *bonitas divina*

11. For Thomas's doctrine of a mixed relation between God and creation, see *ST* Ia, q.13, a.7; see also Emery, "*Theologia* and *Dispensatio*," 525–26; Oliver, *Creation*, 48. The dual aspect of creation's relation to God is expressed well by Hill, who describes the creative act as "a circular dynamism *within* God [which] opens itself as the principle of production of an entirely different kind outside of God." The spatial imagery here is obviously metaphorical, as Hill can reverse the image, saying created reality "exists only 'in' God; in the creative act God empties himself out kenotically, as it were, making room 'within' himself for the nondivine" (*Three-Personed God*, 76n56).

12. Nichols, *Say It Is Pentecost*, 58.

13. Balthasar, *Epilogue*, 51.

"unreservedly" given by the Trinity in creation.[14] Von Balthasar summarizes this kind of ontology beautifully:

> From the very outset God created the worldly image to exist beyond itself and on the way to the archetype, so that all immanence continuously transcends itself toward God. Worldly being is destined to be harbored in Divine Being, worldly time in God's eternally moved eternity, worldly space in the infinite spaces of God, worldly becoming, not in an immobile Divine Being, but in the eternal eventfulness of divine life.[15]

This is so because the gift of created being reflects the structure of divine being, in both its kenotic self-gift and the return, the kenosis of the eucharistic self-giving of the Son back to the Father. Created being moves in the universal motion of kenosis toward that which can (and is) ultimately only attained "through a free self-disclosure by God."[16] Thus, creation, in its very existence, structure, and motion, is always oriented toward the Absolute Good which is only (but yet is!) obtained in the personal missions of God in the Son and Spirit.

Salvation and Union by Divine Love

These personal missions are the personal involvement of the Godhead in a new way (that is, distinguished from the metaphysical relation to created being itself) in the temporal unfolding of the divine gift of love.[17] The focal point of the visible missions is undeniably the Passion, justifying the focus on the relation between the Son's trinitarian person and crucifixion common to Thomas and von Balthasar. Though the acme—to adapt Barclay's terminology slightly—of the missions is the crucifixion and resurrection, the telos of the missions is the unification of God and creation in the Son through the Spirit.[18] It is widely recognized that John's Prologue is a gloss

14. *HA*, 22; see Schindler, *Companion*, 116. This theme of being's transnihilation also raises the question of the nature of sin, evil, hell, and how the privation view of evil held by both Thomas and von Balthasar might be expressed differently within Ulrich's framework of transnihilation, all of which are outside of the scope of this present thesis.

15. *TL2*, 84.

16. Balthasar, *Realm of Metaphysics in the Modern Age*, 14–15; see also Nichols, *Word Has Been Abroad*, 101, 129, 146.

17. For Thomas's discussion of these missions and their invisible and visible aspects in relation to the procession of the Son and Spirit in God, see *ST* Ia, q.43, a.1, 5–7; *LSI* 15.2061.

18. See Barclay, "Kenosis," 22.

on the creation account from Genesis, but if read particularly through the theme of water, the theme of baptism integrates the first three chapters into a presentation of the triune identity as a life of love through the divine act of new creation.[19]

Jesus's discussion with Nicodemus in John 3:1–6 is a classical text read during baptismal liturgies.[20] Jesus specifies that it is by being born ἐξ ὕδατος καὶ πνεύματος, a second birth of divine origin, that one may be born ἄνωθεν into the kingdom of God (John 3:3, 5–7).[21] This alludes back to the first chapter of John's account, where John the Baptizer introduces these two elements of baptism (John 1:24–34), a connection made even more significant because the seeming interruption of the Baptizer in the middle of the Prologue's vivid theological restatement of the creation event from Genesis.[22] While the word spoken in Genesis is hypostatized into an identifiable subject, ὁ λόγος, who both is *with* God and *is* God in 1:1–5, the Spirit who hovered over the water like a bird in Gen 1:2 is not mentioned until the Spirit descends like a dove upon the baptismal waters of the Son (John 1:32; Matt 3:16).[23] Just as the Spirit was present over the waters in the initial act of creation, the Spirit is present over the waters of the new creation in the baptism by which the Father identifies Jesus as the Son of God. The Spirit only seems to be left out of the triune identification if the first eighteen verses are assumed to be disconnected from that which follows, as the traditional title of Prologue suggests.

In this light, the imagery of new birth by water and Spirit, especially as compared with the first birth in 3:4–6, makes sense as the entryway into the kingdom of God (John 3:5) and eternal life (John 3:15). As a new creative act, Christ's ministry of baptism in the Spirit is the eschatological fulfillment of the baptism of the first creation. This creation, which the Father made through the Son by the power of the Spirit, is being beckoned into

19. See Thompson, *John*, 27–30; Moloney, *Gospel of John*, 35; McDonough, *Christ as Creator*, 20.

20. For examples, see *Book of Common Prayer* (1979), 928; Scottish Episcopal Church, *Holy Baptism*; *Catechism of the Catholic Church*, 314; *Order of Baptism of Children*, 20; *Book of Common Prayer* (2019), 162, 168.

21. While the assumed position in the various liturgies mentioned above is that Jesus is speaking of the Christian rite of water baptism, some commentators argue against this interpretation; see Witherington, *John's Wisdom*, 97; O'Day, "Response," 161; see Keener, *Gospel of John*, 547, for further references.

22. Seeing it in this light mitigates the apparent awkwardness of 1:6–8, 15, noted by commentators such as Rae, "Testimony of Works," 301.

23. On the connections between the Spirit in Genesis and John, compare Blocher, *In the Beginning*, 68–69; D. Williams, "Spirit in Creation," 4; Brown, *John: I–XII*, 57; Schweizer, *Holy Spirit*, 68; Moore-Keish, "Creation and New Creation," 80–93.

a new reality, the kingdom of God, by the Son and Spirit. Those who were born of women must also be regenerated, or reborn, of "water and Spirit" (John 3:5) if they wish to enter this eschatological kingdom (John 3:3, 5). This new birth is an entrance into a new reality, one characterized by the abiding presence of the Spirit and the eternal life of the kingdom of God (John 3:15). When Nicodemus struggles to understand this movement from old to new in baptism, Jesus places it within the context of his ascent and descent as the Son of Man (John 3:12–15). The descent is Jesus being sent from heaven to earth in the incarnation, and the ascent is, as verse 14 clarifies, his being raised up upon the cross as the salvation of the world.[24] Both the whence (descent from heaven) and the whither (ascent to the cross as a participation in divine glory) further explain this new birth of the Spirit, identifying its source and goal. The Son was sent from God to usher in the kingdom of God through an eschatological act of new creation in the Spirit, bringing God's people into a new, eternal life with God himself through spiritual rebirth.

At this point, the reason why God has sent his Son and Spirit for the salvation of the world is identified: "For God so loved the world, that he gave his only Son" (John 3:16). The Father has given (ἔδωκεν) his Son out of love for the world, which is the first time the love of God is mentioned in the Gospel of John. This is the reason (γὰρ) for the mission of the Son, which includes the baptism of the Spirit (John 1:32–24; 3:5–9) and his ascension to the cross to secure eternal life (John 3:13–15). God sent his Son because he loved the world, and his love is manifested in the giving of the Son.[25] So, John 3:16 could be paraphrased, "God loved the world *in* giving the Son."[26] That is, the mission of the Son is the expression of the love of God for the world, such that if one were to ask how to characterize divine love, the answer would be found through an investigation into the sending and giving

24. Brown, *John: I–XII*, 145–46. Ridderbos, *John*, 136, links vv. 13 and 14 together to argue that there is "no ascent except by way of descent." Therefore, while these two verses portray the two movements in the opposite order, with ascent coming before descent in v. 13, the perfect verb there (ἀναβέβηκεν) should be read as a gnomic statement rather than in a historic sense. For the cross as the glorification of Jesus in John, see Thompson, *John*, 85.

25. While Ridderbos, *John*, 138, is correct to note that the terminology in this passage may gesture toward the intensity of the love of the Father, another possible meaning of the conjunction οὕτως, the conjunctions οὕτως and ὥστε together express an explanatory relationship between God's love and the gift of the Son, with the latter explaining the manner in which the former is carried out. See also O'Day, "Response," 161.

26. Brown, *John: I–XII*, 133, speaks of "agapan thus expressing itself in action . . . in the Incarnation and the death of the Son."

of the Son to the world and the contents and results of his mission here. Those who accept his testimony (John 3:15–16, 32–33) take his words as the words of God, which is only possible because he has been given the Spirit without measure, permanently abiding with him (John 3:34; cf. 1:33).[27] Not only has the Son received the Spirit from the Father, but the Father loves him and gives him all things (John 3:35). Because of this, the eternal life of rebirth in the Spirit is given through belief in the Son (John 3:36).

The love of God that leads to the missions is the Father's love for the Son, which is placed in parallel with the presence of the Spirit in John 3:34–35, presenting the love of the trinitarian life as that which flows from God to the world. As the means by which one is introduced to the new creation, the liturgical act of baptism ought to be thought of fundamentally as an act of the divine love expressed to creation in the divine missions. Created persons are born ἄνωθεν, recreated or regenerated, through their participation in Christ's own baptism and the enduring presence of the Spirit, and by this are ushered into a reality located within and characterized by the trinitarian relations of love.[28] They are reborn as "children of God" (John 1:12) and as such participate in the life of God, being placed within the patterns of love that characterize the eternal life of Father, Son, and Spirit (John 3:15).

This ethic and its foundation in the divine life are given at the end of Christ's ministry. As those reborn as sons and daughters, Christians are to imitate the love of the Son in their love for one another (John 13:34). They are to keep Christ's commandments because they love him, linked with the Spirit's enduring presence with them, by which both Father and Son will come and "make [their] home with them" (John 14:16–23).[29] They are to

27. Ridderbos, *John*, 150; Thompson, *God of John*, 170–71. For an alternate viewpoint, which exploits the possible parallelism of the Son "speaking" the words of God and "giving" the Spirit of God, see Léon-Dufour, *Lecture de l'Evangile Selon Jean*, 331–33.

28. The two possible interpretations of ἄνωθεν are "again" or "from above." Ridderbos, *John*, 125, is certainly right that it is not "an essential difference . . . . Such a birth is both 'from above' and 'anew.'" If the apostolic text is taken as it is received, the presence of the possible wordplay and apparent misunderstanding of Nicodemus is illuminating rather than contradictory; see also Moloney, *John*, 92; Brown, *John: I–XII*, 138.

Further, the only two occurrences of the word for regeneration (παλιγγενεσία) in the New Testament are Titus 3:5 ("the washing of regeneration") and Matt 19:28, where the NRSV translates it as "the renewal of all things." Coupled with the etymology of the word itself, the connection between the scriptural concept of regeneration, new birth, and new creation is readily apparent.

29. Thompson, *John*, 314, approaches this interpretation when suggesting that the later language of the Spirit's presence will be in terms of the disciples' dependence on and receptivity to Jesus (John 15:1–7), the reciprocity of the friendship (John 15:14–15), and mutual indwelling (John 14:20; 15:5; 17:23, 26). For what seems like an embrace of

abide in the Son's love (John 15:9–10) and to have the love of the Father for the Son in them (John 17:26), by which the Father and Son indwell one another (John 14:10–11; 15:9–10).[30]

So, finally, the end of the divine missions is to unite creatures to the Son by the Spirit who is the Father's love (John 17:22). This unity between God and creation is the divine love that binds together, as Thompson puts it, "because it is self-giving, not self-seeking; it is cohesive."[31] It is, for John's Gospel, a love that is personal yet expresses the very nature and unity of God. It is an ecstatic self-giving to the point of death for the sake of others, yet one in which all are remade and fulfilled as persons. By this love that leads through death, all are reborn to the eternal divine life in which all are called "friends" of the Son (John 15:13–15), loved by the Father, and indwelt by the Spirit. The happiness of seeing God is found only by being brought into the triune life of *amor amicitiae* through the doors of new birth given in the baptism of Christ—water and Spirit, both.

---

a more explicit link between the Spirit and these concepts, see Thompson, *God of John*, 181–82: "[The] Spirit does not replace Jesus, or even become the real presence of Jesus; the Spirit makes the presence of Jesus real." See also Brown, *John: XIII–XXI*, 643–45, 648; Davis, "What Is 'Perichoresis,'" 147–48.

30. See Moltmann, "God in the World," 372–73; Durand, "Perichoresis," 178, 181. For an opposing view, see Crump, "Re-Examining the Johannine Trinity," who argues that the only "perichoretic Trinity" is the Father, the Son, and the believers united to them.

31. Thompson, *John*, 356–57.

Bibliography

Aertsen, Jan. *Nature and Creature: Thomas Aquinas's Way of Thought*. Studien Und Texte Zur Geistesgeschichte Des Mittelalters. Leiden: Brill, 1988.

Anatolios, Khaled. "The Canonization of Scripture in the Context of Trinitarian Doctrine." In *Oxford Handbook of the Trinity*, edited by Gilles Emery and Matthew Levering, 15–26. Oxford: Oxford University Press, 2011.

———. "Personhood, Communion, and the Trinity in Some Patristic Texts." In *The Holy Trinity in the Life of the Church*, edited by Khaled Anatolios, 147–64. Holy Cross Studies in Patristic Theology and History. Grand Rapids: Baker Academic, 2014.

Anderson, James F. *The Cause of Being: The Philosophy of Creation in St. Thomas*. St. Louis: Herder, 1952.

Aquinas, Thomas. *Commentary on Aristotle's Physics*. Translated by Richard J. Blackwell et al. Masterpieces of Philosophy and Science. New Haven, CT: Yale University Press, 1963.

———. *Commentary on the Gospel of John*. Edited by The Aquinas Institute. Translated by Fabian R. Larcher. 2 vols. Latin-English Opera Omnia. Steubenville, OH: Emmaus Academic, 2018.

———. *Disputed Questions on Truth*. Translated by Robert W. Mulligan, James V. McGlynn, and Robert William Schmidt. Chicago: Regnery, 1952.

———. "On Being and Essence." In *Opuscula I: Treatises*, edited by The Aquinas Institute, translated by Robert Miller. Latin-English Opera Omnia. Steubenville, OH: Emmaus Academic, 2018.

———. *On Charity*. Translated by Lottie H. Kendzierski. Milwaukee, WI: Marquette University Press, 1984.

———. *On Love and Charity: Readings from the* Commentary on the Sentences of Peter Lombard. Translated by Peter A. Kwasniewski et al. Washington, DC: The Catholic University of America Press, 2008.

———. *Quaestiones Disputatae de Potentia*. Edited by P. M. Pession. Rome: Marietti, 1949.

———. *Scriptum Super Sententiis Magistri Petri Lombardi*. Edited by Marie Fabien Moos. Paris: P. Lethielleux, 1956.

———. *Summa Contra Gentiles*. Translated by Laurence Shapcote. Latin-English Opera Omnia. Steubenville, OH: Emmaus Academic, 2018.

———. *Summa Theologiae*. Edited by The Aquinas Institute. Translated by Fathers of the English Dominican Province. 10 vols. Latin-English Opera Omnia. Steubenville, OH: Emmaus Academic, 2018.

Ashley, Benedict M. *The Way Toward Wisdom: An Interdisciplinary and Intercultural Introduction to Metaphysics*. Thomistic Studies. Notre Dame, IN: University of Notre Dame Press, 2006.

Augustine of Hippo. "On the Trinity." In *St. Augustin: On the Holy Trinity, Doctrinal Treatises, Moral Treatises*, edited by Philip Schaff and translated by Arthur West Haddan, 3:1–228. A Select Library of the Nicene and Post-Nicene Fathers of the Christian Church, First Series. Buffalo, NY: Christian Literature, 1887.

———. "Sermon 52." In *The Cambridge Edition of Early Christian Writings*, edited by Andrew Radde-Gallwitz and translated by Mark DelCogliano, 311–27. Cambridge: Cambridge University Press, 2017.

Awad, Najeeb. "Thomas Aquinas' Metaphysics of 'Relation' and 'Participation' and Contemporary Trinitarian Theology." *New Blackfriars* 93 (2012) 652–70.

Ayres, Lewis. "Augustine on the Trinity." In *The Oxford Handbook of the Trinity*, edited by Gilles Emery and Matthew Levering, 123–37. Oxford: Oxford University Press, 2011.

Balthasar, Hans Urs von. *The Action*. Translated by Graham Harrison. Theo-Drama: Theological Dramatic Theory 4. San Francisco: Ignatius, 1994.

———. *Creator Spirit*. Translated by Brian McNeil. Explorations in Theology 3. San Francisco: Ignatius, 1993.

———. *Dramatis Personae: Man in God*. Translated by Graham Harrison. Theo-Drama: Theological Dramatic Theory 2. San Francisco: Ignatius, 1990.

———. *Dramatis Personae: The Person in Christ*. Translated by Graham Harrison. Theo-Drama: Theological Dramatic Theory 3. San Francisco: Ignatius, 1992.

———. *Epilogue*. Translated by Edward T. Oakes. San Francisco: Ignatius, 2004.

———. *The Last Act*. Translated by Graham Harrison. Theo-Drama: Theological Dramatic Theory 5. San Francisco: Ignatius, 1998.

———. *Love Alone Is Credible*. Translated by D. C. Schindler. San Francisco: Ignatius, 2004.

———. *Man Is Created*. Translated by Adrian J. Walker. Explorations in Theology 5. San Francisco: Ignatius, 2014.

———. *Mysterium Paschale: The Mystery of Easter*. Translated by Aidan Nichols. San Francisco: Ignatius, 1990.

———. *Razing the Bastions: On the Church in This Age*. Translated by Brian McNeil. San Francisco: Ignatius, 1993.

———. *The Realm of Metaphysics in Antiquity*. Edited by John Riches and translated by Brian McNeil et al. The Glory of the Lord: A Theological Aesthetics 4. San Francisco: Ignatius, 1989.

———. *The Realm of Metaphysics in the Modern Age*. Edited by Brian McNeil and John Riches and translated by Oliver Davies et al. The Glory of the Lord: A Theological Aesthetics 5. Edinburgh: T. & T. Clark, 1991.

———. *Spirit and Institution*. Translated by Edward T. Oakes. Explorations in Theology 4. San Francisco: Ignatius, 1995.

———. *The Spirit of Truth*. Translated by Graham Harrison. Theo-Logic: Theological Logical Theory 3. San Francisco: Ignatius, 2005.

———. *Studies in Theological Style: Clerical Styles*. Edited by John Riches and translated by Andrew Louth et al. The Glory of the Lord: A Theological Aesthetics 2. Edinburgh: T. & T. Clark, 1984.

———. *The Theology of Karl Barth*. San Francisco: Ignatius, 1992.

———. *Truth of God*. Translated by Adrian J. Walker. Theo-Logic: Theological Logical Theory 2. San Francisco: Ignatius, 2004.

———. *Truth of the World*. Translated by Adrian J. Walker. Theo-Logic: Theological Logical Theory 1. San Francisco: Ignatius, 2000.

———. *Unless You Become like This Child*. Translated by Erasmo Leiva-Merikakis. San Francisco: Ignatius, 1991.

Barclay, John M. G. "Kenosis and the Drama of Salvation in Philippians 2." In *Kenosis: The Self-Emptying of Christ in Scripture and Theology*, edited by Paul T. Nimmo and Keith L. Johnson, 7–23. Grand Rapids: Eerdmans, 2022.

Barnes, Michel René. "Latin Trinitarian Theology." In *The Cambridge Companion to the Trinity*, edited by Edward T. Oakes and David Moss, 70–84. Cambridge Companions to Religion. Cambridge: Cambridge University Press, 2011.

Barth, Karl. *Church Dogmatics: The Doctrine of Creation*. Edited by Geoffrey William Bromiley and T. F. Torrance. Edinburgh: T. & T. Clark, 2004.

Basil the Great. *Against Eunomius*. Translated by Mark DelCogliano and Andrew Radde-Gallwitz. The Fathers of the Church 122. Washington, DC: The Catholic University of America Press, 2011.

———. *St. Basil: Letters and Select Works*. Edited by Philip Schaff and Henry Wace and translated by Blomfield Jackson. A Select Library of the Nicene and Post-Nicene Fathers of the Christian Church, Second Series 8. New York: Christian Literature, 1895.

Betz, John R. "After Barth: A New Introduction to Erich Przywara's *Analogia Entis*." In *Analogy of Being: Invention of the Antichrist or the Wisdom of God?*, edited by Thomas Joseph White, 35–87. Grand Rapids: Eerdmans, 2011.

———. "The Humility of God: On a Disputed Question in Trinitarian Theology." *Nova et Vetera* 17 (2019) 769–810.

———. "What's New in the New Trinitarian Ontology? A Commentary on Klaus Hemmerle's *Theses Towards a Trinitarian Ontology*." *Modern Theology* 39 (2023) 131–58.

Bieler, Martin. "*Analogia Entis* as an Expression of Love According to Ferdinand Ulrich." In *Analogy of Being: Invention of the Antichrist or the Wisdom of God?*, edited by Thomas Joseph White, 314–37. Grand Rapids: Eerdmans, 2011.

———. "Introduction." In *Homo Abyssus: The Drama of the Question of Being*, by Ferdinand Ulrich, translated by D. C. Schindler, xv–lv. Washington, DC: Humanum Academic, 2018.

Blocher, Henri. *In the Beginning: The Opening Chapters of Genesis*. Translated by David G. Preston. Downers Grove, IL: InterVarsity, 1984.

Bonaventure. *Commentaria in Quatuor Libros Sententiarum Magistri Petri Lombardi*. Florence: Quaracchi, 1882.

The Book of Common Prayer. New York: Seabury, 1979.

The Book of Common Prayer. Huntington Beach, CA: Anglican Liturgy, 2019.

Bourassa, François. "L'Esprit Saint, 'Communion' du Père et de Fils I." *Science et Esprit* 29 (1977) 251–81.

———. "Sur la Propriété de l'Esprit Saint: Questions Disputées I." *Science et Esprit* 28 (1976) 243–64.

Bouyer, Louis. *Le Consolateur: Esprit-Saint et Vie de Grâce*. Paris: Cerf, 1980.

Brady, Ryan J. "Aquinas the Voluntarist? An Investigation of the Claims of James Keenan, S. J." *Nova et Vetera* 18 (2020) 853–73.

Brown, Raymond E. *The Gospel According to John: I–XII*. The Anchor Bible. Garden City, NY: Doubleday, 1966.

———. *The Gospel According to John: XIII–XXI*. The Anchor Bible. Garden City, NY: Doubleday, 1985.

Buckley, James Joseph. "Balthasar's Use of the Theology of Aquinas." *The Thomist* 59 (1995) 517–45.

Burrell, David B. *Aquinas: God and Action*. Notre Dame, IN: University of Notre Dame Press, 1979.

Canty, Aaron. "Aquinas and Scotus on God as Object of Beatific Enjoyment." In *The Discovery of Being and Thomas Aquinas: Philosophical and Theological Perspective*, edited by Christopher M. Cullen and Franklin T. Harkins, 267–81. Washington, DC: The Catholic University of America Press, 2019.

Carpenter, Anne M. "Analogy and Kenosis." *Nova et Vetera* 17 (2019) 811–38.

Casarella, Peter. "Hans Urs von Balthasar, Erich Przywara's *Analogia Entis*, and the Problem of a Catholic *Denkform*." In *Analogy of Being: Invention of the Antichrist or the Wisdom of God?*, edited by Thomas Joseph White, 192–206. Grand Rapids: Eerdmans, 2011.

Catechism of the Catholic Church. 2nd ed. Vatican City: Vatican, 1997.

Cessario, Romanus. *A Short History of Thomism*. Washington, DC: The Catholic University of America Press, 2005.

Chenu, Marie-Dominique. *Towards Understanding St. Thomas*. Translated by A.-M. Landre and D. Hughes. Chicago: Regnery, 1964.

Clarke, W. Norris. *The Creative Retrieval of Saint Thomas Aquinas: Essays in Thomistic Philosophy, New and Old*. New York: Fordham University Press, 2009.

———. *Person and Being*. The Aquinas Lectures. Milwaukee, WI: Marquette University Press, 1993.

Clement of Alexandria. *Clement of Alexandria: The Exhortation to the Greeks, The Rich Man's Salvation, and the Fragment of an Address Entitled, "To the Newly Baptized."* Translated by G. W. Butterworth. Cambridge, MA: Harvard University Press, 1919.

Coakley, Sarah. *God, Sexuality and the Self: An Essay "on the Trinity."* Cambridge: Cambridge University Press, 2013.

———. "Why Gift? Gift, Gender and Trinitarian Relations in Milbank and Tanner." *Scottish Journal of Theology* 61 (2008) 224–35.

Coda, Piero. *From the Trinity: The Coming of God in Revelation and Theology*. Washington, DC: The Catholic University of America Press, 2020.

———. "The Unity of Reciprocal Love: The Charism of Chiara Lubich and the Theology of Klaus Hemmerle." *International Journal of Philosophy and Theology* 78 (2017) 155–71.

Coleman, Rachel M. "Thinking the 'Nothing' of Being: Ferdinand Ulrich on Transnihilation." *Communio* 46 (2019) 1–17.

Conciliorum Oecumenicorum Decreta. Basil: Herder, 1967.

Crump, David. "Re-Examining the Johannine Trinity: Perichoresis or Deification?" *Scottish Journal of Theology* 59 (2006) 395–412.

Davies, Brian. "The Summa Theologiae on What God Is Not." In *Aquinas's Summa Theologiae: A Critical Guide*, edited by Jeffrey Hause, 47–67. Cambridge: Cambridge University Press, 2018.

Davis, John Jefferson. "What Is 'Perichoresis'—and Why Does It Matter? Perichoresis as Properly Basic to the Christian Faith." *Evangelical Review of Theology* 39 (2015) 144–56.

Davison, Andrew. *Participation in God: A Study in Christian Doctrine and Metaphysics.* New York: Cambridge University Press, 2019.

Denzinger, Henry. *The Sources of Catholic Dogma.* Translated by Roy J. Deferrari. Fitzwilliam, NH: Loreto, 2004.

Dewan, Lawrence. "St Thomas and the Principle of Causality." In *Form and Being: Studies in Thomistic Metaphysics*, 45:61–80. Studies in Philosophy and the History of Philosophy. Washington, DC: Catholic University of America Press, 2011.

Diggs, Bernard James. *Love and Being: An Investigation into the Metaphysics of St. Thomas Aquinas.* New York: S. F. Vanni, 1947.

Dionysius the Areopagite. "The Divine Names." In *Dionysius the Areopagite on the Divine Names and the Mystical Theology*, translated by C. E. Rolt, 50–190. Translations of Christian Literature, Series 1: Greek Texts. London: Society for Promoting Christian Knowledge, 1940.

Dol, Jean-Noël. *L'esprit de Vérité et d'amour: La Pneumatologie de Hans Urs von Balthasar: Esprit Subjectif, Esprit Objectif, Esprit Absolu?* Sed Contra. Paris: Lethielleux, 2016.

Doolan, Gregory T. *Aquinas on the Divine Ideas as Exemplar Causes.* Washington, DC: The Catholic University of America Press, 2014.

Durand, Emmanuel. "Perichoresis: A Key Concept for Balancing Trinitarian Theology." In *Rethinking Trinitarian Theology: Disputed Questions and Contemporary Issues in Trinitarian Theology*, edited by Giulio Maspero and Robert Józef Wozniak, 177–92. London: T. & T. Clark, 2012.

Durrwell, F. X. *L'Esprit Saint de Dieu.* Paris: Cerf, 1983.

Elders, Leo J. *The Metaphysics of Being of St. Thomas Aquinas in a Historical Perspective.* Translated by John Dudley. Studien Und Texte Zur Geistesgeschichte Des Mittelalters 34. Leiden: Brill, 1993.

———. *The Philosophy of Nature of St. Thomas Aquinas: Nature, the Universe, Man.* New York: Peter Lang, 1997.

Emery, Gilles. "Biblical Exegesis and the Speculative Doctrine of the Trinity in St. Thomas Aquinas's *Commentary on St. John*." In *Reading John with St. Thomas Aquinas: Theological Exegesis and Speculative Theology*, edited by Michael Dauphinais and Matthew Levering, 23–61. Washington, DC: The Catholic University of America Press, 2005.

———. "The Dignity of Being a Substance: Person, Subsistence, and Nature." *Nova et Vetera* 9 (2011) 991–1001.

———. "Essentialism or Personalism in the Treatise on God in Saint Thomas Aquinas." *The Thomist* 64 (2000) 521–63.

———. "The Personal Mode of Trinitarian Action in Saint Thomas Aquinas." *The Thomist* 69 (2005) 31–77.

———. "*Theologia* and *Dispensatio*: The Centrality of the Divine Missions in St. Thomas's Trinitarian Theology." *The Thomist* 74 (2010) 515–61.

———. *The Trinitarian Theology of St Thomas Aquinas.* Translated by Francesca Aran Murphy. New York: Oxford University Press, 2007.

Falcon, Andrea. "Aristotle on Causality." In *The Stanford Encyclopedia of Philosophy*, edited by Edward N. Zalta and Uri Nodelman. Metaphysics Research Lab,

Stanford University, 2023. https://plato.stanford.edu/archives/spr2023/entries/aristotle-causality/.

Feser, Edward. *Scholastic Metaphysics: A Contemporary Introduction*. Heusenstamm, Ger.: Editiones Scholasticae, 2014.

Fiedler, Eduard. "Klaus Hemmerle on the Trinitarian Ontology of the Human Person." *Theologica* 11 (2021) 59–75.

Finnis, John. "Object and Intention in Moral Judgment According to St Thomas Aquinas." In *Finalité et Intentionnalité: Doctrine Thomiste et Perspectives Modernes*, edited by Jacques Follon and James McEvoy, 127–48. Paris: Librairie Philosophique, 1992.

Flood, Anthony T. *The Metaphysical Foundations of Love: Aquinas on Participation, Unity, and Union*. Washington, DC: The Catholic University of America Press, 2018.

———. *The Root of Friendship: Self-Love and Self-Governance in Aquinas*. Washington, DC: The Catholic University of America Press, 2014.

Follon, Jacques. "Le Finalisme Chez Aristote et S. Thomas." In *Finalité et Intentionnalité: Doctrine Thomiste et Perspectives Modernes*, edited by Jacques Follon and James McEvoy, 11–39. Paris: Librairie Philosophique, 1992.

Fortman, Edmund J. *The Triune God: A Historical Study of the Doctrine of the Trinity*. Eugene, OR: Wipf & Stock, 1999.

Franks, Angela Franz. "Trinitarian *Analogia Entis* in Hans Urs von Balthasar." *The Thomist* 62 (1998) 533–59.

Franks, Christopher A. "The Simplicity of the Living God: Aquinas, Barth, and Some Philosophers." *Modern Theology* 21 (2005) 275–300.

Friedman, Russell L. *Medieval Trinitarian Thought from Aquinas to Ockham*. New York: Cambridge University Press, 2010.

Gallagher, David M. "Desire for Beatitude and Love of Friendship in Thomas Aquinas." *Mediaeval Studies* 58 (1996) 1–47.

———. "Thomas Aquinas on Self-Love as the Basis for Love of Others." *Acta Philosophica* 8 (1999) 23–44.

———. "Thomas Aquinas on the Causes of Human Choice." PhD diss., The Catholic University of America, 1989.

———. "Thomas Aquinas on the Will as Rational Appetite." *Journal of the History of Philosophy* 29 (1991) 559–84.

Garrigou-Lagrange, Reginald. *Beatitude*. Translated by Patrick Cummins. St. Louis: Herder, 1956.

Geiger, L. B. "Les Idées Divines dans l'œuvre de S. Thomas." In *St. Thomas Aquinas, 1274–1974: Commemorative Studies*, edited by Armand A. Maurer et al., 1:175–209. Toronto: Pontifical Institute of Mediaeval Studies, 1974.

Gilby, Thomas. "The First Way." In *Existence and Nature of God (Ia 2-11)*, 2:191–95. Summa Theologiae. New York: Cambridge University Press, 2006.

Gilson, Étienne. *Elements of Christian Philosophy*. Garden City, NY: Doubleday, 1959.

———. *L'Être et l'Essence*. 2nd ed. Paris: Librairie Philosophique, 1981.

———. *God and Philosophy*. New Haven, CT: Yale University Press, 1941.

———. "*Quasi Definition Substantiae*." In *St. Thomas Aquinas, 1274–1974: Commemorative Studies*, edited by Armand A. Maurer et al., 1:111–29. Toronto: Pontifical Institute of Mediaeval Studies, 1974.

———. *The Spirit of Mediaeval Philosophy*. Translated by A. H. C. Downes. London: Sheed & Ward, 1936.

———. *Thomism: The Philosophy of Thomas Aquinas*. Translated by Laurence K. Shook and Armand Maurer. 6th ed. Ontario: Pontifical Institute of Mediaeval Studies, 2002.

González, Orestes J. Actus Essendi *and the Habit of the First Principle in Thomas Aquinas*. New York: Einsiedler, 2019.

Gregory Nazianzen. *S. Cyril of Jerusalem, S. Gregory Nazianzen*. Edited by Philip Schaff and Henry Wace and translated by Charles Gordon Browne and James Edward Swallow. A Select Library of the Nicene and Post-Nicene Fathers of the Christian Church, Second Series 7. New York: Christian Literature, 1894.

Gunton, Colin E. *Father, Son, and Holy Spirit: Essays Toward a Fully Trinitarian Theology*. London: T. & T. Clark, 2003.

Hankey, W. J. *God in Himself: Aquinas' Doctrine of God as Expounded in the Summa Theologiae*. New York: Oxford University Press, 2004.

Hayes, Zachary. "Introduction." In *Saint Bonaventure's Disputed Question on the Mystery of the Trinity*. Works of Saint Bonaventure 3. St Bonaventure, NY: The Franciscan Institute, 1979.

Healy, Nicholas. "Christ's Eucharist and the Nature of Love: The Contribution of Hans Urs von Balthasar." *The Saint Anselm Journal* 10 (2015) 1–17.

———. *The Eschatology of Hans Urs von Balthasar: Being as Communion*. Oxford Theological Monographs. Oxford: Oxford University Press, 2005.

Heltzel, Peter Goodwin, and Christian T. Collins Winn. "Karl Barth, Reconciliation, and the Triune God." In *The Cambridge Companion to the Trinity*, edited by Edward T. Oakes and David Moss, 173–91. Cambridge Companions to Religion. Cambridge: Cambridge University Press, 2011.

Hemmerle, Klaus. *Thesen Zu Einer Trinitarischen Ontologie*. Einsiedeln: Kriterien, 1976.

———. *Theses Towards a Trinitarian Ontology*. Translated by Stephen Churchyard. New York: Angelico, 2020.

Hill, William J. *The Three-Personed God: The Trinity as a Mystery of Salvation*. Washington, DC: The Catholic University of America Press, 1982.

Holmes, Christopher R. J. "Architectonics Matter: Some Advantages of Treating the Unicity of God in Advance of the Trinity of Persons, in Dialogue with Thomas Aquinas." *International Journal of Systematic Theology* 19 (2017) 130–43.

Holmes, Stephen R. *The Quest for the Trinity: The Doctrine of God in Scripture, History, and Modernity*. Downers Grove, IL: IVP Academic, 2012.

Hoover, R. W. "The *Harpagmos* Enigma: A Philological Solution." *Harvard Theological Review* 64 (1971) 95–119.

Hoye, William J. *Divine Being and Its Relevance According to Thomas Aquinas*. Boston: Brill, 2020.

Ide, Pascal. "'L'Amour Est l'Acte Suprême de l'Être': La Philosophie de Hans Urs von Balthasar: Réception et Chantiers (II)." *Transversalités* 144 (2018) 109–28.

———. "L'Être Comme Amour Chez Balthasar. Approches et Prolongements." In *Chrétiens Dans la Société Actuelle: L'apport de Hans Urs von Balthasar*, 259–304. Magny-Les-Hameaux: Socéval, 2006.

Jenson, Robert. *The Triune God*. Vol. 1 of *Systematic Theology*. New York: Oxford University Press, 1997.

Johnson, Junius. *Christ and Analogy: The Christocentric Metaphysics of Hans Urs von Balthasar*. Emerging Scholars. Minneapolis: Fortress, 2013.

Jordan, Mark D. "The Transcendentality of Goodness and the Human Will." In *Being and Goodness: The Concept of the Good in Metaphysics and Philosophical Theology*, edited by Scott MacDonald, 129–50. Ithaca, NY: Cornell University Press, 1991.

Keener, Craig S. *The Gospel of John: A Commentary*. 2 vols. Peabody, MA: Hendrickson, 2010.

Kenny, Anthony. *Aquinas*. New York: Hill and Wang, 1980.

———. *Aquinas on Being*. Oxford: Clarendon, 2002.

———. *The Five Ways: St. Thomas Aquinas' Proofs of God's Existence*. London: Routledge & Kegan Paul, 1969.

Kerr, Fergus. *After Aquinas*. Malden, MA: Blackwell, 2002.

Kilby, Karen. "Aquinas, the Trinity and the Limits of Understanding." *International Journal of Systematic Theology* 7 (2005) 414–27.

———. *Balthasar: A (Very) Critical Introduction*. Grand Rapids: Eerdmans, 2012.

———. "Hans Urs von Balthasar and the Trinity." In *The Cambridge Companion to the Trinity*, edited by Peter C. Phan, 208–22. Cambridge Companions to Religion. Cambridge: Cambridge University Press, 2011.

Klauder, Francis J. *A Philosophy Rooted in Love: The Dominant Themes in the Perennial Philosophy of St. Thomas Aquinas*. Lanham, MD: University Press of America, 1994.

Knasas, John F. X. *Being and Some Twentieth-Century Thomists*. 1st ed. New York: Fordham University Press, 2003.

———. *Thomistic Existentialism and Cosmological Reasoning*. Washington, DC: The Catholic University of America Press, 2019.

Kosman, L. A. "Substance, Being and Energeia." In *Oxford Studies in Ancient Philosophy*, 2:121–49. Oxford: Oxford University Press, 1984.

Kwasniewski, Peter A. *The Ecstasy of Love in the Thought of Thomas Aquinas*. Steubenville, OH: Emmaus Academic, 2021.

Lafont, G. *Peut-on Connaître Dieu en Jésus Christ?* Paris: Cerf, 1969.

Leamy, Katy. *The Holy Trinity: Hans Urs Von Balthasar and His Sources*. Eugene, OR: Pickwick, 2015.

Lee, Patrick. "The Relation Between Intellect and Will in Free Choice According to Aquinas and Scotus." *The Thomist* 49 (1985) 321–42.

Lefsrud, Sigurd. *Kenosis in Theology: An Exploration of Balthasar's Theology of Deification*. Eugene, OR: Pickwick, 2020.

Léon-Dufour, Xavier. *Lecture de l'Evangile Selon Jean, Vol. 1*. Parole de Dieu. Paris: Seuil, 1988.

Le Pivain, Denis-Dominique. *L'action du Saint-Esprit dans le commentaire de l'évangile de saint Jean par saint Thomas d'Aquin*. Croire et Savoir. Paris: Pierre Téqui, 2006.

Leung, King-Ho. "Transcendentality and the Gift: On Gunton, Milbank, and Trinitarian Metaphysics." *Modern Theology* 38 (2022) 81–99.

Levering, Matthew. "Christ, the Trinity, and Predestination: McCormack and Aquinas." In *Trinity and Election in Contemporary Theology*, 244–73. Grand Rapids: Eerdmans, 2011.

———. "Does the Paschal Mystery Reveal the Trinity?" In *Reading John with St. Thomas Aquinas: Theological Exegesis and Speculative Theology*, edited by Michael

Dauphinais and Matthew Levering, 78–91. Washington, DC: The Catholic University of America Press, 2005.

———. "The Holy Spirit in the Trinitarian Communion: 'Love' and 'Gift'?" *International Journal of Systematic Theology* 16 (2014) 126–42.

———. "Participation and Exegesis: Response to Catherine Pickstock." *Modern Theology* 21 (2005) 587–601.

———. *Scripture and Metaphysics: Aquinas and the Renewal of Trinitarian Theology*. Malden, MA: Blackwell, 2004.

Lingua, Graziano. "Trinity, Number and Image: The Christian Origins of the Concept of Person." Translated by Sarah De Sanctis. *International Journal for the Semiotics of Law* 35 (2021) 1299–315.

Lombardo, Nicholas Emerson. *The Logic of Desire: Aquinas on Emotion*. Washington, DC: The Catholic University of America Press, 2011.

Long, Steven A. "The Doctrine of God and the Analogy of Being." *Nova et Vetera* 17 (2019) 1101–18.

———. "Thomas Aquinas, the Analogy of Being, and the Analogy of Transferred Proportion." In *The Discovery of Being and Thomas Aquinas: Philosophical and Theological Perspective*, edited by Christopher M. Cullen and Franklin T. Harkins, 173–92. Washington, DC: The Catholic University of America Press, 2019.

López, Antonio. "Eternal Happening: God as an Event of Love." In *Love Alone Is Credible: Hans Urs von Balthasar as Interpreter of the Catholic Tradition*, edited by David L. Schindler, 75–104. Ressourcement. Grand Rapids: Eerdmans, 2008.

Löwe, Can Laurens. *Thomas Aquinas on the Metaphysics of the Human Act*. New York: Cambridge University Press, 2021.

Malet, André. *Personne et Amour dans la Théologie Trinitaire de Saint Thomas d'Aquin*. Paris: Librairie Philosophique, 1956.

Mansini, Guy. "*Duplex Amor* and the Structure of Love in Aquinas." In *Thomistica*, edited by E. Manning, 137–96. Recherches de Théologie Ancienne et Médiévale, Supplementa 1. Leuven: Peeters, 1995.

———. "Hegel and Christian Theology." *Nova et Vetera* 14 (2016) 993–1001.

———. "*Similitudo, Communicatio*, and the Friendship of Charity in Aquinas." In *Thomistica*, edited by E. Manning, 1–26. Recherches de Théologie Ancienne et Médiévale, Supplementa 1. Leuven: Peeters, 1995.

Maritain, Jacques. *Three Reformers: Luther—Descartes—Rousseau*. New York: Scribner's, 1950.

Marmion, Declan, and Rik Van Nieuwenhove. *An Introduction to the Trinity*. New York: Cambridge University Press, 2011.

Marsh, Charles. "In Defense of a Self: The Theological Search for a Postmodern Identity." *Scottish Journal of Theology* 55 (2002) 253–82.

Marshall, Bruce D. "Personal Distinction in God and the Possibility of Kenosis." *Angelicum* 98 (2021) 65–104.

Martin, Jennifer Newsome. "The Consubstantial Otherness of God: Divine Simplicity and the Trinity in Hans Urs von Balthasar." *Modern Theology* 35 (2019) 542–57.

Maryniarczyk, Andrzej. "'*Parvus Error in Principio Magnus Est in Fine*': Thomas Aquinas's Reinterpretation of the Understanding of Being and Essence as the Basis for the Discovery of the First Cause as *Ipsum Esse*." *Roczniki Filozoficzne* 67 (2019) 27–52.

Mascall, E. L. *He Who Is: A Study in Traditional Theism*. Rev. ed. London: Libra, 1966.

Maurer, Armand. "Introduction." In *On Being and Essence*, by Thomas Aquinas, 7–27. Translated by Armand Maurer. 2nd rev. ed. Toronto: Pontifical Institute of Mediaeval Studies, 1968.

McCormack, Bruce L. *The Humility of the Eternal Son: "Reformed" Kenoticism and the Repair of Chalcedon*. Current Issues in Theology. Cambridge: Cambridge University Press, 2021.

———. "Karl Barth's Version of an 'Analogy of Being': A Dialectical No and Yes to Roman Catholicism." In *Analogy of Being: Invention of the Antichrist or the Wisdom of God?*, edited by Thomas Joseph White, 88–144. Grand Rapids: Eerdmans, 2011.

McDonough, Sean M. *Christ as Creator: Origins of a New Testament Doctrine*. Oxford: Oxford University Press, 2009.

McGinn, Bernard. *Thomas Aquinas's Summa Theologiae: A Biography*. Lives of Great Religious Books. Princeton, NJ: Princeton University Press, 2014.

McGuckin, John Anthony. "The Trinity in the Greek Fathers." In *The Cambridge Companion to the Trinity*, edited by Edward T. Oakes and David Moss, 49–69. Cambridge Companions to Religion. Cambridge: Cambridge University Press, 2011.

McInerny, Brendan Michael. *The Trinitarian Theology of Hans Urs von Balthasar: An Introduction*. Notre Dame, IN: University of Notre Dame Press, 2020.

Merriell, D. Juvenal. "Trinitarian Anthropology." In *The Theology of Thomas Aquinas*, edited by Rik Van Nieuwenhove and Joseph P. Wawrykow, 123–42. Notre Dame, IN: University of Notre Dame Press, 2005.

Milbank, John. "Can a Gift Be Given? Prolegomena to a Future Trinitarian Metaphysic." *Modern Theology* 11 (1995) 119–61.

———. *The Suspended Middle: Henri de Lubac and the Renewed Split in Modern Catholic Theology*. 2nd ed. Grand Rapids: Eerdmans, 2014.

Miner, Robert. "Thomas Aquinas and Hans Urs von Balthasar: A Dialogue on Love and Charity." *New Blackfriars* 95 (2014) 504–24.

Mirus, Christopher V. "Relation Is Not a Category: A Sketch of Relation as a Transcendental." *Proceedings of the American Catholic Philosophical Association* 93 (2019) 189–98.

Mitchell, Louise A. "Free to Be Human: Thomas Aquinas's Discussion of *Liberum Arbitrium*." *New Blackfriars* 96 (2014) 22–42.

Moloney, Francis J. *The Gospel of John*. Edited by Daniel J. Harrington. Sacra Pagina 4. Collegeville, MN: Liturgical, 1998.

Moltmann, Jürgen. "God in the World—The World in God: Perichoresis in Trinity and Eschatology." In *The Gospel of John and Christian Theology*, edited by Richard Bauckham and Carl Mosser, 369–81. Grand Rapids: Eerdmans, 2008.

Moore-Keish, Martha L. "Creation and New Creation in Baptism." In *Theology in Service of the Church: Essays in Honor of Joseph D. Small 3rd*, edited by Charles A. Wiley et al., 80–93. Louisville, KY: Geneva, 2008.

Moser, Matthew A. Rothaus. *Love Itself Is Understanding: Hans Urs von Balthasar's Theology of the Saints*. Minneapolis: Fortress, 2016.

Moule, C. F. D. "Further Reflections on Philippians 2:5–11." In *Apostolic History and the Gospel*, edited by W. Ward Gasque and Ralph P. Martin, 264–76. Exeter: Paternoster, 1970.

Mühlen, Heribert. *Der Heilige Geist Als Person*. 2nd ed. Münster: Aschendorff, 1966.

Nichols, Aidan. *Balthasar for Thomists*. San Francisco: Ignatius, 2020.

———. *No Bloodless Myth: A Guide Through Balthasar's Dramatics*. Introduction to Hans Urs von Balthasar. Edinburgh: T. & T. Clark, 2000.

———. *Say It Is Pentecost: A Guide Through Balthasar's Logic*. Washington, DC: Catholic University of America Press, 2001.

———. *The Word Has Been Abroad: A Guide Through Balthasar's Aesthetics*. Introduction to Hans Urs von Balthasar. Edinburgh: T. & T. Clark, 1998.

Nimmo, Paul T., and Keith L. Johnson, eds. *Kenosis: The Self-Emptying of Christ in Scripture and Theology*. Grand Rapids: Eerdmans, 2022.

Nygren, Anders. *Agape and Eros: A Study of the Christian Idea of Love*. London: Society for Promoting Christian Knowledge, 1932.

Oakes, Edward T. *Pattern of Redemption: The Theology of Hans Urs von Balthasar*. New York: Continuum, 1997.

Oakes, Kenneth. "Gathering Many Likenesses: Trinity and Kenosis." *Nova et Vetera* 17 (2019) 871–91.

O'Callaghan, Paul. "Can God Be Enriched? On the Metaphysical Underpinnings of Von Balthasar's Theology." *Irish Theological Quarterly* 84 (2019) 175–94.

O'Day, Gail R. "Response." In *Life in Abundance: Studies of John's Gospel in Tribute to Raymond E. Brown, S.S*, edited by Raymond E. Brown and John R. Donahue, 158–67. Collegeville, MN: Liturgical, 2005.

O'Donnell, John. *Hans Urs von Balthasar*. Collegeville, MN: Liturgical, 1992.

O'Donovan, Oliver. *The Problem of Self-Love in St. Augustine*. New Haven, CT: Yale University Press, 1980.

Oliver, Simon. *Creation: A Guide for the Perplexed*. New York: T. & T. Clark, 2017.

———. "Love Makes the World Go 'Round: Motion and Trinity." In *Love Alone Is Credible: Hans Urs von Balthasar as Interpreter of the Catholic Tradition*, edited by David L. Schindler, 176–88. Grand Rapids: Eerdmans, 2008.

———. *Philosophy, God and Motion*. Routledge Radical Orthodoxy Series. New York: Routledge, 2005.

———. "Trinity, Motion, and Creation Ex Nihilo." In *Creation and the God of Abraham*, 133–51. Cambridge: Cambridge University Press, 2010.

Olsen, Cyrus. "*Exitus et Reditus* in H. U. von Balthasar." *Heythrop Journal* 52 (2011) 643–58.

The Order of Baptism of Children. Collegeville, MN: Liturgical, 2020.

O'Regan, Cyril. *Balthasar and the Spectre of Hegel*. Vol. 1 of *The Anatomy of Misremembering*. Chestnut Ridge, NY: Crossroad, 2014.

Owens, Joseph. *St Thomas and the Future of Metaphysics*. Milwaukee, WI: Marquette University Press, 1957.

———. *St Thomas Aquinas on the Existence of God: Collected Papers of Joseph Owens*. Edited by John R. Catan. Albany: State University of New York Press, 1980.

Papanikolaou, Aristotle. "Person, Kenosis, and Abuse: Hans Urs von Balthasar and Feminist Theologies in Conversation." *Modern Theology* 19 (2003) 41–65.

Penido, M. T.-L. "*Cur Non Spiritus Sanctus a Patre Deo Genitus*." *Revue Thomiste* 35 (1930) 508–27.

Phelan, G. B. "The Existentialism of St Thomas." In *Selected Papers*, edited by Arthur G. Kirn, 67–82. Toronto: Pontifical Institute of Mediaeval Studies, 1967.

Pitstick, Alyssa Lyra. *Light in Darkness: Hans Urs von Balthasar and the Catholic Doctrine of Christ's Descent into Hell*. Grand Rapids: Eerdmans, 2007.

Poirel, Dominique. "Scholastic Reasons, Monastic Meditations and Victorine Conciliations: The Question of the Unity and Plurality of God in the Twelfth Century." In *The Oxford Handbook of the Trinity*, edited by Gilles Emery and Matthew Levering, 168–81. Oxford: Oxford University Press, 2011.

Rae, Murray. "The Testimony of Works in the Christology of John's Gospel." In *The Gospel of John and Christian Theology*, edited by Richard Bauckham and Carl Mosser, 295–310. Cambridge: Eerdmans, 2008.

Reichel, Hanna. "The End of Humanity and the Beginning of Kenosis." In *Kenosis: The Self-Emptying of Christ in Scripture and Theology*, edited by Paul T. Nimmo and Keith L. Johnson, 289–308. Grand Rapids: Eerdmans, 2022.

Richard of St. Victor. *Richard of Saint Victor, "On the Trinity": English Translation and Commentary*. Translated by Ruben Angelici. Eugene, OR: Cascade, 2011.

Ridderbos, Herman N. *The Gospel According to John: A Theological Commentary*. Translated by John Vriend. Cambridge: Eerdmans, 1997.

Riedl, Matthias, ed. *A Companion to Joachim of Fiore*. Brill's Companions to the Christian Tradition. Leiden: Brill, 2018.

Rousselot, Pierre. *The Problem of Love in the Middle Ages: A Historical Contribution*. Translated by Alan Vincelette. Marquette Studies in Philosophy 24. Milwaukee, WI: Marquette University Press, 2001.

Russell, Heidi. *The Source of All Love: Catholicity and the Trinity*. Maryknoll, NY: Orbis, 2017.

Sabathé, Martin. "L'Originalité de la Doctrine Trinitaire de *Commentaire de l'Évangile Selon Saint Jean* Par Saint Thomas d'Aquin." *Revue des Sciences Philosophiques et Théologiques* 99 (2015) 217–37.

Sarisky, Darren. "Tradition II: Thinking with Historical Texts—Reflections on Theologies of Retrieval." In *Theologies of Retrieval: An Exploration and Appraisal*, edited by Darren Sarisky, 193–209. New York: T. & T. Clark, 2017.

Schindler, D. C. *A Companion to Ferdinand Ulrich's* Homo Abyssus. Baltimore: Humanum Academic, 2019.

———. "Does Love Trump Reason? Toward a Nonpossessive Concept of Knowledge." In *The Catholicity of Reason*, 85–115. Grand Rapids: Eerdmans, 2013.

———. "Towards a Non-Possessive Concept of Knowledge: On the Relation Between Reason and Love in Aquinas and Balthasar." *Modern Theology* 22 (2006) 577–607.

———. "What's the Difference? On the Metaphysics of Participation in a Christian Context." *The Saint Anselm Journal* 3 (2005) 1–27.

Schmitz, Kenneth L. "Enriching the Copula." *The Review of Metaphysics* 27 (1974) 492–512.

Schroeder, H. J. *Disciplinary Decrees of the General Councils*. St. Louis: Herder, 1937.

Schultz, Janice L. "Love of Friendship and the Perfection of Finite Persons in Aquinas." In *Medieval Masters: Essays in Memory of Msgr. E.A. Synan*, 209–32. Thomistic Papers 7. Houston: Center for Thomistic Studies, 1999.

Schweizer, Eduard. *The Holy Spirit*. Philadelphia: Fortress, 1980.

Schwöbel, Christoph. "Christology and Trinitarian Thought." In *Trinitarian Theology Today: Essays on Divine Being and Act*, edited by Christoph Schwöbel, 113–46. Edinburgh: T. & T. Clark, 1995.

———. "The Eternity of the Triune God: Preliminary Considerations on the Relationship Between the Trinity and the Time of Creation." *Modern Theology* 34 (2018) 345–55.

———. "The Generosity of the Triune God and the Humility of the Son." In *Kenosis: The Self-Emptying of Christ in Scripture and Theology*, edited by Paul T. Nimmo and Paul T. Johnson, 267–88. Grand Rapids: Eerdmans, 2022.

———. "God Is Love: The Model of Love and the Trinity." *Neue Zeitschrift Für Systematische Theologie Und Religionsphilosophie* 40 (1998) 307–28.

———. "'Taking the Form of a Servant': Kenosis and Divine Self-Giving in Thomas Aquinas and Martin Luther." *Angelicum* 98 (2021) 43–66.

———. "The Trinity Between Athens and Jerusalem." *Journal of Reformed Theology* 3 (2009) 22–41.

Scottish Episcopal Church. *Holy Baptism*. Edinburgh: General Synod Office, 2006.

Servais, Jacques. "Balthasar: Proponent and Beneficiary of the Thought of Ferdinand Ulrich." *Communio* 49 (2022) 182–217.

Sherrard, Joseph H. "Review of *Advancing Trinitarian Theology: Explorations in Constructive Dogmatics*." *Themelios* 40 (2015) 336–38.

Siewerth, Gustav. *Die Abstraktion Und Das Sein Nach Der Lehre Des Thomas von Aquin*. Salzburg: Müller, 1958.

———. *Der Thomismus Als Identitätssystem*. 2nd ed. Frankfurt: Patmos, 1961.

Slotemaker, John T. *Trinitarian Theology in Medieval and Reformation Thought*. Cham, Switz.: Palgrave Macmillan, 2020.

Smith, Timothy L. *Thomas Aquinas' Trinitarian Theology: A Study in Theological Method*. Washington, DC: The Catholic University of America Press, 2003.

Solignac, Laure. "Les Personnes Selon Saint Bonaventure." *Revue des Sciences Philosophiques et Théologiques* 94 (2010) 451–80.

Sonderegger, Katherine. *The Doctrine of God*. Systematic Theology 1. Minneapolis: Fortress, 2015.

———. *The Doctrine of the Holy Trinity: Processions and Persons*. Systematic Theology 2. Minneapolis: Fortress, 2020.

Soskice, Janet Martin. "Aquinas: Philosophical Theology as Spiritual Practice." In *Naming God: Addressing the Divine in Philosophy, Theology, and Scripture*, 165–96. New York: Cambridge University Press, 2023.

———. "Being and Love: Schleiermacher, Aquinas and Augustine." *Modern Theology* 34 (2018) 480–91.

———. *The Kindness of God: Metaphor, Gender, and Religious Language*. Oxford: Oxford University Press, 2008.

Spencer, Archie J. "Causality and the *Analogia Entis*: Karl Barth's Rejection of Analogy of Being Reconsidered." *Nova et Vetera* 6 (2009) 329–76.

Speyr, Adrienne von. *The World of Prayer*. San Francisco: Ignatius, 1985.

Tabaczek, Mariusz. "A Trace of Similarity Within Even Greater Dissimilarity: Thomistic Foundations of Erich Przywara's Teaching on Analogy." *Forum Philosophicum* 23 (2018) 95–132.

Tertullian. *Latin Christianity: Its Founder, Tertullian*. Edited by Alexander Roberts, James Donaldson, and A. Cleveland Coxe and translated by Peter Holmes. The Ante-Nicene Fathers 3. Buffalo, NY: Christian Literature, 1885.

Thompson, Marianne Meye. *The God of the Gospel of John*. Grand Rapids: Eerdmans, 2001.

———. *John: A Commentary*. The New Testament Library. Louisville, KY: Westminster John Knox, 2015.

Torrell, Jean-Pierre. *Saint Thomas Aquinas: Spiritual Master*. Translated by Robert Royal. Vol. 2. Washington, DC: The Catholic University of America Press, 2015.

Tourpe, Emmanuel. "Dialectic and Dialogic: The Identity of Being as Fruitfulness in Hans Urs von Balthasar." In *Love Alone Is Credible: Hans Urs von Balthasar as Interpreter of the Catholic Tradition*, edited by David L. Schindler, 318–27. Ressourcement. Grand Rapids: Eerdmans, 2008.

———. "La Positivité de l'Être Comme Amour Chez Ferdinand Ulrich à l'arrière-Plan de Theologik III: Sur un Mot de Hans Urs von Balthasar." *Gregorianum* 89 (2008) 86–117.

———. "Le Thomisme Ontologique de Gustav Siewerth, Ferdinand Ulrich et Hans André à l'arriére-Plan de la Pensée Balthasarienne." *Revista Española de Teología* 65 (2005) 467–91.

———. "«Thomas d'Aquin Est le Penseur de l'Être Comme Amour» À Propos de Deux Livres Récents: II. l'Être Comme Amour Selon Heinrich Beck." *Revue Philosophique de Louvain* 106 (2008) 545–55.

Townsend, Luke Davis. "Deification in Aquinas: A *Supplementum* to *The Ground of Union*." *Journal of Theological Studies* 66 (2015) 204–34.

Ulrich, Ferdinand. *Homo Abyssus: The Drama of the Question of Being*. Translated by D. C. Schindler. Washington, DC: Humanum Academic, 2018.

———. *Leben in Der Einheit von Leben Und Tod*. Frankfurt am Main: Knecht, 1973.

———. *Der Mensch Als Anfang: Zur Philosophischen Anthropologie Der Kindheir*. Einsiedeln: Johannesverlag, 1970.

Van Nieuwenhove, Rik. *An Introduction to Medieval Theology*. Introduction to Religion. Cambridge: Cambridge University Press, 2012.

———. "Trinitarian Indwelling." In *The Oxford Handbook of Mystical Theology*, edited by E. Howells and M. McIntosh, 388–403. Oxford: Oxford University Press, 2020.

Velde, Rudi te. *Aquinas on God: The "Divine Science" of the Summa Theologiae*. Ashgate Studies in the History of Philosophical Theology. New York: Routledge, 2006.

———. *Participation and Substantiality in Thomas Aquinas*. Leiden: Brill, 1995.

Vincelette, Alan. "Introduction." In *The Problem of Love in the Middle Ages: A Historical Contribution*, by Pierre Rousselot, 11–75. Translated by Alan Vincelette. Marquette Studies in Philosophy 24. Milwaukee, WI: Marquette University Press, 2001.

Vogel, Jeffrey A. "The Unselfing Activity of the Holy Spirit in the Theology of Hans Urs von Balthasar." *Logos* 10 (2007) 16–34.

Vollenweider, Samuel. *Horizonte Neutestamentliche Christologie*. Tübingen: Mohr Siebeck, 2002.

Wadell, Paul J. *The Primacy of Love: An Introduction to the Ethics of Thomas Aquinas*. New York: Paulist, 1992.

Waldstein, Michael. "The Analogy of Mission and Obedience: A Central Point in the Relation Between *Theologia* and *Oikonomia* in St. Thomas Aquinas's *Commentary on John*." In *Reading John with St. Thomas Aquinas: Theological Exegesis and Speculative Theology*, edited by Michael Dauphinais and Matthew Levering, 92–112. Washington, DC: The Catholic University of America Press, 2005.

Walker, Adrian J. "Love Alone: Hans Urs von Balthasar as a Master of Theological Renewal." *Communio* 32 (2005) 517–40.

Walter, Gregory A. "Trinity as Circumscription of Divine Love According to Friedrich Schleiermacher." *Neue Zeitschrift Für Systematische Theologie Und Religionsphilosophie* 50 (2008) 62–74.

Ward, Graham. "Kenosis: Death, Discourse and Resurrection." In *Balthasar at the End of Modernity*, by Lucy Gardner et al., 15–68. Edinburgh: T. & T. Clark, 1999.

Wawrykow, Joseph P. "Franciscan and Dominican Trinitarian Theology (Thirteenth Century) Bonaventure and Aquinas." In *The Oxford Handbook of the Trinity*, edited by Gilles Emery and Matthew Levering, 182–96. New York: Oxford University Press, 2011.

Webster, John. "'Love Is Also a Lover of Life': Creatio Ex Nihilo and Creaturely Goodness." *Modern Theology* 29 (2013) 156–71.

———. "*Non Ex Aequo*: God's Relation to Creatures." In *God and the Works of God*, 1:115–26. God Without Measure: Working Papers in Christian Theology. New York: T. & T. Clark, 2016.

———. "Perfection and Participation." In *The Analogy of Being: Invention of the Antichrist or the Wisdom of God?*, edited by Thomas Joseph White, 379–94. Grand Rapids: Eerdmans, 2011.

———. "Principles of Systematic Theology." *International Journal of Systematic Theology* 11 (2009) 56–71.

———. "Theologies of Retrieval." In *The Oxford Handbook of Systematic Theology*, edited by Kathryn Tanner, John Webster, and Iain Torrance, 583–99. Oxford Handbooks in Religion and Theology. Oxford: Oxford University Press, 2009.

Weinandy, Thomas G. *The Father's Spirit of Sonship: Reconceiving the Trinity*. Edinburgh: T. & T. Clark, 1995.

Westberg, Daniel. "Did Aquinas Change His Mind About the Will?" *The Thomist* 58 (1994) 41–60.

White, Thomas Joseph. "Divine Simplicity and the Holy Trinity." *International Journal of Systematic Theology* 18 (2016) 66–93.

———. "How Barth Got Aquinas Wrong: A Reply to Archie J. Spencer on Causality and Christocentrism." *Nova et Vetera* 7 (2009) 241–70.

———. *The Incarnate Lord: A Thomistic Study in Christology*. Washington, DC: Catholic University of America Press, 2015.

———. "Introduction." In *Analogy of Being: Invention of the Antichrist or the Wisdom of God?*, edited by Thomas Joseph White, 1–31. Grand Rapids: Eerdmans, 2011.

Wigley, Stephen D. *Balthasar's Trilogy: A Reader's Guide*. T & T Clark Reader's Guides. London: Continuum, 2010.

Williams, David T. "The Spirit in Creation." *Scottish Journal of Theology* 67 (2014) 1–14.

Williams, Rowan. "Balthasar and the Trinity." In *The Cambridge Companion to Hans Urs von Balthasar*, edited by Edward T. Oakes and David Moss, 37–50. Cambridge Companions to Religion. Cambridge: Cambridge University Press, 2004.

———. "Interiority and Epiphany: A Reading in New Testament Ethics." *Modern Theology* 13 (1997) 29–51.

———. "What Does Love Know? St Thomas on the Trinity." *New Blackfriars* 82 (2001) 260–72.

Wippel, John F. *Metaphysical Themes in Thomas Aquinas II*. Studies in Philosophy and the History of Philosophy 47. Washington, DC: The Catholic University of America Press, 2007.

Witherington, Ben, III. *John's Wisdom: A Commentary on the Fourth Gospel*. Cambridge: Lutterworth, 1995.

Wittman, Tyler R. "The Logic of Divine Blessedness and the Salvific Teleology of Christ." *International Journal of Systematic Theology* 18 (2016) 132–53.

Wood, Jordan Daniel. "The Father's Kenosis: A Defense of Bonaventure on Intra-Trinitarian Acts." *Pro Ecclesia* 30 (2021) 3–31.

Zizioulas, John D. *Being as Communion: Studies in Personhood and the Church.* Contemporary Greek Theologians 4. Crestwood, NY: St Vladimir's Seminary Press, 1997.

Subject Index

Scripture Index

www.ingramcontent.com/pod-product-compliance
Lightning Source LLC
LaVergne TN
LVHW090518110826
845146LV00003B/898

* 9 7 9 8 3 8 5 2 4 4 0 7 2 *